EATING THE MOON

Mark David Campbell

A NineStar Press Publication

www.ninestarpress.com

Eating the Moon

© 2021 Mark David Campbell
Cover Art © 2021 Natasha Snow

This is a work of fiction. Names, characters, places, and incidents are either the product of the author's imagination or are used fictitiously. Any resemblance to actual persons living or dead, business establishments, events, or locales is entirely coincidental.

All rights reserved. No part of this publication may be reproduced in any material form, whether by printing, photocopying, scanning or otherwise without the written permission of the publisher. To request permission and all other inquiries, contact NineStar Press at the physical or web addresses above or at Contact@ninestarpress.com.

Printed in the USA

ISBN: 978-1-64890-271-0

First Edition, May, 2021

Also available in eBook, ISBN: 978-1-64890-270-3

CONTENT WARNING:

This book contains sexually explicit content, which may only be suitable for mature readers. Depictions of alcoholism and murder.

What if it were the other way around, and homosexuality was the norm and heterosexuals were pushed into the shadows?

During his twice-weekly sessions, Guy, a sixty-seven-year-old anthropologist, tells Richard, his thirty-two-year-old psychiatrist, a fantastic tale about a society where almost everyone is homosexual and sex is considered the most basic form of communication.

As a young man, on a cargo ship that sinks in the Bermuda Triangle, Guy is saved by the first mate, Luca, and they wash up on the shore of an uncharted tropical island. There, Guy must undergo a brutal initiation ritual and swim across shark-infested waters in order to win the love of a local man. Meanwhile, Luca, unable to accept his sexuality, becomes obsessed with being rescued and soon degenerates into drug dependency. Serious trouble ensues when Luca discovers that the locals have a large stash of gold, and he devises a plan to steal it. When Luca's scheme falls apart, Guy must choose between remaining on the island with the man he loves or saving Luca's life.

Could there really be such a society, or does it only exist within the fantasy of a lonely old gay man?

Dedicated to my husband.

Prologue

"The usual, Brad," Guy called out as he walked up to the front bar.

"I was wondering if you'd be in tonight." Brad scooped up a glassful of ice, then swung around. His trapezoid muscles flexed beneath his camouflage print undershirt as he reached up and took a bottle of Canadian Club Whisky from the shelf. He turned back, and with an exaggerated motion, poured a double into the glass.

"Sleep well?" Guy said casually.

"Like a baby." Brad winked, leaned forward, and placed the glass on a cardboard coaster in front of Guy.

Guy sniffed. "I see you found my cologne." He picked up the glass and threw back a quick gulp.

"Yeah." Brad smiled. "But it smells better on me than it does on you." His brown eyes sparkled as he looked directly into Guy's.

"Can't argue with that." Guy reached up and gently patted Brad on the cheek. "Just don't go making yourself too comfortable in my cave."

Brad pulled back. "Guy, has anyone ever told you what a miserable old bastard you are?"

Guy chuckled. "So often I'm starting to answer to it."

Brad shook his head. "You never let anyone in, do you?" He went to serve an elderly man who was perched on a stool at the corner. The elderly man watched intently as Brad grabbed a moist bottle of beer by the neck, popped off the cap, and plunked it down in front of him.

"Keep the change." The man was almost salivating as he handed Brad a ten.

Sailors was like any number of pubs in downtown Toronto—turn-of-the-century sandblasted red-brick exterior, oak-and-brass-accented interior. It was Thursday, and those getting a jump on the weekend would be out—less choice, better chance of scoring. Right now it was too late for the after-work rush and too early for the drag show. The DJ hadn't even set up yet. It was mostly the old boys, like Guy, looking to stake out a barstool before the younger crowd came clambering in. Guy took a swig of his whisky. It was the summer solstice, and it didn't really matter if nobody else was celebrating. As soon as the booze and E kicked in, he would party on his own.

Guy went to the far end of the bar and climbed onto his favorite stool, swiveled it sideways, and leaned back against the exposed brick wall. From his vantage point, he had all the strategic zones in the main room within his scope: the back bar, the dance floor and stage next to it, even the washroom and the entrance to the dark room in the farthest corner to the right. No one could come or go; nothing of importance could happen without him observing. A Madonna remix droned on in the background, but the front bar was far enough away from the main room you could still carry on a conversation. Not that Guy wanted to converse, but he liked to listen in on what other people had to say, especially when they didn't realize he was eavesdropping.

Guy looked toward a thin young man perched on a barstool facing the door—his spidery legs crossed, left elbow braced on the bar with one knuckle delicately pressed against his cheekbone, a Manhattan grasped in his right hand. He reminded Guy of someone he had known long ago and hadn't particularly liked. But that was a world away from here.

The young man turned suddenly and shot a sneer at Guy, as if to say, "You've got to be kidding, old-timer."

Guy smiled and shrugged. Back on the island, that similar-looking man had almost killed someone just to get noticed.

A cool blast of air blew in as another young man pushed open the fake stained glass panel door. Guy watched him as he stood there and tried to smooth his T-shirt over a little bulge of fat riding up along the waistband of his underwear.

The thin man at the bar rolled his head toward the door with a look of practiced tedium. "Don't just stand there like a debutant." His high-pitched voice rose well above the music. "Close the bloody door, darling."

The chubby young man smiled nervously, let the door swing closed, and walked up to the thin man. "Hi," he chirped. "I was a little worried you might stand me up again."

"Well, you know how busy my schedule is." He placed his glass on the bar and made a zigzag motion with his forefinger in front of the chubby man's chest. "New Armani tee?"

"Yes, I got it for ten percent off." He beamed.

"Love the clearance table." The thin man reached out and lightly whisked the chubby man's sleeve, as if to remove grime acquired from the touch of bargain shoppers.

The chubby man's smile withered. "Hey, I thought this was supposed to be the first day of summer. I'm freezing my tits off." He hugged himself and shivered. "How do they know when it's summer anyways?"

"It's astrology, you know, like star signs."

Guy shook his head and took another drink of his whisky.

"By the way, I read your horoscope on the internet today," the thin man announced loudly. "It said, *Crossing paths with a mysterious stranger could lead to a defining moment in your life.*" He turned toward Brad. "Another Manhattan, no cherry in mine. And one for my friend."

"What did yours say?" the chubby man asked eagerly.

"Oh, the usual—love, happiness, and riches."

The chubby man leaned against the bar while Brad placed two glasses near them and flashed a fluorescent smile.

"Honey, pay the man. You know I'm saving up for my trip down to P-town at the end of July, and I'm short of cash."

The chubby man dug in his pocket, pulled out a twenty, and handed it to Brad.

"Keep the change, Bradley," the thin man cooed.

The chubby man nodded hesitantly.

As Brad turned toward the cash register, Guy caught his eye and made a circle in the air with his finger. Brad nodded and poured another whisky.

The chubby man watched as Brad carried the glass over to Guy. Then he leaned in close and whispered something into the thin man's ear, who immediately swung his head around and stared at Guy.

"Very subtle," the chubby man puffed. "Why don't you just call him over here?"

"Oh, don't pay any attention to him. That's just Jungle Jim. He's probably deaf anyways." The thin man recomposed himself, combing the side of his gelled hair behind his ear with his fingertips. "He's a friend of Brad. Otherwise I'm sure they wouldn't let him in. Completely nuts, you know, but I hear he's rich. Drives a Kompressor."

"My mother drives a Kompressor," said the chubby man.

"Your mother drives a Golf," the thin man scolded.

"Volkswagen, Mercedes, no big difference."

"Not until someone sees you in one, my dear."

The chubby man frowned and began chasing the cherry around the bottom of his glass, trying to stab it with his stir straw. Having no success, he reached in, grabbed it with his fingers, and popped it into his mouth. "You know, you should get some rich old boyfriend," he said while still chewing on his cherry.

"Me? You know how wrinkle-phobic I am," the thin man scoffed. "But what about you? Why don't you find a sugar daddy?"

The chubby man giggled nervously. "I'm not really sure."

The thin man surveyed the room. "Take your pick. It's like *Jurassic Park* in here tonight." He clicked his tongue against the roof of his mouth. "I wish they'd play some real dance music and chase the dinosaurs out of here."

Just then the DJ in the main room cranked up the music, and a low, throbbing techno beat drowned out the rest of the conversation. More people came in and shuffled past the front bar toward the main room. Guy slouched comfortably with his forearm resting on the bar, holding his glass. On the far wall, under a pair of crisscrossed rower's paddles, hung a framed photo of the *Titanic*. He stared at the photo for a while and thought about the sinking of his own ship, the *Crescent Moon*. He shivered, took a large sip of whisky, and a warm glow began to flow through him. It wasn't quite the same glow he used to get from the grog back on the island, but it was good enough for this place. A gas bubble rose up in his chest, bringing with it the taste of his dinner. Roasted chicken—when done right, it was almost as good as baked iguana. That was so long ago, but those memories kept gurgling up, and sometimes it felt as if it had only been yesterday. The flickering flame from the tea candle on the bar caught Guy's eye, and he thought of burning torches under a starlit tropical sky. He closed his eyes, leaned his head back against the wall, and floated away with the images.

He imagined himself swimming in a beautiful sea, the water crystalline and warm. In the distance, he could see a beach so white it shimmered in the sunlight. On the beach, there was a young man calling and waving to him.

He was brown and beautiful and naked except for a white loincloth. Guy couldn't quite make out what he was saying, but he saw him smiling and understood he wanted him to come and play. Then another man appeared next to Guy in the water. Guy tried to convince the man to swim toward the beach with him, but the man told him to swim in the opposite direction. Guy didn't know what to do, so he just bobbed up and down, treading water. Suddenly, underneath him he saw the shadow of a huge shark. Frantically, he swam toward the beach. As he looked back over his shoulder, he saw its enormous dorsal fin only a few feet behind him. He could almost feel rows of teeth ready to bite off his lower half. The man on the beach ran into the surf, grasped Guy's arm, and pulled him forward just as the shark lunged and—

Someone bumped his leg, and Guy opened his eyes with a start. He was panting, and his forehead was damp. Maybe he had dozed off for a moment or two. He looked around. The place was now packed full of men, young and old, but mostly young. He spotted the thin man and his chubby friend making their way through the crowd toward the dance floor. Guy drained his glass, stood up, and followed. He wedged himself past the loners clutching their beers for courage and pressed between the little clusters speaking into one another's ears with cupped hands.

Guy pushed his way onto the center of the dance floor. The strobe lights spun, and the music throbbed. The beat reverberated through his chest, and he began to dance. His feet floated, and his muscles undulated with each wave as he gyrated and swayed like a snake. Naked torsos swam through flickering strips of golden torchlight all around him. His body became moist with sweat, and he, too, pulled off his tank top and tucked it into his waistband. This was what he'd come here for—to remember what it had felt like to be lost within the rhythm. He inhaled the scent of warm bodies mixed with jungle spices and the humid Caribbean breeze. At last he was back on the island.

Then the peripheral darkness began to close in on him, and the music echoed as if it were coming from a tunnel. His body went rubbery, and he sank downward in slow motion. In the distance he heard someone yell, "Call 911! Guy's out again."

And all went black.

Chapter One

Intake

Guy looked at the yellow laminate plaque on the concrete wall next to the door. The name *Richard Bowing, MD, PhD* was written in black marker on a strip of medical tape, covering the engraved name of a previous occupant. Guy glanced up toward the Exit sign at the end of the corridor and yawned loudly while scratching his ass through his hospital drawstring pants.

The nurse escorting him pressed his baby-shaved cheek against the frosted glass panel of the door, listened, then knocked twice. He looked back at Guy with puppy eyes and touched his forearm. "Don't worry. You'll like Dr. Bowing. He's very nice."

Guy nodded. "How nice to know he's nice."

A deep voice within said, "Come in."

The nurse opened the door and stepped in. Guy followed him like a robot.

"Good morning, Dr. Bowing," the nurse said. "This is Mr. Palmer, your next appointment."

A handsome man in his early thirties with dark hair and a strong chin was seated at a desk in the corner at a right angle to the window. "Thank you, Armando," he said while still staring at his computer screen.

"Take a seat over there." Armando gestured toward a blue vinyl sofa pushed against the wall under the window. "You're in good hands." He turned and left.

The room was small, with basic Canadian public medicine decor: ocher concrete walls, institutional windows, and sparse furnishings—bright, but not happy.

Dr. Bowing looked up from his screen and smiled at Guy. "Good morning, Mr. Palmer." His eyes were hazel, and his teeth said he came from a good middle-class Canadian family with a dental plan. He stood up and held out his gym-callused hand across the desk. He was tall, athletic, and well put together.

Guy looked at his outstretched hand but stood there limply. "The name's Guy," he said and planted himself on the sofa.

"Okay, Guy, you can call me Richard." He picked up a clipboard and a pen, walked over to a half-egg-shaped swivel chair facing the sofa, and sat down. The crease in his linen pants was impeccable. His socks were fine cotton and his shoes Italian.

"Tell me something about yourself." Richard leaned forward, toward Guy.

Guy slid back as if he were trying to let the sofa swallow him. "I'm a sixty-seven-year-old tattooed homosexual man they found half-naked, passed out on the dance floor of a gay bar," Guy said flatly.

"And how are you feeling this morning?" Richard's expression was sympathetic.

"Like somebody put a sweater on my tongue."

"It's good to see you have a sense of humor." Richard grinned.

"Yes, all us crazy folks have a great sense of humor." Guy dug his finger into a tear in the vinyl armrest. "But you're the brain drainer here, so I guess it's your job to decide if I'm looney tunes or not, isn't it?"

"I see you know where you are and why you're here."

"Toronto Metro Psych Ward, right?" Guy cupped the sides of his head and began to massage his temples slowly.

"Do you know what day it is?"

"Of course, I do. Do you?" Guy sneered.

"And do you know where you live?"

"Apartment 1502, sixty-six Isabella Street, just off Church." Guy returned to massaging his temples.

"What do you do, Guy?"

"You mean besides smoking, drinking, and recreational drugs? I guess you could say I'm a semiretired professor at Toronto University. I give a few classes and do a bit of research."

"Interesting. What do you teach?"

"Anthropology." Guy looked at Richard with eyes that pleaded for him to stop the interrogation.

"Fair enough." Richard held up his hand. "You don't have Alzheimer's. They checked you out last night. Physically you're okay. Actually, you're in great shape, considering."

"Yes, yes, I know." Guy pressed his temples and moaned. "Why don't you give me something stronger than that Tylenol shit? Maybe some Percocet. My head is splitting."

"Well," Richard said. "I don't want to lecture you, but you do smoke, drink, and use drugs. That can't be good for you."

"Thank you, Mommy Dearest, but I've had these headaches for years." Guy half closed his eyes and slowed his breathing.

"What do you do for them? Take anything?"

"Nothing works, really. Whenever the weather changes, my head throbs." Guy pointed out the window at the blackening sky. "Lately it's gotten worse."

"That's rough." Richard sat upright in his chair. "Have you seen a neurologist or had a CAT scan?"

"Yeah, I've been through all of that."

"Well, you were pretty dehydrated last night. That's why you collapsed." Richard shifted in his chair and crossed his legs.

"E can do that." Guy shrugged slightly.

"Do you want to tell me about it?"

"Not really."

Richard sat quietly, looking at Guy.

"Okay, fine." Guy huffed. "Last night was the summer solstice. It was supposed to be the best night of the season: feasting, dancing, and sex until dawn."

Richard furrowed his brow. "Summer solstice?"

"June twenty-first. Some people celebrate Christmas, Ramadan, or Chanukah. I celebrate the solstice and equinox. Or at least I used to. But that was some other place and time."

Richard nodded.

Guy rolled his eyes. "Let's just say instead of celebrating, I got high alone on some shit chemicals, then spent the night in hospital. Some festival, eh?" He stretched his arms out along the back of the sofa. An array of tattoos, like graffiti on the side of a subway train, poked out from the sleeves and V-neck of his standard-issue hospital T-shirt.

Richard studied Guy. His clipboard was positioned on his lap with a pen in his hand, but he still hadn't written anything.

"Doc, this is not my first time here," Guy said, shaking his head. "I know the drill: check me out, dry me out, then ship me down to the psych ward to make sure I'm not a danger to myself or society."

"That's pretty much the drill."

"Listen, it's nine o'clock in the morning. Could we drop the clinical crap, get a coffee, and I'll answer all your questions?" Guy's eyes pleaded.

"Well, there's a coffee machine down the hall." Richard swiveled around in his chair and tossed his clipboard onto the desk.

"I'll pass. I don't think my guts could take coin-drop java this morning."

"Look, it's obvious to me that you're fine, and you're free to go, of course. But before you take off, I'd like to make a suggestion." Richard interlocked his fingers and stretched them.

"Shoot." Guy leaned forward, and the stiff vinyl sofa groaned.

"It appears to me that perhaps there are a few things you might want to get off your chest." Richard's voice was relaxed and casual. "The way the system works is like this. You've been checked in, and so the government is footing the bill. If you agree, but only if you agree"—Richard now spoke with a kind of conspiratorial enthusiasm—"I can recommend further therapy and they'll go on paying for it."

"Nice try, Doc." Guy forced a smile. "Unless I'm mistaken, you just started here, didn't you?"

"Yes, a couple of weeks ago." Richard nodded.

"Just as I thought. You're a twinkie, fresh out of grad school, and you need to get your case study quota up and put your publication record in shape. So you're slumming it down here in the public sector for a couple of years before you get a university position or move on to a lucrative private practice in the north of the city. Am I right?"

Richard uncrossed his legs, placed both feet flat on the floor, and sat back in his chair but said nothing.

"How old are you anyway? Twenty-eight? Thirty?"

"I'm thirty-two, as a matter of fact." Richard crossed his arms. "And you're right. I just graduated this spring."

"So, make me an offer, Dr. Peachfuzz." Guy propped his elbows on his knees and rested his chin on his knuckles. "What's in it for me?"

Richard held his palms out. "I can't offer anything, just a sympathetic ear. Come in twice a week and talk for an hour and I'll listen."

Guy scratched his head and blew out a puff of air. "What time?"

"I have slots Mondays and Fridays at nine in the morning."

"Mondays and Fridays, eh?" Guy tapped his finger on the arm of the sofa. "And you'll write me a medical certificate so I can get out of my dreadful Monday-morning steering committee and the Friday-morning departmental meetings?"

"I could do that."

Guy looked over and surveyed the books on the shelf over Richard's desk, focusing on the worn spines of Freud's *Three Essays on the Theory of Sexuality* and Bion's *A Memoir of the Future*. "Are you sure you have the balls to put up with me?"

Richard uncrossed his arms and leaned toward Guy. "I don't want you ending up facedown on a dance floor again."

Guy rubbed his chin and thought for a moment. "Before I agree to be your couch gerbil, I want to clarify something." Guy looked directly at Richard. "You're homosexual, right?"

The expression drained from Richard's face. His chair squeaked as he sat back, crossed his arms again, and cleared his throat. "And why would that be important?"

"I don't want to waste my time playing word games with some muffin head who's read about repressed homosexuality and castration anxiety." Guy paused and grinned like an innocent child. "But you.... You're a man who knows what it's like to have a dick in his mouth, aren't you?"

"You're very direct, Guy." Richard scrunched up his face, and his eye twitched. "Actually, I have a girlfriend." There was a subtle playground sneer in his voice.

"Ahhh, of course you do." Guy leaned his head backward against the sofa and slapped his forehead. "You're one of those bookworm-sexuals, aren't you?"

"What's that supposed to mean?"

"Nothing. It's a term I invented for nerds like you who study other people's sexuality and intellectualize their own so they can remain hidden within the safety of the academic closet."

Richard balked. "You don't know anything about me." He looked as if he were trying to contain his anger.

"Of course, I don't, and I'm sure your girlfriend has the best boyfriend in the world—thoughtful, attentive, and considerate. Besides, real passion is overrated anyway. She's not missing out on anything."

"Enough about my personal life, please," Richard said with a tone of clinical authority. Then he breathed in deeply, uncrossed his arms and softened his expression and voice. "Don't worry. I'm not looking to mess with your head or your sexuality, but I am someone you can talk to. And if I'm not mistaken, you could use a friendly ear."

"Okay, then, I'll do it." Guy looked at Richard ambivalently.

"And one other thing," Richard said cautiously. "I want to ask your permission to record our sessions."

"Why not?" Guy flipped his hand in the air like he was swatting at a fly. "I just agreed to be your lab rat, didn't I?"

Richard got up, took the recorder from his desk, and returned to his swivel chair.

As he fumbled with the buttons, Guy continued to speak. "Doc, you see me now. I'm a semibald, loose-skinned old man, but I was once young like you."

"Everybody gets old." Richard lightly touched the salt-and-pepper hair at his temple.

"Yeah, but getting old really sucks if you're gay." Guy scrunched up his face. "I guess it wasn't much easier when I was young." Guy stared back at Richard but said nothing more. The wall clock ticked, and sounds from outside crept into the room.

After a few minutes, Richard shifted in his seat. "This is where you're supposed to tell me something about growing up."

"Yeah, yeah, Doc. I know how head shrinking works." Guy yawned. "Well, here goes. I grew up in a rural, redneck Ontario village. I was an only child, and my parents were almost forty when they had me. I came as quite a shock. My mom and dad owned the only general store, and our house was above it. My folks put in long hours in the store—from eight in the morning till ten at night, six days a week. They had a big dream of retiring early and spending their winters in Florida. I guess when I came along, I spoiled their dream."

"Did you feel unwanted?"

"Hmm, maybe not unwanted but certainly not wanted. Growing up, I spent a lot of time alone. I used to read comic books. I guess it was my way of hiding from reality. Tarzan was my favorite."

Richard chuckled. "Tell me about it."

"During the long cold winters, I would spend hours submerged in a hot bath. That's when I first created my little fantasy world: a steamy tropical jungle, crystal pool, and half-naked natives. Old Tarzan films and National Geographic specials were like clues that other realities were not only possible, but maybe they really did exist." Guy furrowed his brow. "Maybe that's why I chose to study anthropology in the first place."

Richard cocked his head. "Because of old Tarzan films?"

"You could say that." Guy smiled. "Perhaps I was looking for my own gay jungle or a homo Shangri-la."

Richard nodded.

"My folks had a little cottage on a lake north of our village, and during the summers, whenever possible, I would escape to the privacy of the woods, strip off my clothes, and lie naked in a sunny patch or steal away to a secluded little pond and skinny-dip. I was Tarzan's Boy, swinging with him, side by side from vine to vine through the jungle." Guy paused. "That's how I discovered masturbation." He tugged at his T-shirt and scratched his neck. "Do they wash these things in a special soap just to make them itchy? Anyway, as I was saying, I wasn't ashamed of wanking, you understand. I knew other boys did it. More than anything, it was my growing desire that frightened and isolated me. Everything I knew back then told me that my fantasies were sick."

"Well, I'm sure you know fantasies are a sign of a healthy, creative mind." Richard rested his chin on his knuckles.

"Yes, isn't that lovely." Guy gave him a pained smile. "But if you are a lonely, confused gay kid, living in a homophobic village, fantasies are all you have. And that's the problem. Queers build their lives on fantasy."

"Why do you say that?"

"Because reality sucks, and we don't have many other choices."

"It's true that some queer kids have it pretty rough growing up." Richard cocked his head. "But things are getting better."

"Oh, thank you, Pollyanna. I'll remember that."

Richard clenched his jaw.

"Doc, what if things were the other way around? If queers were in control and the heteros were the freaks?" His tone sounded more like a challenge than a question. "Do you think such a society could exist, or is it just a ridiculous fantasy?"

"You tell me," Richard said. He folded his hands on his lap.

"Yes, yes, I know," Guy said. "The analyst enters into the delusional world of the patient in the absence of containment. The patient projects his unbearable emotions onto the analyst, who, capable of understanding these emotions, contains, elaborates, and gives them back to the patient in a form in which he can think and dream about—essential to the coherent construction of his personal emotional history and tolerable truth." Guy rattled off the phrase, then paused.

Richard looked at Guy curiously. "You've read Bion?"

"Well, that's a very crude summary of Bion." Guy shrugged. "But more importantly, you've read Bion?" He grinned.

"Of course." Richard raised his eyebrows. "He's required."

Guy tapped his head with his forefinger. "A friend of mine once wrote, 'Freud gave us the road map to the human unconscious, and Bion challenged us to take a journey within.'" Guy held up both hands, as if he were praying. "Listen, Doc. I want to take you on a little journey, tell you a story I've never told any other living soul."

"You can confide in me." Richard's expression was sincere, almost hopeful.

"Okay, here goes. A long time ago, I discovered a place which was like no other place I could have ever dreamed of or imagined." Guy held out his hands like a man pleading for salvation. "It's real. I swear it is. I've kept it secret my entire life, but now—I don't know why—I need to tell someone about it."

"Maybe you need to validate it in some way?" Richard rested his elbows comfortably on his knees. "Remember, I'm here to listen, not to judge you."

Guy slumped into the sofa. "Because of my own stupidity and greed, I lost it. And I've spent almost fifty years trying to find my way back."

"And where is this place?"

"Hang on. I haven't even started telling you my story yet." Guy reached back and scratched his nape. Then he stared at the far wall and began.

*

I'm twenty-two years old. My body is hard, my smile white, and my eyes bright. I've just finished my final year at the University of McGill in Montreal—the year is 1970.

That's also the spring my parents die in a car accident driving home from their first winter in Florida. My folks were never very good at accounting, so there is no life insurance policy, and after the lawyers clean up their debts, mortgage on the store, and my school fees, there really isn't much left. With no job, no money, and nothing to tie me down, I say to myself, why wait for someone else's permission to see the world? Why not go down to the docks and get my own ticket to adventure?

Mind you, I'm no stranger to the docks. I know my way around. Back then the gay bars were as dangerous as the docks, if not worse. I'm familiar with certain nighttime passageways and shadowy nooks. I know how a casual glance and a pause can start a game of lead and follow. I know how to initiate a touch without words. I know a flash of five fingers and an open palm cements a deal. Sailors are lonely and have money, and I need money and more.

I ask around a bit and find a tramp freighter, the *Crescent Moon*, Liberian registry, leaving Montreal and sailing south. The captain of the *Crescent Moon* is an old German guy who smells of booze. I say old. He seems old. I don't know, he must be fifty or something. He tells me most of his crew are Chinese and he's sick of steamed rice and stir-fry. Then he asks me two questions: Am I running from the law, and can I boil a potato? I answer no to the first and yes to the second. Maybe he likes me because he sees himself when he was young. For whatever reason, he offers me passage as cook, cabin boy, and deckhand. All I know about being a sailor is from books and movies, Kipling and Doyle, *Mutiny on the Bounty*, and stuff like that.

The *Crescent Moon* is carrying fertilizer and farming equipment, or so I believe, heading for Cuba and some of the smaller Caribbean islands. We sail at 4:00 a.m. on a brutish spring morning and head down the St. Lawrence River and out into the Atlantic, past the fishing banks and beyond the territorial limits. Of course, we can't enter American waters since the US has an embargo against Cuba—our first stop—so we make a wide sweep out past Bermuda.

At first, it's all very exciting, and I take every chance I get to look outside, not that I see very much apart from deep blue rolling waves. I have a canvas hammock strung in a kind of anteroom behind the galley with no window, but I don't get to spend much time there anyway. When I'm not preparing meals for the captain and the first mate, I'm washing dishes, cleaning heads, bringing coffee to the bridge, and generally running errands. For never more than an hour at a time, I manage to crash in my hammock, only to be summoned from my brief sleep for some chore or other. It isn't long before I start to think maybe I've made a big mistake, but it's too late to change my mind.

The captain and crew are decent enough and treat me well, although I can't say we have very much in common other than sharing space on this old rust bucket, and many of the crew barely speak English. To the crew, I'm sure I'm just some stupid kid who has signed on for adventure, and they know I'll jump ship at the first semidecent port.

The first mate, an Italian-American guy named Luca, is the only one on board I make friends with. He's not much older than I am, twenty-four to be exact. The Chinese crew assumes we are brothers. Sometimes they even confuse us, calling us by each other's name.

The funny part about it is, we are really quite similar in appearance. We are about the same height and build. Luca sort of looks like a more muscular version of me, I guess. Of course, he's slightly darker, and he has blue eyes while mine are green. He could be my big brother or a cousin, maybe. Luca thinks it's a joke and says his great-grandpa must have been in my great-grandmother's underpants.

Most nights, we have coffee together during his watch. He complains about my coffee while he explains the ship and shows me various charts and things, but he never really tells me much about his personal life, and I don't ask too many questions. It's understood that men on a ship like this usually don't talk about their personal histories. I sense Luca has a dark side I'm not sure I want to discover.

After about five days out at sea, as we arch past Bermuda and turn toward Cuba, we hit rough weather. I don't know whether it's particularly bad or just the kind of nasty storm that the Atlantic is famous for. At first, it's exciting, with mountains of water all around. Even the sky has now become sea. The rusty old bucket of a ship booms, groans, and echoes with each pounding wave, and I'm sure the sea will rip us apart. None of the crew appears to be particularly worried. Instead, they go about their business, coping with each lurch and toss of the ship as if this is normal and expected. I try my best to do the same. Their smirks and grins tell me I'm not deceiving anyone with my false nonchalance. By nightfall, my stomach begins to churn and my head starts to ache. Next thing I know, I'm hanging on to the toilet bowl for dear life. I moan, "Oh God, kill me."

It's difficult to say how long the storm continues. I've already emptied my stomach of everything and am dry heaving when, little by little, my nausea and headache begin to clear, and I suspect I might actually survive. I remain facedown in the toilet awhile longer as my strength slowly returns. Once I am able, I grab the door latch and the bilge pipe and pull myself up onto my rubbery legs and try to stand. As I do so, I realize not only has the tempest in my stomach eased, but the ship is no longer being buffeted and tossed.

In the way that a sudden silence following a great commotion can be alarming, my first reaction to the calm is that something is wrong. Then I feel the vibrations and low hum of the ship's diesel engines, and I know we are still moving. I lumber out of the head, steadying myself along the wall railings. I pass through the galley and stand in the open aft doorway breathing in the fresh salt air and gazing out to sea, looking for lights or a horizon or something. The sea is dead flat, and a strange fog surrounds the ship about fifty meters out, masking any signs of horizon or sky or stars. After the vastness of sea and sky, then the anger of water and waves, this closeness and calm are entirely unexpected. It feels as if the ship has entered an enormous room that both protects and traps us. I shiver.

As the fog in my head clears, I realize I am a disgusting mess, and I dearly want a cup of hot coffee to wash the taste of my earlier ordeal out of my mouth. I return to the galley and put on a large pot to brew, supposing the crew will also want hot coffee now that the storm is over.

Somewhat apprehensively, I go back into the head and do my best to clean it and myself. Mind you, the standards for what qualifies as clean on board this floating piece of junk are somewhat relaxed. I drink a cup of coffee, and then, feeling almost shipshape and presentable, I fill the small enamel coffeepot to take to Luca, who I know will be waiting expectantly on the bridge. In a naïve kind of way, I'm quite proud of myself for weathering the storm and remaining reasonably intact. This is the first exciting episode on my great adventure, and now that it is over, or so I think at the time, I feel a little cocky.

As I climb the outside stairs to the bridge, I make out a small patch of sky overhead through the fog where a cluster of stars shines unnaturally bright. To me the newness and strangeness of everything at sea gives me a sense of wonder and magic, although I'm sure a seasoned sailor would only laugh at me.

On the bridge, Luca and I share the pot of coffee.

"A little bit of rough sea. How did you weather the waves?" he asks with a kind of wicked gleam in his eye.

"Absolutely no problem, if you disregard my clinging to the loo and begging for an early death." I shrug. "So, am I to understand this was not really a big one?"

"Sorry." He shakes his head. "Just a little pissing about, not even enough to cause the captain to rise from his bunk. 'Course, he's had his fill of cheap Russian vodka by now, so I doubt even Hurricane Mary could have raised him up."

"I'm sure you won't mind, when I retell this story to my grandchildren, if I upgrade the storm a notch or two. I could have you save the ship and crew from imminent death," I jest.

"I'd be happy to be your hero." He throws a flirtatious grin back at me and flexes his eyebrows.

I feel my face flush red. Perhaps Luca can tell by looking in my eyes; I'm not as naive as I pretend to be. As my mother was fond of saying, sooner or later you get the face you deserve. I try to smile innocently and look out the window at the night sky. Even though we are still entirely surrounded by thick fog, the sky directly ahead of us is now clear.

"Where are we, exactly?" I sound like a lost tourist asking for directions.

"Well, according to the compass, we are heading two hundred thirty degrees southwest, just off the lower tip of Bermuda," he says, pointing to the chart spread out on the desk.

"Right here?" I put my finger on the map.

"Yes, but if you don't trust that, just look up—see that group of stars? Those five stars form the *W* called Cassiopeia." Luca points at each star.

I follow his gestures with my eyes.

"Cuba's in that direction." Luca stretches out his arm and takes aim as if he's looking along the sight of a rifle.

"Doesn't sound too accurate to me," I say, trying my best to look down the line of sight along his arm.

"That's why we have charts and a compass." He shrugs and drops his arm. He turns back to the chart table, leaving me staring out the window.

"How do we know how far away Cuba is?"

"That's easy. The height of the North Star over the horizon"—Luca points with his thumb over his shoulder toward the stern of the ship—"is equal to our degrees in latitude." He takes a swig of his coffee and swallows. "It's a simple formula, and when you can see the North Star, it works pretty well."

"And those other three stars just below"—I scribble my finger up and down in the air—"are they part of Cassiopeia too?"

Luca looks up from his coffee cup and squints, then returns to my side. "No, strange, I've never really noticed them before. Probably just some minor stars that are particularly bright tonight. The sea and fog reflect light in strange ways."

Luca and I stand there for fifteen minutes or more gazing out to sea as we sip our coffee. I become transfixed by the three stars, and even though my eyes water, I can't bring myself to blink. Whether it's an illusion or actual, the stars appear to grow in size and brightness, paling Cassiopeia. By the time I speak, the three stars have illuminated the sky the way a full moon might do on a particularly clear night.

"Is that normal?" I ask. But before Luca can respond, I hear a great boom, and I'm thrown forward. My head slams against the steel bulkhead, and that's all I remember of being aboard the *Crescent Moon*.

*

Guy stared at the place where the ceiling tiles met the corner. The tick of the mechanical, institutional clock on the wall dominated the room.

After a few minutes of silence, Richard said gently, "What are you thinking?"

"There is a tiny brown spider making a web in the corner of your ceiling," Guy said without breaking his stare.

Richard swiveled around in his chair and looked. "Does that have any particular meaning for you?"

"Well." Guy dropped his stare and turned his head to meet Richard's eyes. "Obviously, it means you have bugs in here to feed it." Guy shrugged.

Richard tensed his jaw. "Okay, I get it. You don't want to be analyzed. I'll restrain myself."

Thunder cracked outside, the air felt full of static electricity, and raindrops pattered against the window. Guy stretched to look out the window behind him. The thunder boomed again, and the pattering rain became a symphony.

"Ahh, finally, relief." Guy held his temples with both hands.

"Headache better?"

Guy nodded.

"Glad to hear it. It's a quarter to ten. Do you need a moment to compose yourself?"

"No, I know the drill." Guy grunted as he pushed himself off the sofa and stood.

Richard rose. "Will I see you this time Monday, then?"

"Why not? See you Monday." Guy started for the door.

"Oh, one more thing," Richard said.

Guy stopped. "What's that?"

"You're right. The vending machine stuff is dreadful." Richard threw Guy a cocky smile. "On Monday, you can do us both a favor and bring the coffee from the Tim Hortons next door. Cappuccino for me."

Guy rolled his eyes. "I guess Freud was right."

Richard tilted his head to one side. "How so?"

"The fee is part of the therapy." Guy winked and left the office.

Chapter Two

The *Crescent Moon*

It was Monday morning. Guy sat on the hard yellow seat, jiggling his foot and watching the cleaner push and tug the cleaning machine back and forth across the blue linoleum floor in the main reception hall. Guy checked his watch and rubbed his hands nervously. The trickle of people coming through the tinted sliding glass doors had become a flow, as staff and patients hurried toward the elevators or down one of the various corridors. Guy checked his watch again. He stood and darted out. Ten minutes later, he returned with a cup of coffee in each hand. He walked through the reception hall, turned right, and entered the wing of the Addiction and Mental Health Unit.

Up ahead, around the corner, he heard the squeak of rubber soles on the freshly polished linoleum. When he reached Richard's door, he stopped and sniffed. Among the odors of cleaning fluids and hospital disinfectants, he detected the faint scent of Adidas Sport cologne—the same cologne the young nurse, Armando, had been wearing last Friday. Guy smiled and knocked.

"Come in."

Guy entered. "Good morning, Doc. Here's your cappuccino." He placed a foam cup on the corner of the desk and sat on the sofa.

"Thanks." Richard stood up, went over with his coffee, and sat down in the swivel chair in front of the sofa.

"Did you ever notice the little plastic cup covers now have warnings on them?" Guy popped off the lid with his thumbs and looked around for a place to put it. "Caution, contents may be hot." Richard signaled to the wastepaper bin next to the corner of his desk, and Guy tossed the lid in. "I hope it's hot. Coffee is supposed to be hot."

"I guess it's just so people don't accidentally burn themselves." Richard carefully peeled the plastic lid off his cup, leaned over and placed it in the bin.

Guy blew on his coffee then took a large sip. "You know, Doc, it seems like everything has a warning label on it nowadays. Nobody wants to take responsibility for anything or anyone." Guy leaned forward and placed his coffee on the floor near his feet.

"Is that what you are doing here? Taking responsibility?" There was no tone of accusation in Richard's voice.

Guy was silent for a moment, then said flatly, "People should come with warning labels." He paused. "I guess we do, really. It's just nobody ever takes the time to read them until it's too late."

"I'm not sure I follow you."

"You know, use with caution." Guy pointed toward his own chest with both hands. "Crazy old faggot inside.

Oh, I forgot we're not supposed to use that word anymore."

"Use whatever words you want. It's just the two of us here."

Guy reached down, picked up his coffee, and took another drink. He leaned back, stared at the blank wall behind Richard's head as if he were watching something, and began to speak.

*

I lie there struggling to stay unconscious, but reality comes crashing in like the waves that are crashing in all around me. I'm disoriented, confused, and I feel like a large spike has been driven through my left temple behind my eye sockets. I curl up tight like a frightened animal and reach for something to hang on to. I slow my breathing, and the throbbing eases a little to where I can focus my eyes. All at once, I realize I'm in the stern of a lifeboat and Luca is near me, rowing like a wild man.

Clinging to the gunwale, I rise to my knees and yell with as much force as my splitting head will allow, "What the hell's going on?" A wave spills over the side, drenching me, and I sputter and cough.

Luca yells back, "Hold tight! She's gonna blow!" He rows with even greater force, his arms and shoulders straining against the oars.

A large round wave looms up behind and slips under us, and our small craft rises and accelerates. I see terror in Luca's eyes as he struggles to position us with the wave. I grip the gunwale harder.

"Rudder! Rudder!" he hollers as he digs in the oars.

I look around in panic, knowing whatever it is he wants me to do, our lives depend upon it. Then I spot a wooden rudder at the stern, directly behind me. Our lifeboat, like the ship, is from another era. I swivel around, clutch the tiller, and attempt to steer. I had spent many summers at the lake sailing my parent's Albacore skiff, and this is not so very different. Somehow, between my steering and Luca's brute strength, we manage to ride out the passing wave.

I still have no idea why we are in a lifeboat in the middle of a tempest and not onboard the *Crescent Moon*. I venture a glance over my shoulder from where we flee. Suddenly, as if in answer to my bewilderment, there's an ear-splitting crack, and I lurch forward, almost losing my grip on the tiller. The sky and water light up with a sickly red and orange glow that's eerily beautiful. A burning white light engulfs the ship, and I can almost feel the heat on my spray-drenched face. Over the crash of waves and wind, I hear a long, slow groan of buckling steel, like a death cry from some prehistoric beast. Two more explosions send white flares shooting into the night sky. Then, with a final throaty boom and a belch of air, the *Crescent Moon* slips below the inky surface of the sea and all is dark.

"What the...?"

"We hit a rock, a shoal or something, dead-on. Not on the charts!" Luca screams back.

"Where's the captain? Where're the others?"

"I don't know! Everyone was below deck when we hit. She was burning. There was no time to warn them. I barely got us into the lifeboat." He digs in and pulls hard but loses his grip, slips, and slams the oars against the side of the boat.

"Burning? I don't understand. Why was it burning?" Tears are now streaming down my face.

"We were carrying explosives." Luca sets the oars and pulls back firmly.

"Explosives? I thought we were carrying fertilizer and farm supplies." I wipe the tears from my eyes and the snot running down my mouth and chin.

Luca's expression turns to stone, and he continues to row. For the next hour or so, he fights to keep our craft true with the oars while I do my best to steer. We ride out each passing wave, one after another, and little by little the waves lose their crests and become rolling hills of water. As the sea subsides, I can tell from Luca's face and slumping shoulders he, too, is relaxing slightly, or perhaps he's just exhausted. I guess even though we are not out of danger yet, we are no longer likely to capsize.

"Those crates marked farm instruments? Munitions for Castro, courtesy of the Soviets." Luca trails his oars in the water. "Besides, fertilizer is highly combustible. When we hit ground and the fertilizer caught fire, I knew it was only a matter of minutes before the whole thing blew." His eyes fill with tears, and he looks at me as if he were begging me to tell him something.

"And the others, what about...?"

"There was nothing I could do." Luca drops his head, promptly releases his right hand, and crosses himself. He takes hold of both oars again, trailing them in the water.

The wind in our ears and the slap of the water against our tiny craft are the only sounds as we drift aimlessly along the rolling surface of the night sea. Eventually Luca lets go of the oars and they drag listlessly, banging lightly against the side of the boat. Neither of us speaks nor looks at the other. Our ship is gone, our shipmates drowned, and we're alone in the middle of the sea. I continue to hang on to the tiller and steer with the waves, not knowing what else to do. My breathing slows to match the roll of the sea, an emptiness fills my mind, and I fall asleep.

When I awake, I find myself curled up in the stern. A glow of light from the horizon tells me it must be early morning. Luca is stretched out ahead of me with his legs spread and his head resting backward against the wooden rowing bench. I focus my sleepy eyes on him and realize his pants are wide open and he is slowly stroking himself.

At first, I'm surprised. Then, considering what we have just been through and our present situation, it seems to make sense somehow. When we are found, there will certainly be an inquiry into his responsibility. He is the first mate, and it was on his watch that the ship sank. He abandoned ship while the rest of the crew perished. He will probably be found guilty and go to prison for a very long time. But I can't judge him. He was courageous and strong at a time when I was panic-stricken. He saved my life. I want to thank him, but I don't have the words to express what I am thinking and feeling.

I remain still for a few minutes, not wishing to disturb him, and then in an exaggerated, somewhat theatrical way, I stir as if I've just awoken, giving him ample time to cover himself and avoid any mutual embarrassment. He continues stroking himself, not shifting his position nor raising his head. I move hesitantly, with great slowness and care, watching for signs of aversion. None come. In crab-like fashion, I creep over to him until my face is inches from his crotch. He stops stroking and puts his free hand on the back of my head, gently guiding my mouth over his glans. It's warm and moist and tastes both bitter and salty. I know what to do and how to do it well.

It doesn't take long before he flinches twice and comes. I swallow and clear my throat. Then I gently kiss the underside of his balls and slide myself upward, kissing his hairy belly and chest as I rise. Hovering over him, supported by my arms on the bench, I look into his eyes and smile apprehensively. He smiles back briefly. Then his face sours to a frown.

Oh shit, I think, *I've just made a big mistake.* But before I can retreat, tears fill his eyes and I know it's not revulsion I see. Lowering myself onto the bench, I lie next to him and cradle his head in my arms. He surrenders, and his tears become sobs, streaming down my chest.

"Shh, shh, we're alive" are the only words I have to offer him as I stroke his hair. We cling to each other until we both fall asleep again.

I don't know how long I've been asleep, when suddenly my eyes open to the blinding light of day. I sit up guardedly and blink in the intense noonday sun, expecting to see only sea and sky before me. Instead, I'm greeted by an exquisitely lush, green volcanic island, framed by an azure sky and turquoise sea. At first I think I must be hallucinating. But if my eyes deceive me, so too do my nostrils. Mixed with the marine scent of salt and seaweed, the breeze carries a spicy jungle perfume. Our ship must have hit a small islet that was part of a larger island group, and in our panic and confusion as we made our escape, we hadn't realized we were actually only a few miles offshore.

"Aha!"

"What is it? What do you see?" Luca stirs, rubbing his face and pushing himself upright.

"Land ho!" I call out boyishly.

Luca grabs the gunwale to steady himself with one hand and shields his eyes from the sun with the other. "Oh my God!"

"We're saved. We're saved," I yell. Laughing and without forethought, I grab Luca and kiss him hard on the lips. But rather than a passionate outpouring of wet emotion, his lips are firm and closed. He doesn't refuse me, although he doesn't engulf me either. That's how it had been with the men I had known at the docks in Montreal—sex but no intimacy. For now, the only important thing is that we have survived.

With Luca rowing and me steering, we head straight toward the island.

"Look, just over there. Past the bay and behind that hill, isn't that smoke?"

Luca stops rowing and stares in the direction I'm pointing. "It sure is." And he continues to row with increased vigor. A barrier reef lies about a mile offshore, and Luca heads us toward a break in the reef. As we approach, we pass through a floating ribbon of charred debris and greasy diesel fuel that has been carried in by the current: pieces of wood and polystyrene, a partial life ring, and a plastic Chinese rice bowl. I can almost feel the intensity of the blast that ripped our ship apart, and I suppose that most of it, being iron and steel, is now lying on the bottom of the sea. None of the other crew could have possibly survived, and I pray we don't come upon the bodies. Luca rows our small craft through the debris, and we pass in silence, the way people do at a funeral procession.

The sea is gentle, and we traverse the reef with ease. Once inside, the water is probably only forty feet deep at most and crystal clear. I gaze down into a marine garden. Schools of yellow jack move as one and change direction in perfect unison with each passing wave. My eyes follow as a giant manta ray silently glides across the seascape like a visitor from a shadow world. A nurse shark slowly swaggers along the sandy bottom at the base of a large head of brain coral. I feel more like a tourist on a sightseeing tour than a survivor of a shipwreck.

The water becomes shallower, and eelgrass covers the sandy bottom. Luca digs in hard with the oars, and our boat comes to a gentle swooshing halt on the sand.

I brace my hands on the gunwale and leap out onto the beach, but as I stand up straight my head begins to throb and I become dizzy.

"Oh, I must've lost my land legs," I joke. Moments later I topple face-first into the sand.

"Guy! Are you all right?"

"Yes, it's just my head."

"Stay put." Luca jumps out and comes to my side. "You're as white as a ghost." He holds my chin and examines the goose egg on my forehead.

"Let me lie here for a few." I roll over. I'm cold and shaking and dripping with sweat.

"Can you make it to that tree over there? You'll be out of the sun."

"Give me a minute," I slur. "I'm not much of a real man, I guess." Drool is running out my mouth and nose.

A few minutes later, Luca helps me stagger over to the tree. He retrieves a small piece of driftwood and places it under my head. After stripping off his shirt, he returns to the water's edge, soaks it, and comes back and washes my face and chest. The warm seawater evaporates, leaving my skin cool.

"I have to secure the boat." Luca scrounges around and finds some driftwood logs to wedge under the keel. With great effort, he rolls the boat well up onto the beach and ties it to the trunk of the tree under which I lie.

"We desperately need to find water. I'm going to see where that smoke is coming from. You'll be safe here. Sleep. I'll be back soon."

"Don't leave me."

"You're okay for now." He bends over and kisses me lightly on the forehead.

I know he's right. I'm not capable of moving.

"I'll be back soon. Don't worry," he calls as he trots off down the beach.

I'm alone with only the rustle of the palm fronds in the breeze, the rhythmic swoosh of the water on the sand, and the high-pitched zing of cicadas from the tropical forest behind. I pass out.

*

Guy stopped speaking and gazed at Richard as if to say, "Oh, you're still here." He leaned back in the sofa, stretched his arms over his head, and yawned loudly. "So, what do you think so far?"

Richard blinked like a man who had just been interrupted while watching a story on television. "Very interesting. I think you've raised a number of important issues we should explore."

"Such as my difficult breastfeeding relationship with my mother?"

Richard squinted suspiciously at Guy. "Such as why this narrative is so important to you and why you have such a strong desire to share it with me."

Guy smiled in a way that said he was pleased but also holding something back. "I just want to tell you a story. That's all."

"That's our deal, isn't it?" Richard sat forward. "You talk and I listen." He glanced at his watch. "But our time is almost up. We'll have to continue with this on Friday."

Guy stood up. "Ironic, isn't it?"

"What's that?"

"In the age of globalization, you can no longer set out to see the world with only a change of socks and underwear and a few bucks in your shoe."

"Times have changed," Richard said.

Guy yawned. "I don't know. Maybe you still can. It's just me who's gotten old and frightened."

Richard rose. "You don't appear to be a man who's frightened by very much."

"Looks can be deceiving."

"What is it that frightens you the most?"

Guy gave Richard a dodgy smile. He walked across the room, then paused at the door and looked back toward Richard. "Living, Doc. That's what frightens me." He opened the door and left.

"You can pick up your medical certificate from the nurses' station," Richard called after him.

Chapter Three

Waning of the *Crescent Moon*

Armando was positioned behind the nurses' station counter reviewing some charts on the computer screen. He looked up as Guy passed, blinked, and then smiled with recognition. "Good morning, Mr. Palmer. Dr. Bowing is ready to see you. Go on in."

Guy was already partway down the hall, heading toward Richard's office.

"Good morning." Richard looked up from his computer screen as Guy marched through his doorway.

Guy didn't respond. He placed the cappuccino on the edge of his desk and sat down on the sofa as if he were a passenger on a bus waiting for it to depart. Then he held his nose up and sniffed the air—a faint odor of chlorine. Richard's hair was slightly damp, and a gym bag was wedged in the corner behind his desk. "Back or breast?" Guy said.

Richard jerked his head and squinted. "Excuse me?"

"Your swim stroke: back or breast?"

"Mostly back, but I throw in twenty lengths of breast at the end of my workout."

Guy nodded. "I swim every day at noon." He slapped his left pec. "But I'm strictly freestyle and fly. Always like to see where I'm going."

Richard furrowed his forehead. "How did you know I just went swimming?"

Guy rolled his eyes but didn't respond.

Richard got up from behind his desk, walked over to the swivel chair with the recorder in his hand, and sat down. "Why don't you continue to tell me about your home life and growing up?" Richard clicked the Record button, and the little red light turned green. He reached over and placed the machine on the edge of the desk.

Guy leaned into the sofa and made a low groan in the back of his throat. "What more is there to tell? My mom was the tough guy. Dad mostly ignored me." Guy paused. "Sometimes I felt like inventory in their store."

"Do you resent them?" Richard leaned forward, resting his elbows on his knees and his chin on his knuckles.

"Not really." Guy shook his head. "They worked hard to put me through school. I had a lot more than most of the other kids in my village, I guess—certainly more than Luca, who grew up in that orphanage and had nothing and no one."

"This is Luca from the ship, right?"

Guy nodded.

"He's very important to you, isn't he?"

"He used to be."

"And where is he now?"

"Good question. It depends on which lifetime we're talking about." Guy relaxed his face and looked off into the distance. He stared at the wall and began to tell his tale.

*

I must have been unconscious for a long time. Even though I open my eyes, I have no idea where I am. I am trapped halfway between a very bizarre world of dreams and a confused reality. I imagine my old professor visiting me. He's naked to the waist and lecturing me loudly, but I can't understand his words. I cry out.

Then I'm back in the lifeboat, lying on my back gazing up at the burning ship. The crew is standing on deck looking down at me, seemingly unaware and unconcerned about the fire behind them. Luca is crouching above me trying to insert what I think is his hard penis into my mouth. I refuse to spread my lips or open my teeth.

"Take it," he commands. "You need it. Take it."

"Yes, yes, yes," the crew chants. "Take it. Take it."

I fight hard. Luca pries open my lips while others hold my head. He shoves whatever it is into my mouth, and cool water pours down my throat. I cough.

Finally, I am on the docks in Montreal, lying on some boxes and old sacks in a dark corner of one of the warehouses. I realize I'm not alone as, one by one, men wearing towels around their waists appear out of the darkness.

Two of the men move down and grab my legs and spread them apart. They lift my legs upward while another man rubs grease on my ass. I struggle, but now I am surrounded by men holding me down. The man who greased me takes what I think is a large gas nozzle and tries to insert it into me. I fight harder but can't move. After a few seconds of discomfort, the nozzle slides in smoothly, without pain. Then I feel a warm fluid flow into me, and all I can smell and taste is almonds. It's wonderful. I open my mouth to ask for more, and someone fills my mouth with a thick liquid that tastes like licorice. A wave of heat sweeps through my body, and my skin tingles. Everything and everyone surrounding me glows and then melts into colors that flow like a lava lamp. I feel as if my mother's old beaver-fur coat has folded in around me, cloaking me in soft furry darkness, and I sleep.

When I finally wake and completely open my eyes, the torturous throb in my head is gone. I am nestled in a large hammock, and an orange evening light is coming through an open doorway. I lie there, gently swinging, and survey my surroundings. The room, from what I can see, is entirely white plaster, with a variety of rectangular platforms jutting out from the walls. Some of the platforms are piled with cushions and cloths, while others have clusters of odd-shaped decorated ceramic pots, bowls, and jugs arranged on them. Numerous large wooden beams traverse a high-peaked thatched ceiling above me. Brightly colored banners of gauzelike cloth hang from the beams and wave in a warm breeze that wafts in through the doorway. I float back to sleep.

Later, I awake to the sounds of drums, xylophones, whistling flutes, and laughter coming from outside. They are strange sounds, wild and primitive and at the same time gentle and comforting. My first thought is, there's a party outside, and confined here to my hammock, I'm missing it. I swing back and forth listening, reassured I'm not alone, and doze off to sleep again.

Sometime during the wee hours of the morning, I hear Luca snoring. I look over and see him curled up on a platform bench near me, amongst a pile of cushions and cloth. I'm still very weak but can no longer sleep, so I lie there in the rare light and watch him. His face is strong and well-defined, with touches of pretty around his eyes and lips—not angelic, but perhaps once kissed by an angel. All the strain I saw on his face in the lifeboat is now gone.

It's full morning before he stirs. He opens his eyes and smiles at me. "Welcome back, Kiddo," he says as he might say to a kid brother he shares a room with.

"It's good to be back," I say, returning his smile. "How long was I gone?"

"Long time. I thought I was going to lose you." Luca stands up and stretches.

I know he has a good body since I've already seen him with his shirt off, but now as I see him, full-length, almost naked, I'm taken aback by his lean, muscular Mediterranean physique, elegant and agile. He's wearing some kind of elaborate loincloth embroidered with shiny beads and shells.

He sees me looking and grins. "You must be feeling better."

"Did you go native or have to borrow a pair of underwear from a passing showgirl while I was out of head?"

He blushes. "Yes, you're definitely feeling better, 'cause now you're getting nasty."

"Where exactly are we? This doesn't look much like a hospital."

"Well, that's a little hard to explain. I'll show you later, but for now, rest. You're gonna need all your strength." He smirks like he's holding back a joke or something.

"What? What is it?"

Just as I ask, someone outside the door whistles, and I jump.

"Relax, Kiddo." Luca laughs and gently slaps me on the shoulder. "I assure you, you're gonna love it. Do you think you can eat something?"

"God yes, I'm famished."

A silhouetted figure steps partially in through the doorway. Because of the contrast in light, I can only discern he's a squarely built man of medium height. He's carrying a wooden tray he holds out into the shadowy light of the room. It's piled with fruit, nuts, stacks of little cakes that look like fat tortillas, and tiny steaming decorated bowls. The tray is adorned with tropical flowers.

"What's this, room service?" I ask, both surprised and impressed at the same time. "Don't tell me. We washed ashore at some fancy tropical hotel?"

"Not exactly, but first, let's eat. You need to start back on solid food. Look at you. You're skinny as a rail."

I reach down and rub my ribs. "I lost a few pounds, didn't I?"

"A few! Check out your bony ass."

"I guess I have to thank you a second time for saving my life." My eyes water as I begin to well up.

"Well, now don't get all sappy on me. Let's get a few things straight. The first time was more by accident and duty than anything else, and I'm not the one you need to thank this time. They are." Luca gestures toward the man standing motionless by the door.

As I look up at him, he slowly steps toward us. The slats of light beaming through the doorway seem to ripple rhythmically down his body like dominoes falling in succession. He's about my age or slightly younger, I guess. His skin is light brown, and he's muscled without being bulky. He has a broad barrel chest, forested with glistening black hair. On the center of his chest, he has a butterfly tattoo the size of a plate. His shoulders are square and his arms powerful, not long and skinny like my own. His hands and feet are large and broad. He's wearing a plain white loincloth, a simple pair of woven grass sandals, and he has a pink shell strung around his neck with a cord.

I lie there in my hammock staring as he turns and squats to place the tray on one of the platform benches along the wall. His thighs are strong and hairy, and his buttocks are an architectural marvel. I breathe in slowly and feel dizzy.

Ironically, in all his physical perfection, it's his face that captivates me most. It's round, both boyish and manly at the same time. His broad nose is sharply defined at the bridge. His cheekbones are high, almost protruding, and he has big brown eyes that seem to sparkle. His jaw is not sharp and angular like mine, but it supports the rest of his face well. I spot a dimple in the middle of his button chin, and gooseflesh ripples up my arms and across the back of my neck.

"Guy, this is your nursemaid, Nando." Luca smirks. "He's the one you need to thank."

At the mention of his name, he looks at me and smiles in a way that is pure and genuine, as if he has never learned to temper his sentiments with a stranger. I guess, really from his perspective, after spending countless days and nights attending to me, I'm not a stranger to him at all.

My face flushes red. "Thank you for um... I mean, *gracias, muchas gracias.*"

"*De nada,*" he humbly replies.

"*Dónde estamos en Cuba?*"

"*No, no estamos en Cuba.*" He smiles again and bows as he backs, almost floating, out of the room.

"Hey, I didn't know you could speak Spanish," Luca says brightly.

"Well, a little school Spanish," I say, feeling quite proud of myself.

"Great! But Nando is not Latino, and he speaks American English quite well."

"Oh shit," I groan.

"Idiot," Luca says, laughing.

"Hey, leave me alone. I'm a sick person, and I'm hungry as a bear."

As we eat and banter with each other, Luca tells me very little about where we are and who our hosts are.

"Don't worry yourself about it. When you're strong enough to get out of that hammock, you'll know everything. Right now, your job is to eat and sleep. You have to stay put!"

After breakfast or lunch, or whatever it is, Luca disappears for the day. I sleep through the morning, but I'm becoming quite restless, and I want to see where I am. I know there are others around because I hear children outside speaking an unfamiliar language.

That afternoon Nando returns and, even though he speaks English well, our conversation is difficult. When I ask him any direct questions, he seems deathly shy. Since I've always been a good talker when I want to be, I press on.

"Nando, where did you study English? In school?"

"No, not at school."

"Well, did you learn it from tourists or something?"

"I learned it from my daddy."

"Is your father English?"

"He is American, like you."

"I'm not really American. I'm Canadian."

"Oh," Nando says with an expression that indicates he doesn't understand the distinction.

There's an uncomfortable pause, and Nando begins to nervously clean and straighten the room.

"Nando." I shift myself upright in my hammock for the first time. "I'm curious to see outside, and the truth is I really need to go to the bathroom."

"Bathroom?"

"Washroom? Um, the loo?"

Nando frowns, obviously not comprehending.

"Pee-pee?" I venture and put my hands together at my crotch and make a swooshing sound.

"Ah!" Nando's face lights up. "You need to take a leak."

"Yes, I need to take a leak. I'm about ready to explode."

"I will help you." Nando rushes over and steadies me as I climb out of my hammock.

I'm entirely naked, and as I stand, Nando surveys my body.

"Pretty skinny, eh?" I say, a little embarrassed.

"Oh yes, very pretty." He exhales the words. "All plaster white."

"Thanks, I think," I say and laugh. "But I really have to go."

Nando, with his hand secure under my armpit, directs me. I'm a little wobbly at first, but it feels good to be on my feet again, and I promptly find my balance and strength as we cross the room.

There, in the far corner of the room behind a wooden screen, is a small basin with a drain, hollowed into the plaster floor. It's painted around the edge with a bright design. I pause for a moment, wanting to be sure that this is, in fact, the toilet and not a washbasin, or some kind of ceremonial bowl, or something.

"Take your piss here, or do you need to take a dump?"

I laugh again. "Man, your father really taught you American English well, didn't he?"

"Thank you." He smiles sweetly, not realizing I'm poking fun at his lexicon.

And then again, there is an uncomfortable silence as I wait for him to release me and give me some privacy.

"Oh, please forgive me," he says. "You need help." He reaches over and gently takes my penis and aims it.

"Oh, oh, no, no!" I jump. "I think I can manage this one by myself." I brush away his hand just as I feel myself becoming chubby. Nando says nothing, nor does he make the slightest move to leave or look away. I've always had a philosophy about doctors and hospitals: leave your dignity at the door. I guess it applies here too, so I pee out of necessity—under Nando's full inspection.

"Good, good," he says like some kind of very strange coach encouraging a trainee. "The color is bright. You are well."

Although I'm not completely confident of Nando's professional credentials, I have to admit he has nursed me so far, and I'm relieved by his diagnosis and the opportunity to pee.

"Do you wish to take food outside?"

"Absolutely, a fine idea, a picnic on the veranda. But first, I think I need my pants. I don't want to frighten the neighbors."

"You are embarrassed by your disfigurement?"

"My disfigurement? I may be a little skinny, but I'm hardly disfigured."

"No." Nando blushes. "I mean this." And he takes my penis in his hand once again. "You have no cover for your glans."

I pause, taken off guard by his casual attitude toward touching me. To be honest, I like it. Just before I become uncontrollably hard, I turn slightly and slide my cock out of his hand.

"I'm circumcised."

"Circumcised, what is that?"

"They remove the foreskin, er, cover, at birth."

"Why, why would anyone do such a horrible thing to a baby?"

"I've often wondered that myself."

"Is it an offering or a sacrifice to your gods?"

"Well, not my god. I guess it's just a tradition."

"Oh, how sad, to take your beautiful cock and cut it like that."

"Don't worry. I can't remember if it hurt, and it works just fine."

"You are very brave." Nando furrows his brow and purses his lips. Then after a moment, he says, "Your eyes are so green. You must wear this green cloth to match your eyes." Nando holds out a folded cloth he has retrieved from a pile on one of the benches. "Like the green of the forest."

"Can't I just wear my own pants?"

Nando looks nervous. "Umm, your old clothes are not here."

Strange, I think.

"But do not worry," he quickly adds. "I have many things for you to wear."

He hands me the green cloth, and I wrap it around my waist. "I hope people don't mind me running around in only a towel."

"Oh no. This is what we wear," Nando says as he puts a pair of grass sandals at my feet.

"Okay," I say reluctantly, slip on the pair of sandals and head for the door.

As I step through the doorway, I'm immediately blinded by the bright sunlight, so I pause waiting for my eyes to adjust. I blink rapidly, and little by little, I am able to focus on the panorama spread out before me. I reach out and grab the doorframe to steady myself. I must still be hallucinating.

*

Guy stopped talking. The sound of footsteps and voices in the corridor wafted through the office door.

"And what did you see out the doorway?" Richard asked.

Guy held up his forefinger. "You'll have to wait until Friday to find out."

Richard rubbed his chin. "Okay, so far in your story, Luca has brought you to safety, and Nando has nursed you back to health. Is that correct?"

"Yes."

"It's very curious." Richard studied Guy for a moment. "Luca looks enough like you to be mistaken for your brother, and Nando is your complete physical opposite—yet you describe both of these men as beautiful, while at the same time, you describe yourself in much less flattering terms."

"Are you saying I saw myself as inferior to them?"

"I'm saying these two men are models of perfection—one very similar to you and the other is your opposite."

Guy hunched his shoulders and scoffed. "Yeah, so what?"

"Idolizing a supermodel or fantasizing about someone exotic in a faraway place is safer than risking involvement with someone who might be more present and obtainable."

"And what about becoming involved with someone who is simply present and obtainable because you are expected to?" Guy said. "By the way, how's your girlfriend?"

Richard's face soured. "I'm not the one in analysis here."

"Okay, fair enough, Doc." Guy spread his arms back and stretched.

Richard's expression became professional. "So, was it just sex between you and Luca, or was there something more?"

"Cut the relationship, group-hug shit, Doc." Guy scowled as he got up from the sofa. "You know as well as I do—making a friend, falling in love, painting a picture, writing a musical score, cliff diving, scoring a goal, or sticking your penis into a wet hole—it all comes down to the same thing." Guy cupped his groin and jostled himself. "Sex! It's always sex." Then he grinned widely. "But it's never *just* sex." And he walked out the door.

Chapter Four

Welcome to the Village

Guy walked up to the nurses' station balancing two cups of coffee, one on top of the other. "Good morning, Armando."

Armando looked up suddenly. "Oh, good morning, Mr. Palmer."

"Padre Pio?" Guy stared at the tiny gold medallion hung where the low V-neck of Armando's scrubs exposed curly wires of chest hair.

"Oh, this." Armando blushed and touched the medallion. "I'm not really religious," he said, looking like an ex-smoker caught carrying a concealed pack of cigarettes. "It's just my mom's got...." He stopped, his face twitched, and his Adam's apple bobbed as he tried to swallow.

Guy reached over the counter with his free hand, touched Armando on the shoulder, and nodded sympathetically. "Whatever helps, big boy," he said gently. Then he turned and walked down the corridor toward Richard's office.

"Sorry if I'm late." Guy walked directly in. "Was just chatting with a friend." He handed Richard a coffee.

"Thanks. No, you're right on time." Richard clicked on the tape recorder and took a sip of his cappuccino. "Do you have a lot of friends?"

"This is the closest thing I have to what you might call a social life." Guy laughed. Stretching his arm over his head and cracking his neck, he added, "I'm sure I'm not your only looney who feels that way." Guy sat down on the sofa.

"Have you tried getting out and meeting people?" Richard asked as he got up from his desk and sat down on the swivel chair.

"Oh yes," Guy said as if he knew the correct answer to a quiz-show question. "I met a guy last night."

"Tell me about him." Richard leaned back into the chair.

"Early thirties, a little chubby. Likes Madonna, lives in the burbs, not out to his family. Never had a long-term relationship but is attracted to older guys. I've seen him and his skinny friend hanging around Sailor's Pub before. Looks like last night he was out on his own."

Richard smiled. "Where did you meet him?"

"At the Black Eagle." Guy sat forward, resting his elbows on his knees. "You know, tourist night, mixed crowd, not too hard-core." Guy made no attempt to explain Thursday night was the night when the curious and those who just wanted to say they had been there, went to the notorious S&M leather bar on Church Street.

"And?" Richard said with an almost adolescent lilt to his voice.

"That's it," Guy said. "He was looking for an older man with a little bit of status and cash. I guess I fit the bill." Guy stuck out his chin and shrugged. "But I didn't want to be his daddy."

"How can you be so sure he was looking for a daddy? What did he say?" Richard placed his coffee on the desk, and sat upright.

Guy frowned and jiggled his foot impatiently. "We didn't actually talk," he said, enunciating each word.

"You didn't talk?" Richard's voice cracked as his hand flew up involuntarily.

Guy grabbed the gray tufts of hair at his temples. "Doc, I fucked him for ten minutes in a dark room!" He spread out all ten fingers, as if Richard needed to count them. "That was more than enough to tell me everything I wanted to know." Guy tilted his head back and focused on the wall behind Richard. "As I was telling you...."

*

My eyes water, and I blink rapidly as I step through the doorway into the blinding sunlight. As soon as I'm able to focus, I discover the stone cottage sits on top of a long, raised stone-and-earth terrace about fifteen feet above the ground below. The walls of the cottage are covered with white stucco, and bands of decorative relief painted black and orange wrap around it like a belt. A gentle ocean breeze teases my locks and rustles the dried leaves of the large thatched roof. Looming in front of me is an enormous stone-and-earth terrace mound, like a crude pyramid, about forty feet high, with a grand stone stairway up the center. My mouth hangs open as I bend my head back and scale the steps with my eyes. It looks like a photo from one of my textbooks of some ancient archaeological site.

I turn completely around and run my eyes along the array of stone-and-thatched cottages sitting atop terraces that circumscribe a large oval plaza about the size of a soccer field below me. In the center of the plaza is a round raised pool.

On every terrace, there are flowers, flowering vines, and pots filled with flowering plants. There are even flowers floating in the central pool.

I scrunch up my face in disbelief and look back over my shoulder at Nando, who is standing patiently behind me. If this is not a hallucination, maybe it's some kind of theme park or movie set. But surely it can't be real. Where the hell am I?

"Do you like our little village?" Nando says as I stand there with my mouth hanging open.

I stutter, trying to find words. "It's—it's truly marvelous... not like anything I've ever seen before."

Nando smiles, obviously pleased with my reaction.

"And the flowers, there are flowers everywhere." Oh great, I am standing in front of the most wondrous sight I've ever seen in my life and the only thing I can think of saying is to compliment my host on his petunia patch.

"Oh yes, people always say, give a woman good soil and she will grow corn and potatoes. Give a man good soil and he will plant a flower," Nando says.

I immediately think of old Mr. Simpson back in my village. People always said he was a little queer, but he did have the best rose garden in the whole county. I breathe in deeply and savor the perfumed air. "It feels so good to be upright and outside. What a fabulous day, flowers, sun, and birds singing. It's like paradise."

"We have a song the children like to sing on days like this." And Nando, without the slightest indication of self-consciousness, proceeds to sing a hauntingly beautiful little tune. The words are completely foreign to me, even though many seem to mimic the sounds of nature. This is the first time anyone, especially a young man so enchanting, has serenaded me. Although I know it's corny, I feel like I've just stepped into a romantic scene from the Rodgers and Hammerstein musical, *South Pacific*.

"It's such a beautiful song. What do the words mean?"

"Oh, the words are the loveliest part. I will translate them for you. 'Birds sing, flowers bloom, and fish jump. Sound, smell, color, and dance are the language of life. Every animal and plant has its own way to say I want to fuck.'"

I choke at his last line, and if it had not been for the sincere expression on his face, I would have assumed he was joking with me. I smile at him. "Well, it certainly captures nature's intent, doesn't it?"

"Oh yes, we have many such beautiful songs about sex."

Although I want to continue talking about sex, I suddenly notice that, except for an old man and a few children at the far end of the plaza, the village looks quite deserted. "Where is everybody?"

"It's past midday. The women are up at their fields, and the men are down at the beach with their boats. Some of us remain here to look after the old people and the children."

"Ah." I think about my economic anthropology course back at university—*sharp sexual division of labor*. But no anthropology course could have prepared me for what I have yet to discover.

"Please, sit down and eat." Nando holds out his hand, pointing to a pile of cushions and mats and the picnic lunch arranged on the platform behind me.

While I'm seating myself, a small girl with golden wiry hair and coffee-brown skin, who is playing with the little group of children in the plaza, looks up and runs toward us. As she climbs up the stone steps of the terrace on all fours, she squeals with delight, "Doe, Doe."

Nando smiles, waves, and calls back something completely incomprehensible to me. When she reaches us, she leaps into Nando's lap and buries her face in his stomach.

"This is Lisha. I am her favorite today." At the mention of her name, she squirms and buries her face deeper into Nando's stomach.

"She is timid, and you are a stranger," he whispers. "They do not see many strangers."

That's odd, I think. They must have contact with other people, because the children look as if they might have come from every corner of the globe. "Is she your daughter?" I ask.

"No, she is not mine."

"Do you have any children?"

Nando looks to the ground, crestfallen. "No, I am not able." He rises to his feet, lifting Lisha in his arms. "I must put her to rest now."

Nando hurriedly climbs down the steps with Lisha and disappears into a cottage on a lower platform.

I suck in air through my teeth. "I guess that was a faux pas," I say out loud to myself. I sit there picking at the food. Suddenly a wave of dread flows over me, and I feel lost and alone. I wanted a big adventure, but now I have no idea where I am, and nobody from home knows where I am either. The only person I know is Luca, and I don't really know him that well. I'm not even sure if I'm a guest or a prisoner here. How the hell am I ever going to get back home?

*

Guy suddenly looked at Richard. "Are you bored yet?"

"No," Richard said. "Your description is fascinating." He paused for a moment. "But I'm still contemplating what you told me about having sex with that young man in the Black Eagle."

Guy wrinkled his brow. "Doc, have you ever noticed with some people you begin a conversation and become bored after a few minutes? While with somebody else the conversation becomes enthralling and lasts for hours. Some people intrigue you and others don't. It's not so different with sex, is it?"

"Yes, but how can you accurately assess a person after ten minutes of casual sex in a dark room?" Richard said flatly.

"Words are inaccurate, and people often lie. They tell you what they think you want to hear. Even worse, they tell you what they want to believe about themselves." Guy picked up his coffee cup from the floor and took a drink. "With sex, you can learn all you really want to know if you're perceptive." Guy rolled his head. "Is he repressed or clingy, a social climber or a gold digger? Is he looking for a friend, a lover, a daddy? What does he like, need, and fear? And that's only for starters."

"And how do you know you're not just projecting?" Richard squinted.

"Isn't projection essential to all forms of communication?" Guy held out the palm of his hand.

Richard raised an eyebrow and looked skeptically at Guy.

"Don't worry, Doc. Most people don't understand the language they speak. I'm sure nobody is aware of that little dark secret you have sitting out there in plain view." Guy flexed his eyebrows and grinned wickedly.

"Are you practicing psychology now?" Richard gestured toward the bookshelf.

"Call it what you want." Guy shrugged. "Sex is the most basic form of communication." He stood up. "It makes words redundant. Nothing more, nothing less." He left the room.

Chapter Five

Coming Out

"You know, Doc, coffee is always better with a cigarette," Guy announced as he walked into the office balancing two foam cups, one on top of the other, in his right hand while he shut the door with his left.

Richard turned away from his computer screen and glanced at his watch. "Well, you know the rules."

"I remember when we used to smoke everywhere." Guy placed both coffees on the desk. He handed the top one to Richard and sat down on the sofa. "Trains, buses, even in movie theaters."

With his coffee and the tape recorder in hand, Richard moved to the swivel chair. "I smoked for a few years in grad school but gave it up." He curled his lip in a way that looked a little self-righteous, a little nostalgic.

"I have to admit things are cleaner and smell better than they used to... well, except me perhaps. It's Big Brother looking over my shoulder I don't like." Guy bobbed his head and pointed to the door with such intent that Richard swiveled around and looked.

"Are you being a little paranoid?" Richard switched on the recorder.

"Yes, of course, I am. But you know how they started out with the warnings on the packages about cancer and lung disease and all that stuff?" Guy spoke in a measured tone as if he was about to reveal a conspiracy plot. "Then they decided to really scare kids, so they also added pictures of disgusting teeth and rotten organs and wrinkles and stuff?"

"Yes, I've seen them. They're not pretty." Richard sat back in his chair and crossed his leg over his knee.

"Well, I collect them, have them all," Guy said quickly, then returned to his slow conspiratorial tone. "I've noticed something a little strange."

"What's that?" Richard took a long sip of cappuccino and raised his eyebrow as if to signal he was listening.

"Well, on the pack that warns you about smoking and erectile dysfunction...." Guy paused, his mouth open and his palm spread out. "There's no picture!"

Richard snorted a laugh and shook his head. "I'm not sure anyone would buy a pack of cigarettes with a picture of a limp dick on it," Richard said summarily, as if he expected Guy to shift topics.

"That's my point! The fastest way to scare a teenage boy away from smoking is to show him a limp dick."

"I can't argue with that."

Guy dropped all sense of irony from his voice. "Tits and twats are decorative, but dicks and balls are dangerous." Then he said with a lyrical tone, "Speaking of male genitals, let's pick up where we left off."

*

It's dusk by the time Nando returns carrying a large bundle. He's as attentive and bright as before. He must have forgiven me for asking him if he has any children. All the same, I think maybe it's best not to ask too many personal questions for now.

"Come now. We must get you ready for the feast," Nando says.

"Feast?" An image from those old black-and-white Hollywood films, where the intrepid explorers are not only the dinner guests but also the main course, flashes through my head.

"Yes, yes, you must be introduced to the village. There is much excitement among the men. It is said that the Red brothers will take you, but the Blue brothers claim that they will have you."

"Whoa! What do you mean they will take me? Take me where?"

"Oh no, no. Do not be afraid. I mean take you as a brother. Everyone belongs to a brotherhood."

"Well, I don't know how long I'll be here. Do I have to join one of these brotherhood groups?"

"No, but almost everyone does. After you are introduced, you can choose."

"What brotherhood are you in?"

"The Green, my daddy's, of course. We have the honor of hosting the feast because we found you. The Green brotherhood is small compared to the mighty Blues and the Reds, but we can still make a good party. Do not worry. I promise you will enjoy."

Nando places his bundle on one of the platform benches, unties it, and spreads it open.

"I will make you so splendid that everyone will wish to have you as their brother."

And Nando, like a frenzied Italian designer, goes to work on me, instructing me to stand with my arms spread while he wraps a long, green, patterned cloth around my waist, then expertly loops it in the back, feeds it up between my legs, adjusts my nuts, and fastens it in the front. I begin to breathe heavily and make a slight moan. Just as I prepare myself for a venture into ecstasy, he gently pats me on the bum, like a parent might do to a child, and steps away to retrieve one of the other articles he has come with. I look over to try to see if Nando also has a boner, but with the bib of his loincloth hanging down in front of his crotch, I'm not really sure.

"Too tight? Too loose?"

"I don't know. I've never worn a loincloth before," I say meekly.

Nando examines and adjusts the waist. "Loose enough to dance in, tight enough to stay on while wrestling," he pronounces with satisfaction.

"Wrestling! I hope I'm not going to be wrestling," I say anxiously. But Nando ignores me and continues with his creation.

"It's a shame you have no holes in your ears or nose for jewels."

Something I must remember to do when I get back to Canada, I think but don't say out loud.

Next, he fastens a cape made of cloth and green parrot feathers around my shoulders.

"You are skinny, but you have a nice chest and shoulders, so the cape will hang properly." Then he produces a large jade necklace and slips it over my head. It's really more like a breastplate and weighs at least two pounds.

Perhaps I have misinterpreted Nando's attention. Does he see me as a man, or am I an exotic pet to be cared for and fussed with? One thing is certain. I'm only a guest, so I decide to play along. "If this isn't a costume ball, I'm going to look like a royal ass," I say. But Nando is so intent he doesn't answer. I hope he knows what he's doing.

Just then, Luca comes in, looking disheveled and staggering slightly, his loincloth with all its shells askew. I sigh in relief. "Just in time. Thank the stars, I won't have to go through this alone."

Luca stares at me, snorts, then falls onto one of the benches in a fit of laughter.

I sneer at him. "What happened to you? Truck hit you and you forgot to get the license plate number?"

"What about you?" he says, sputtering through a gasp of laughter. "Circus leave town and left you behind?"

"Very droll. Help me. I can't go out in public like this. I look like a birdman."

Nando, ignoring us, proceeds to attach green feathers to locks of my hair.

"Don't be such an old lady. They're gonna love you." Luca tries to regain control. "You'll have the time of your life. Hey, I had to go through it. It's just that it looks a lot funnier on you than it did on me." He bursts into laughter again.

"What's all this business about choosing a brotherhood?"

"Stop worrying. It's like a boy's club—you know, the kind of thing they do at those private schools. I joined the Reds last night. Those boys are crazy. Just wait till you get to know the Reds."

"Yes," Nando says somberly. "The Red brotherhood is the largest."

"Come on. You're not gonna leave me alone for this," I half beg, half command.

"Sorry, Kiddo, got a hammock party down at the beach tonight, and I'm not gonna miss it."

"A what?"

"You'll find out in good time. Now get yourself prettied up, and off you go to your party."

In the meantime, Nando is carefully placing a decorated grass bag diagonally over my neck and shoulders.

"What's this for?"

"Tributes and gratuities." He beams, producing a pair of grass sandals, of course decorated with beads, shells, and small feathers.

I sit on the edge of the bench and dutifully put them on.

"Now stand up and let me see," he says.

As I stand there, Nando inspects his creation, preening the feathers and adjusting my loincloth and cape.

"Beautiful, absolutely beautiful," he says, but I don't know whether he is referring to the feathers or me.

"Man, I wish I had a camera so I could send the folks back home a picture of you," Luca says, giggling like a hyena. "Okay, Bird Boy, I'm off."

"No, no, wait! You can't abandon me like this."

"Oh yes, I can," he scoffs and jaunts out the door, leaving me in full feathers alone with Nando.

"Bastard!" I mutter. Outside I hear flutes, percussion instruments, and laughing.

"Couldn't I just wear my normal clothes?" I whine.

"No, no," Nando says. "You must be properly introduced."

I can tell from the firm tone in his voice and the sulky expression on his face this is not negotiable, and he is losing patience with me. I acquiesce.

"What are you wearing?" I offer brightly. "Something equally as, er, elegant, I hope?"

"No, I do not dress. I serve. But do not worry, I shall remain close until you know what to do."

Now I'm convinced I'm an exotic pet, or at least some kind of performing act.

"What do they expect of me?"

"Only to eat, drink, and get to know the men of the village, the ones you desire to know. Oh, be careful with the, um, beer. It can be very strong." And he smiles in a reassuring, motherly way.

I feel like a five-year-old all dressed up for my first Halloween party but frightened to go. I stand there frozen in the doorway. I'm pissed at Luca for leaving me alone, and I'd rather rot in the cottage than go out in public dressed like this. But I guess if I'm ever going to figure out where I am and just what is going on, I need to go.

Nando takes hold of my arm firmly. "Wait for the drums." As he speaks, the light flutes and tinkling xylophones cease, and deep drums begin to pound. "You walk ahead." Nando slides behind me and takes hold of the trailing edge of my feathered cape.

I draw in a deep breath and muster my courage. I grit my teeth and step through the doorway of the cottage out into the night. Drums pound and torchlights flicker all around me. I have the same disoriented feeling one has when first stepping out of the darkness onto the strobe-lit dance floor of a disco. At first, I can only see the blue-and-orange silhouettes of clusters of men in the plaza below. I stand shyly on the platform at the top of the terrace steps. I guess it's time to put my anthropology into practice—observe, interact, and participate. "Dorothy, say good-bye to Kansas," I mumble to myself.

"Do not be shy," Nando whispers in my ear. "I have told everybody about your missing glans cover, so they will not be shocked."

"What!" My sandal catches on the corner of my cape, and I lurch forward. If Nando had not caught me by the arm at the last minute, I surely would have tumbled down the steps to my death, feathers, cape, and all.

*

Guy stopped talking. The old institutional clock on the wall clicked. After a few minutes, he turned his head toward Richard. "You know, Doc, at the end of the day sex is our only line of defense. Strange old queers like me, leather daddies, and outrageous drag queens, we're the ones who keep the heteros at bay. And even so, they still come flooding in. First, it starts with a few fags bringing in their fag hags. Next the trendy chicks show up with their boyfriends in tow. Soon the dark room is closed, and you can't find space on the dance floor. The fags have to move on."

Richard leaned his head to one side and studied Guy. "The world is not really divided so neatly into two mutually exclusive camps, you know. I think you need to reflect on some of the reasons why you feel so threatened by heterosexuals."

"You're right. Why should I care if what little space we have is colonized by the heteros?"

"But I think you do."

"Why?" Guy pushed himself up in the sofa. "Now I don't need to hide in the closet. I can go out and get married, buy a minivan, a house in suburbia, and adopt someone else's mistake. After work, I'm off to the supermarket to pick up more milk and cereal before the PTA meeting, then home for a meal in front of the television before falling asleep on the sofa."

"And why does this scenario bother you so much?"

"What happened to the gay movement?"

"The gay movement has changed and evolved."

"Yes, but where's the sex? We've been domesticated and castrated. We've become bad copies of the most dreary heterosexuals!" Guy barked. He sat, jiggling his foot, his face tense. Then he closed his eyes and said in a melancholy tone, "I miss the days when we were perverts, and only we occupied the shadowy corners and were party to the secrets that dare not be named."

"Things are getting better, you know," Richard said as he checked his watch. "It's time. Do you need a moment to compose yourself?"

"No. Do you?" Guy snapped and stood up. "Listen, Doc, if things are so much better, then why am I here!" He stomped out the door.

Chapter Six

Introductions

"Live fast and die young before you get old," Guy said loudly as he pushed the door open.

Richard looked up from his copy of the *American Journal of Psychoanalysis* and swiveled around in his chair. "Good morning, Guy."

Guy fumbled with the door, making sure it was securely shut.

"You seem very agitated this morning," Richard said.

"AIDS, cancer, or even being beaten to death in some back alley." Guy took his place on the sofa. "None of those things are as horrifying as the prospect of becoming a lonely old faggot."

"That's pretty harsh, don't you think? Not every gay person is lonely in their old age."

"What do you know?"

"Is there something specific that's bothering you this morning?" Richard clicked on the recorder, which was sitting on the corner of his desk.

"No, nothing." Guy paused. "And everything."

"Do you want to tell me about it?"

Guy made a low growl in the back of his throat. "It's those moralistic pseudo-intellectuals at the university who've got my jockey shorts in a knot."

"What happened?"

Guy pursed his lips and clenched his fist. "Yesterday, the Human Subjects Committee rejected my research proposal."

"That's too bad. Do you know why?"

"Yes, I wanted to study why poppers are so much a part of gay culture, while they're almost unheard of among heteros." Guy squirmed on the sofa, trying to find a comfortable position.

"Ahh, amyl nitrate." Richard lightly rubbed the stubble on his chin. "And why was your proposal rejected?" Richard took a long drink of his coffee.

Guy hunched his shoulders innocently, almost like a child. "Obviously, the link between gay culture and poppers is sex."

"I still don't see why the proposal was rejected."

"Methodology." Guy sat back and folded his arms. "Specifically, participant observation."

"Oh." Richard sat upright. "Now I see where the problem is."

"Exactly!" Guy spread his hands, palms upward like a preacher about to give a sermon. "We can theorize about human sexual activity as long as we don't actually observe it firsthand or, God forbid, participate in it. Look—" Guy sat forward again. "How am I supposed to study gay people without sexually interacting?" He spoke through clenched teeth.

"Mr. Palmer, do you mean to tell me you didn't know the ethics committee wouldn't accept your proposal if it included sex with your subjects?"

Richard shot Guy a look that seemed to say, *Cut the crap.*

Guy curled his lip and grumbled, "The same little politically correct fascists who rejected my proposal are at this very moment extolling the virtues of participant observation as the cornerstone of anthropological research to their naive undergraduates. Fuckin' hypocrites."

"Yes, but sex with your subjects? Surely, there was more to your research than just that."

Guy twitched his foot nervously and scowled.

Richard continued, "You need to ask yourself why you set yourself up to be rejected in the first place."

"Gay people are so nice as long as we don't have sex," Guy said sarcastically. Then he blew out a lungful of air as if he had just been deflated. "Can we talk about something less negative now?"

"For example?" Richard interlocked his fingers.

"Parties!"

*

Nando and I descend the stone steps to the beat of drums and cross the plaza. I do a quick survey of the figures sitting cross-legged and lounging on mats and cushions arranged on the lower steps of the pyramid mound. Strange, no women, only men. And I feel as if all the men are waiting for me. Nando escorts me to the first platform of the pyramid mound, and I sit in the center of the group on a large cushion. True to his word, Nando remains close to my side whispering explanations and instructions.

The men cluster around me. From old to young, they are almost every size, shape, and tone one can possibly imagine. Some are tall and lean, although many are shorter and more robust, like Nando. Some have dark hair, eyes, and complexions, while others are paler. All, however, from the big ones to the small, have a natural muscle tone, typical of people who move, work, and play—more like the sailors I knew at the docks and not at all like the spongy-bodied hothouse plants or contrived gym-rats at university.

Once we're seated, the flutes and xylophones play again while small groups of young men—adolescent boys really—dressed in plain white, like Nando, appear, carrying what seems like an endless stream of food: steamed fish wrapped in banana leaves, pots of meat stew, loaves, buns, and flat tortillas, and arrays of roasted corn on sticks, mounds of potatoes, sweet potatoes, and other roots I've never seen before. There are piles of red and orange tropical fruit of all sizes and shapes, which—to my northern eyes—look like fruit from another planet.

Splayed out on a large platter is a stuffed baked snake with the skin still on. Someone puts a bowl in front of my face—large roasted rhinoceros beetles floating in a slimy-looking bluish sauce. I flinch in horror at its contents, my stomach rolls, and I start to gag. But rather than offending my hosts, my squeamish reactions entertain them, and they laugh and jeer with one another.

"It's probably best you don't tell me what I'm eating until tomorrow," I whisper to Nando. "Or better yet, never tell me."

Nando hands me a gourd. "Here, drink this."

I hold the spout to my lips, tip my head back, and take a sip. The beer or the wine, or whatever it is—I'll call it grog—is warm, thick, and viscous. I recognize the taste instantly from when I was ill. More than the sweet herbal taste, I recall the warm swaying feeling of bliss. After a few swigs, my initial discomfort flows away and I feel completely at ease, safe and secure, like I have just been reunited with all my dear old friends, rather than in the center of a strange ceremony amongst strangers.

I'm about to take another large swig when Nando gently taps the grog gourd in my hand. "Tsk, tsk." He clicks his tongue. "Drink slowly. There is much more feast yet to come."

I smile, amused at his ever-watchful maternal care, and continue to pick at what looks like a baked potato.

As the feast progresses, the men shift their seats, continually changing position and moving ever closer and closer to me. Little by little Nando slides back on the platform until I lose track of where he actually is. I assume he's somewhere nearby. Almost imperceptibly, the men sitting around me and against me begin to lightly touch and stroke my feathers, hair, and shoulders. Whether it's the natural easiness of the environment or the effect of the grog or both, I feel no apprehension or shyness. Their brushes and fleeting touches progress to caresses along my arms, legs, back, and stomach. All this touching somehow seems to compensate for our inability to speak directly. At some point, a radiant young man's face appears inches from my own. With his hands gently on my cheeks, he captures my mouth with his kiss. From then on, I'm, shall I say, lost. As his tongue moves in and out of my mouth, I feel my entire body being engulfed by licks and kisses, while my feather cape is being loosened and my loincloth unfolded. I do not resist. I lie backward on the platform, ready to give and receive.

Up until then, I had only experienced illicit gropes, furtive masturbation games, and drunken desperate liaisons in dirty dark hideaways, down at the docks in Montreal. Here, under an open sky and flickering torchlights in front of whomever cares to watch and join in, I have sex. It's more than organs rubbing and penetrating following a hormonal imperative. It's whole masculine bodies—warm, wet, hairy, and smooth—touching, exploring, and communicating. I swim through a sea of probing tongues, entwining limbs, and writhing torsos, all moving with the same desire to please and be pleased. Moans and grunts and animal sounds blend with drums, flutes, and percussion. And just as I surrender to complete sensuality, content to remain in this hedonistic state forever, I feel my body tighten, and an enormous wave of orgasm flows through me.

The man who is sucking me at the time bears down, and I grasp his head with both my hands and pump vigorously until I can no longer hold it. I shoot into his mouth.

Immediately after licking the last of my spurts, he rises to his feet and dashes off. I assume he's going to spit.

All around me, half beneath me, half on top of me, men are grunting and moaning their arrival. Hungry mouths engulf cocks, and as with me, once the suckers have their mouths full, they spring to their feet and disappear around the corner of the platform.

I should take more notice, but by now, a herd of pink elephants flying by wouldn't rouse more than my passing attention. I lie there amongst the heap of sweaty, musky, and slippery men, and I'm one of them. For the first time in my life, sex does not feel dirty.

After resting awhile, some of the men began to stir, and water and grog are passed around. The drums begin again, and one by one the men get up to dance. They float in rhythmic unison like schools of fish. Their movements and gestures are like words from a poem in a foreign tongue. They slip in and out of the shadows, wrapping their bodies around one another as if they were snakes.

One young man with fiery red hair and freckles takes my arm and pulls me to my feet. I protest lightly, but admittedly I have never missed an opportunity to dance. I soon discover, however, that my stiff two-step attempts to follow the music leaves everyone in gales of laughter. Just as I'm about to resign myself to observer and not participant, two muscular men sandwich me between their bodies, rolling me like a wave. Like everything so far, all I'm required to do is relax and allow myself to be swept along. And I do. Floating through the night, dancing, drinking, and sex are my only measures of passing time.

But no party lasts forever. By the time the squawking birds announce the coming of dawn, I'm in no condition to stand, much less return to the cottage on my own. All at once I realize that the man whose chest and abdomen I've been reclining on is Luca.

"Time to go home, party boy," he says. "Kizo will carry you." A giant of a man, who has a body that appears to be carved out of stone, lifts me into his arms.

"Pico, give us a hand," Luca says, and a smallish man with a wiry body and an oversized head hangs on to my arm as he struggles to carry the bundle of costume I shed earlier.

Once inside my cottage, the little guy carefully sets my stuff in the corner. The giant places me into my hammock, and Luca rocks it. I try to kiss them to thank them, but I'm unable to find the strength, and I simply smile. Nando is fast asleep in a hammock near mine. Luca, Kizo, and Pico flop down together on a pile of pillows, curl up like a litter of puppies, and fall asleep.

I lie in my hammock swinging gently—still floating from the grog—and admire Luca's face and body as he sleeps. But more than that, I admire the way he always seems at ease and in control of everything and everybody around him—including me.

I don't know if I love him, but I do know I want to be like him.

*

Guy leaned back comfortably in the sofa. "Doc. Let me say that in my lifetime, I have been to many parties: circuit parties, grand balls, theme parties, and orgies, with VIPs, royalty, common folk, and riffraff. But none have ever compared to that night I joined the Green brotherhood. God, what a night—and I was the life of the party." Guy raised his hand triumphantly. "No, I was the party!"

Richard tried unsuccessfully to suppress a smirk.

Guy slowly lowered his hand. "And after that night—" He grinned. "—I walked like a turkey for days!"

Richard's lips parted, and he broke into laughter. "You know, of course, the cardinal rule of psychoanalysis," Richard said, still giggling. "Never laugh at your patients, at least not to their faces."

Guy beamed with satisfaction.

"Feeling better?" Richard said.

"As a matter of fact, I am. Thanks, Doc." Guy raised his cup to take a drink but stopped. "I just wish I could turn it off—this junk that keeps rattling around in my head—or at least turn the volume down a little bit."

"That's what we are trying to do here—make you more comfortable with whatever it is that is so difficult." Richard glanced over to the recorder on the desk. The green light was still on.

"My problem is," Guy said softly, "I'm no longer sure if the line between reality and fantasy is so absolute." He rose to his feet and left.

Chapter Seven

Fitting In

Guy walked into the office humming. He placed the coffee on the corner of Richard's desk and sat down on the sofa, still humming to himself.

Richard looked up from his email and smiled. "Good morning."

"Sorry," Guy said too loudly as he pointed to the earphones in his ears. He removed them and then said in a quieter voice, "I like to listen to music when I'm out in public. It gives me a little space, protects me."

"What do you like to listen to?" Richard fumbled around his desk until he found his tape recorder. He got up, went over, and sat down on the swivel chair facing Guy.

"Mostly simple pop tunes. In amongst the fluff and stuff, I always find one song that has something to say."

"And what are you listening to this morning?"

"'Y.M.C.A.'"

"'Y.M.C.A.'?" Richard laughed. "My old aunt makes me dance that song with her at every family wedding."

"Yes, but apart from being the anthem for tasteless breeding rituals"—Guy waved his hand dismissively—"that song has two of the four principles of lying."

"I'm sure you're going to tell me about it."

"Oh yes." Guy held up one finger. "First, give the people what they want to see and hear, and they will believe it. See, back in the eighties this group of clowns appeared on the scene dressed up like every gay cliché in the book, and everybody loved them—one big joke."

Richard nodded in agreement. "Okay, I'm with you so far."

"And second." Guy held up two fingers. "The best way to hide something is in plain view. Even if it was nothing more than a marketing scheme, finally here was a song that spoke directly to us fags."

"I guess gay people have come a long way since the Stonewall riots."

"Have we?" Guy sneered. "So why are you still hiding?"

Richard's expression went flat.

Guy continued, "Anyway, it was as if they were sending an encoded message in that stupid song that said there is a place where you can go where you will be safe."

Richard interlaced his fingers and swayed the chair back and forth for a second, then stopped. "And where's your safe place, Guy?" he asked as if he were making a challenge.

"I think we both know the answer to that, don't we?" Guy smiled coyly. "Shall we go there?"

*

The morning following the party, I feel self-conscious and don't know how to react, but everyone I run into is so casual and friendly—like we are old mates—in no time my shyness disappears. For the next few weeks Luca and I become caught up in some kind of tropical erotic fantasy. We plan our days and nights around sex: on the pyramid mound, in the jungle, on the beach, in just about every imaginable place and with every imaginable combination of men. We are the new boys in town: a curiosity, outsiders to this small community, no real threat to anyone, and therefore of interest to almost everyone. Since we can't speak their language, we let our dicks do the talking, at first gorging ourselves on the most beautiful men, like Den the ebony-skinned angel and Lalli, who looks like Michelangelo's *David*.

Living arrangements are quite casual, and men pretty much seem to stay wherever and with whomever they want, provided they are welcome. I feel welcome with Nando, so I stay put. Actually, maybe I'm falling for him, even though he seems to be the one man on the whole island who won't have sex with me. Meanwhile, Luca moves in with Kizo the Giant. In that silly old battered Spanish conquistador helmet and breastplate he always wears to ceremonies, Kizo looks kind of like a very big, little boy playing pirate or superhero. Maybe it's the contradiction between his imposing physical strength and his sweet nature that excites Luca. At first, I'm a little jealous, but try as I might to the contrary, I can't help liking Kizo too.

Pico, the skinny, spidery man who helped deliver me home after my welcoming ceremony, is a constant presence at Nando's—popping in suddenly, staying for as long as he pleases, and darting off just as suddenly. I figure he's either Nando's brother or best friend. They don't seem to distinguish much between the two, and even when I ask, I don't get a straight answer.

Of course, life on the island is more than one grand sex orgy, and the daily routine has a funny way of making everything, no matter how exotic or unusual, seem normal. For the most part, the pace is slow and rhythmic, like a delicate Caribbean breeze, and the land and sea provide all that's needed. However, collecting nature's abundant gifts requires hours of manual labor, and it's not long before Luca and I start going out fishing with Kizo and Pico every morning.

It's still a good hour before dawn. Nando is up stoking the fire, making fresh corn cakes, and brewing coffee by the time Pico and I flop out of our hammocks. We wander out to the front veranda, yawning and scratching our bums. Nando smiles and passes me a gourd full of hot coffee. Then with his fingertips he gingerly picks a corn cake off the flat roasting rock and hands it to me.

"Watch. It is hot."

I lightly toss it up and down until it's cool enough to eat. Pico leans over and spears a roasting cake with a stick, holds it to his mouth, and blows on it.

I pop a piece of corn cake into my mouth, chew a couple of times, and speak with my mouth half-full. "When are you going to come out fishing with us?"

"I told you. I must stay and mind the children." Nando looks a little irritated.

"I know," I say. "It's just that it would be more fun if you came along." I cringe a little, hoping I haven't revealed my growing feelings too much.

"I cannot, but if you bring home a big fish, I will forgive you for abandoning me." Nando smirks and winks.

Pico grabs hold of my elbow and pulls me toward the steps. "It's a deal." I down my coffee and hand the empty gourd to Nando.

"Wait! Don't forget your hat and sun cream."

I wriggle my arm from Pico's grip as Nando passes me a shallow basket and a coconut shell filled with a greasy white compound. Pico and I hurry down the steps and along the trail.

By the time we reach the beach, the men are already gathered, preparing their nets, yawning, and discussing the day's strategies. Kizo and Luca are waiting with the canoe in the water—net, hooks, and spears ready. "Hurry, hurry. We can't trade old fish for new potatoes," Kizo calls.

Luca holds the canoe steady as Pico jumps in the bow and I climb in the center facing the stern. Luca gets in beside me. Kizo gives the boat a strong shove, hops into the stern, and paddles us out toward the reef.

As we glide out of the sandy bay and into deeper water, I gaze back at the dark silhouette of the hills. Halfway up, I spot a procession of torches, like a giant glowing centipede. I can just hear singing over the sound of the surf, and I smile. It must be the women heading up to their plantations. At first, I think it strange that Luca and I haven't met any of the women, but by now it's quite clear that there is a distinct separation between the men's world and the women's.

I turn and look ahead toward the reef and the melon-stained horizon. With every undulation of the sea, the morning becomes a little brighter. Soon the blistering sun will climb into the sky and beat down on my delicate skin. I take the coconut shell filled with a concoction of coconut butter, white clay, aloe, and herbs Nando prepared for me. Precariously balanced in the center of our tippy dugout canoe, I twist and shift as I spread greasy cream over even the tiniest piece of exposed skin.

"You look like a big mayonnaise sandwich." Luca scoops out some cream and spreads it on my back. My skin tingles under his strong, gentle touch.

"Better a sandwich than burned toast," I say as I fasten my basket on my head with a string tied under my chin.

Now, covered white, tip to end, with a basket tied to my head, I'm ready to greet the sun. I look at the other three, majestically posed in the canoe, the early morning light caressing their half-naked, tanned bodies, and I feel like a white toad sitting amongst gods.

Kizo paddles us out to our usual spot at a break in the reef. While he fishtails his broad paddle to steady the canoe, Luca stands straddling the gunwale and gathers the net in pleats. Then with a smooth sweeping gesture, he flings it out into the air. I watch it spread like the wings of a butterfly and settle flat on the surface of the water, making a gentle splatter. The weights pull one side of the net down while the row of corks tied to the other side bob on the surface, and the net floats into place like a curtain. Kizo maneuvers the canoe away from the net, and all we have to do is wait for fish. Pico hangs over the bow, playing with his fingers in the water and singing a little song to himself, while Luca and I lean against each other and doze with the gentle rocking waves.

After an hour or so, Kizo senses the time is right and paddles close to the floating net. While Kizo steadies the canoe, Luca grabs the leads and straddles the gunwales. Then he pulls the net closed like a giant purse and hauls in our catch: yellow jack this time. As he hauls, Pico and I grab the slippery fish behind their gills, trying to avoid getting stuck by their dorsal spines as we untangle them and toss them into a couple of large baskets before they can wriggle from our hands back into the water.

By late morning, we have filled our baskets with yellow jack, and we return to the bay along with the other canoes of men who have also been fishing out on the reef. Kizo beaches the canoe, and while he and Luca spread out the nets along the sand and carefully check for and repair any tears, Pico and I haul the baskets of fish up to a shady spot under a coconut tree. We plunk down on the sand and with our fishing knives—which are really obsidian blades hafted into a wooden grip—we gut and scale the fish. By now the sun is sitting high in the sky and the air is heavy and humid. The men wander away from the beach back to their cottages a few at a time, carrying their baskets filled with cleaned fish.

Once we have secured our boat, hung our nets up to dry, and cleaned all our fish, Pico and Kizo cart the baskets to the village. Meanwhile, Luca and I steal off to a little spot on top of the cliff overlooking the bay where the fishing boats are beached, to enjoy the breeze from the sea.

Luca is my only connection to the outside world, and I'm his. Actually, he's more than that. He's the first man in my life with whom I feel I can share my secrets, fears, and desires. In a sense, he's the first man I've ever talked to, I mean really talked to. And once I get started, I can't stop. I talk his ear off like a born-again Christian who has discovered the path to paradise and wants to share the road map, and I tell him every mundane detail of my boring life.

"You know, one Sunday when I was thirteen, I told my folks I had too much homework to do so I couldn't go to church. I stayed home and spent the whole morning wanking."

"Back at St. Mike's Boy's School, I held the wanking record, ten times in six hours."

"Wow." I look out at the thin white line where waves break against the barrier reef and think of how far away Canada is. Then I lie back on the flat rock next to where Luca is sprawled. "I never imagined there could be a place like this," I say as I stare up at the cloudless powder blue sky. "A place where sex is so free and open. It's like paradise."

Luca's expression becomes somber. "Let me tell you a little secret about how the world works, Kiddo. Long time ago, back at St. Mike's, I quickly figured out that I needed something from them, and they wanted something from me. So, I played along as best as I could and put out when they wanted me to. In exchange, I got a roof over my head, food in my belly, and an education. Maybe this place feels like paradise, but underneath it all it's no different than any other place."

"Luca," I say in a serious tone, "what really happened at St. Mike's?"

"Not a lot I want to remember and less I want to tell you about. I walked out of that hellhole and never looked back," Luca says sternly. Then his voice softens. "I miss the other boys. They were all the family I've ever had." He props himself up on his elbows and looks at the horizon as if he is studying it.

I run my eyes along his body. He looks just like a superhero without a costume.

He turns his head, smiles, and rolls over, resting his chin on my chest. "Hey, but now I've got you, Kiddo. Right?"

I lift my head and look at him. "Just like Batman and Robin?"

"As long as I get to be Batman." Luca laughs.

Everyone in the village assumes Luca and I are brothers—the brother I've never had. Right now, I need a brother more than I need a lover. Maybe Luca does too. But my feelings for him are something more than brotherly.

"Where do you think we are?" I say, tossing a stone off the edge of the cliff and watching it arc downward and plunk into the sea below.

"Marooned on a tropical island, assumed dead," Luca says as he sits up and leans backward on his outstretched arms.

"No, no I mean, where do you think this island is?"

"Don't have the slightest idea. Somewhere off the coast of Cuba, I think. I've asked Kizo and the others, but nobody's talking." Luca's voice and face indicate he's read too many detective stories as a boy.

"You don't think they're hiding something, trying to keep us here, do you?" The idea both frightens and excites me.

"We come across all these people living here on this island and they hardly have any contact with the outside world. You've got to admit, that's a little strange."

"They certainly seem honest and open." Now I sound like one of those naïve women in the detective comics who are just about to fall prey to the evil villain. "They don't act like they're trying to hide anything."

"Did you notice the amount of gold these boys wear? They even use it for fishing lures and net sinkers. Where do you suppose they got all that gold from?" Luca says, almost whispering.

"How would I know? Maybe they brought it with them or found it or something." Now I sound like a country bumpkin who wouldn't know gold from tin, and it's true.

"Or something. Try to find out and let me know. We might be able to go back rich." Luca's tone slips from detective to scheming villain.

"What? You're planning to rip them off?"

"Come on." Luca cops a dirty grin. "Maybe we can trade for some of it."

"With what, sex?" Now I have the rare chance to belittle Luca, and I plunge in my dagger. "Your tongue has already been over every square inch of this island."

Luca looks at me with an exaggerated expression of tedium. "Thanks for bringing our conversation back to sex. Maybe we could focus on our big problem: how to get off this rock." He swings around and faces me, cross-legged. "We've got to do something to get back home," he says, almost pleading.

"Home? We just got here," I say with a touch of whine in my voice.

"Yes, home," he says sternly.

"Neither one of us has much of a home to go back to. Remember, there'll be a court hearing about the *Crescent Moon*, and you'll probably face charges. Have you thought about that?"

"How bad can prison be? No worse than St. Mike's. But right now, I don't care. We can't stay here."

I stare out beyond the reef to the empty horizon. I feel no melancholy for what I've left behind.

"Look, Kiddo," Luca says, "you've got to finish your little adventure, go back, and start your life. Get married, have children, buy a home. We certainly can't spend the rest of our lives here playing hide the weenie on the beach."

"I don't want a wife or children or any of that shit, and I don't believe you do either. For the first time in my life, here on this island, I'm happy." I clear my throat loudly and spit over the edge.

Luca is silent for a few minutes. Then he begins in a slow and persuasive tone. "Listen, all the boys played with one another at St. Mike's. It doesn't mean anything—really."

I wonder who Luca is trying to convince—me or himself. "Well, it means something to me, and I think it does to you too."

Luca leans forward, puts his hands on my shoulders, and looks directly into my eyes. "When they find us, you can stay if you want. What about Nando? You two seem to be getting awfully cozy together."

I break his stare and blush. "Ha! Nando thinks I'm a house pet, not a man. Every time I try to touch him, he slides away. Maybe the guy's frigid or something? No, forget I just said that."

"Maybe he's just shy." Luca grins at me.

"Yeah, right. I don't even think they have a word for shy!"

"Well, maybe he doesn't want to do it with the biggest whore on the island." He hangs his mouth open and beams one of his superb smiles straight into my heart. I hate that he can manipulate me, but I crave it all the same.

"Oh, look who's calling who a whore!" I say, trying to protect myself with a vain show of ambivalence. "How many did you do in the hammock last night?"

"Four, but you're only a whore if you take it up the ass, and unlike you, I never take it up the ass!" He sticks out the tip of his tongue at me.

"Who told you that shit?" I spit out with as much contempt as I can feign.

Luca, as always, knows he has me and goes in for the kill. "Everybody knows that, and that makes you a whore. Me, I'm just a pig. Hey! Most men are pigs." Luca swivels back around and stretches the full length of the rock with his hands serving as a pillow behind his head.

I think about how he saved my life on the *Crescent Moon*. I picture him lying in the lifeboat when we were at sea—the first time I touched him. I lap up his beauty and confidence and wish I were more like him. "Enough, enough." I wave my hands. "What do I have to do?"

Luca gets up on his haunches. "We've got to keep a constant watch out for a ship or plane or smoke on the horizon. This spot's a good one." He sweeps his hand in an arc. "Build a signal fire and always keep it smoldering. You're going to have to build a lean-to to protect it from the wind and rain. Get some of the boys to help you if you can stop fucking long enough."

"Come on."

"No, I'm serious. You've got to keep regular lookouts and be prepared. You understand me, right?" He continues to gesture emphatically.

"I understand you." I hunch submissively. "I said I would help. What are you going to do?"

"I've already explored this side of the island, and I haven't seen a damn thing. I'm going to head off to the far side. Maybe I can see something from there. At least we'll know if this really is an island or not. I'll be gone about three weeks."

"What happens if you get into trouble or something?"

"Kizo will tag along."

"That's 'cause he's in love with you."

Luca looks away and speaks, almost whispering. "I'm not the sort of man anyone should fall in love with."

"Why would you say that?"

Luca is silent for a moment, and then he turns and faces me. His face is hard. "Don't worry about me. Just make sure you're prepared." He gets to his feet and starts down the little path. "See you in a few, Kiddo," he says, but he doesn't make eye contact.

I turn and stare out to sea. My whole life, from my little village to university, I've been searching for somewhere I belonged. And finally, I might have found just such a place. I don't know what the future will bring, but for now if my luck holds, we won't see a ship or plane anytime soon. Then I shiver, thinking about Luca and the gold. I didn't need to study anthropology to know what happens to a native population after they have been "discovered," especially if they have anything of value. If these people do, in fact, have a stash of gold, our rescue might very well be their demise. And I would be responsible—their angel of death.

*

Guy spread his arms wide, stretched them over his head, and yawned loudly. Still yawning, he said, "In the Garden of Eden, it takes a little more work to feed yourself than just picking an apple off a tree. Besides, apples don't grow in the tropics, and who wants to eat apples all the time, anyway?"

Richard nodded. "And so, you found your gay paradise, but you're faced with a dilemma. Luca wants to leave, even though he knows he will pay a price if he does. There'd certainly be an inquiry into the death of the captain and crew. And then there's Guy, the weaker of the two, who wants to stay within the fantasy where he feels safe and not return to reality."

"Yep," Guy said. "That pretty much sums up the story so far."

"Apart from the story line, I'm more concerned about how this describes you. Part of you is unwilling to leave the safety of this fantasy, and part of you recognizes that even though reality has consequences, at some point you must leave the fantasy behind."

"The island feels like it's drifting farther away, and time is running out."

"And you're afraid of living without it?"

"Precisely." Guy chewed his lip. "Without it, what would I call home? Where would I be safe?" Guy pushed himself forward and planted his feet.

"We still have a few minutes left. And you haven't told me what the other two principles of lying are."

"That's easy." Guy rose to his feet. "Number three, space is your easiest alibi, but time will always give you away."

Richard swiveled around in his chair and watched as Guy moved toward the door. "And the fourth principle?"

"It doesn't really matter if other people believe your lie. It's only important that you do." Guy paused for a moment in the doorway and glanced back at Richard. "Ask yourself, Doc, how many of those principles do you use?"

Guy walked down the corridor half whispering, half singing the words to the Y.M.C.A. song.

Chapter Eight

Where is this Place?

Guy sat down on the sofa and stretched out his legs. "A while back, almost twenty years ago, I guess, I did a psychological assessment. It was part of one of my rehab programs."

"And how were you assessed?" Richard said as he got up from his desk and moved over to the swivel chair.

"Well, I did all kinds of little tasks and answered questionnaires. I don't really remember the details except for one task they asked me to do."

"What was that?" Richard took a sip of his cappuccino.

"They gave me a pile of magazines. I was told to imagine what my life was about, then quickly leaf through the magazines and tear out any pictures I thought were representative and arrange and paste them on a large sheet of paper. It was supposed to be my personal story."

Richard nodded. "And did this technique help you to visualize your story a little better?"

"That's the thing, Doc. I still have the stupid collage. Here, I brought it for you to look at." Guy dug in his pocket and pulled out a large, crinkly sheet of paper. He unfolded and smoothed it on his lap, then passed it to Richard. "What do you think?"

"Fish?" Richard said with a tone of surprise. "Pictures of fish?"

"Yeah, and don't miss the can of tuna down here. That represents me. You know, canned fish."

Richard studied the collage carefully. "And why did you choose fish?"

"Because I like fish."

"Obviously you do." Richard smiled. "And what was your story?"

"Fish are swimming all around me, but I'm trapped in a can."

Richard examined the picture again and furrowed his brow. "That's it?"

"Yep, that's it."

"Curious." Richard continued to study the collage.

Guy gazed at the wall and began to tell his story.

*

I keep my promise to Luca. First thing each morning and last thing each evening, I climb the trail up the cliff with some heavy logs from the beach and throw them onto the smoldering coals of the signal fire. So far we haven't had much nasty weather, but Nando, Pico, and I construct a thatch lean-to to protect the fire from wind and rain, just in case. I pass each long, lonely evening sitting at the signal fire, staring out to sea looking for a passing ship or airplane, and praying for Luca's safe return.

When I'm not tending the signal fire, I'm either down at the seaside with Pico, who is teaching me how to catch crabs, or up in the village with Nando, who is trying to teach me their language. It's nothing like English, French, or Spanish, and I don't have the benefit of a textbook, so I struggle through the best I can. Overall, my progress is slow and painful for me and everyone around me. Luckily Nando is a very patient teacher, and quite a few people seem to know a little Spanish, which leads me to believe they must have some contact with the outside world. Pico, on the other hand, never says more than one or two words at a time, but he always listens.

"Yes, if you say it that way, with the long sound, it means a woman fish with eggs." Nando splays open the fish he is cleaning for dinner and scoops out the red roe in its belly. "But if you make the sound short, it means all fish in general, because it is a man's word."

"How can fish be masculine then change to feminine when they have eggs?"

"Not the fish. The word!"

"I'm never going to get it." I reach over and steal a bit of roe and pop it into my mouth.

On my second pass, Nando slaps my hand away. "Sure, just remember, men do the fishing, so fish is a man's word, and women grow the potatoes, so potato is a woman's word."

"Okay, now, if I understand you correctly, there are only two time periods." I try to clean some fish roe out from between my cheek and teeth with my tongue.

"Right. It is the same for something yesterday or today because they are both real."

"So if I say today is a nice day or yesterday is a nice day, I use the same form." I glance over at the fish.

"Yes, you just tell when it happens." Nando waves his bamboo knife. "Stay away from my fish until I have cooked it."

"And if I want to say tomorrow will be a nice day, I use the other form—the imaginary one—because it hasn't happened yet, right?"

"Now you understand." He scoops some roe with his index and middle finger and holds it up to my mouth.

"I guess that makes sense if you think about it." I open wide and lick his fingers clean.

"Of course, it does. It's very easy."

"And if I want to tell someone that I think I'm falling in love with him?" I stare deeply into Nando's eyes.

He pauses for a moment, then turns his head away. "It depends if that love is real or a fantasy."

I drop my head. "I'm never going to get it."

That evening as I sit alone tending the signal fire on the cliff, strange sounds and words float around inside my head. As anyone who has endured a language immersion program can testify, speaking in your own tongue with a fellow native speaker is like the cigarette you sneak out for when you know you are supposed to be at your desk studying or the beer you and your best friend share when you cut class and hide out down at the railway tracks. Luca is my cigarette and my stolen beer. It's been almost a moon now since Luca has been away with Kizo exploring the far side of the island. I dearly miss talking good old American slang with him, but mostly I miss just being with him. I stare out at the horizon and whisper, "Come home soon, Boy Scout."

Late the next evening, Nando and I are sitting outside the cottage on the platform watching the sinking sun stain the horizon the color of a ripe mango. Great numbers of white cattle egrets squawk and fuss in the treetops beyond the silhouette of the pyramid mound.

"Where is this place? How did people get here?" I say as I spread my arms and sweep them back and forth in the air.

Nando's face seems to glow, and he gazes far off, as if he can see something in the sky beyond the trees. "It was long ago," he says, speaking slowly and delicately, drawing his words from somewhere deep inside—like he's telling a story that has been told to him many times before. "So long ago that no one knows when we first came here from the great cities far away. At that time the Daughter of the Moon had left her home in the wetlands to join with Feathered Serpent, the ruler of the drylands in the north. She traveled by seafaring canoes with fifty-two of her divine sisters. The canoes were paddled by fifty-two of the strongest, most beautiful men who, although common men, had forsaken the touch of women and given themselves only to the service of the Moon."

Nando pauses. I study his face as he continues to stare upward, as if in a trance. I shift a little, and he goes on with his story.

"Two weeks out at sea the grand party is lost. Then they came across a large band of smaller war canoes.

These were the Island people who had made many raids along the coastal towns of the wetlands. The Island people immediately recognized the Daughter of the Moon and offered her and her party safe passage. Since they were low on fresh water and had lost their bearings, the Daughter of the Moon accepted the hospitality of the Island people."

"Probably not the wisest thing to do," I say.

Nando shakes his head slowly, then continues, "The Island people led the sea canoes to their island, where they fell upon the Daughter of the Moon and her party, slitting many of the men's throats and taking the women prisoner. That night, as the Island people feasted, the full moon suddenly disappeared and everything became dark."

Nando smiles and sniffs. "The Island people fell to their knees, fearing they had stolen the moon from the sky. That's when, in the cover of darkness, the Daughter of the Moon and her surviving sisters fled from the village and escaped in one of her canoes. When the moon appeared once again, the chief saw that he had been deceived. He swore to recapture the Daughter of the Moon and set out after her."

Nando breathes in deeply and continues. "The Daughter of the Moon's great canoe was faster than the smaller Island canoes in open sea, but it was overloaded. Closer and closer, the Island canoes came. At that moment, just as they feared the Island people would catch up with them and they would all perish, a strange curtain of fog appeared."

I lie back on the patio floor with my head resting on my hand and gaze up at the darkening dome. The sun has dipped below the horizon, draining the sky of its yellows and oranges. Purple shadows from the great pyramid mound and forest are creeping across the plaza toward us. A chorus of frogs serenades the incoming tide of darkness.

Nando lies beside me and continues to stare upward, as if he is reading a text written in the heavens. "The Daughter of the Moon and her canoe slipped into the thick fog where they were hidden from the Island people. They had escaped but were lost with many wounded, and they still did not have any fresh water or food. Then a small patch of clear sky with three bright stars appeared ahead of them to guide them through the darkness."

"Wait a minute!" I jerk my head up. "That sounds like what happened to us just before our ship sank."

Nando rolls his head toward me and smiles. "Of course, it is." He looks back toward the sky and continues his tale. "By dawn, the canoe emerged from the fog, and there, shimmering in the morning light, the people saw the most beautiful islands they had ever seen. They knew that these three islands were actually the three stars that had seen the Daughter of the Moon in peril and laid themselves down on the sea. 'This is where we shall live, on the Islands of the Stars,' said the Daughter of the Moon."

Nando pauses and sniffs again, then he rolls his head toward me, looks directly into my eyes, and says, "And that is how we came to this place."

The shadow of the pyramid mound has now engulfed the plaza, scaled the steps, and crept across the terrace, leaving the two of us blanketed in darkness. I gaze back at Nando, my heart pounding in my chest. I say nothing, not wanting to break his spell. Here I am, marooned on the Islands of the Stars—held prisoner by Nando's brown eyes.

*

Guy continued to stare at the far wall then breathed in deeply and yawned and stretched. "We are strange creatures, indeed." Guy looked directly at Richard. "We spend our lives trying to get close to one another, but for most of us, sex is as close as we ever get."

Richard held Guy's stare. "And who are you close to?"

Guy's mouth hardened, and he blinked rapidly, his eyes watery. "No one." He stretched his neck and swallowed. "Doc, since the future doesn't exist yet, a promise like 'I will always love you' has no meaning at all."

"It expresses how you feel at the time and the desire for that feeling to last forever, don't you think?"

"Yeah, but forever comes with an expiry date."

Richard rested his chin on his knuckles. "As does everything in life."

Guy forced a melancholic smile. "As does life." He got up from the sofa and walked toward the door. Then he stopped and turned back to Richard. "Doc, do you think truth also comes with an expiry date?"

"What do you mean?"

"You're thirty-two years old. You don't get a second chance to be young." His expression was compassionate, and his tone was fatherly. "Isn't it about time you stopped trying to live up to everyone else's expectations and started living your own truth?" Without waiting for a response, Guy turned and left.

Chapter Nine

The Birds and the Bees

Guy burst into the office. "Yep, it's right there in the anthropology textbooks. The nuclear family is the basic human social unit—just Dad, Mom, and the kids. Ridiculous!"

Richard, who was looking out the window, swiveled around in his desk chair and gave Guy a forced smile that seemed to say both *hello* and *Here we go again.*

Guy lowered the volume of his voice and continued as he claimed his usual place on the sofa. "Even within our society, families are highly fluid: single parents, gay parents, collectives, divorce, adoption, and remarriages. We pretty much fuck who we can, and everything else are variations in the game, full stop."

"So why does some out-of-date textbook have you so agitated this morning?"

"Because they expect me to teach that heterocentric, hegemonic crap!"

"Mr. Palmer." Richard spoke with a slight tone of condescension as he got up and moved over to the swivel chair. "Correct me if I'm wrong, but isn't it your job as an anthropologist to present people with new tools and concepts so that they can think differently?"

"I'm just sick and tired of narrow-mindedness." Guy spit out the words.

"I'm sure you are more than capable of giving a lecture about changes to the concept of the family. Or do you prefer to teach only to the converted?"

Guy clamped his jaw. Then he curled his lip and sneered at Richard. "You know, Doc, I hate it when you're right."

Richard had a rather smug look on his face.

Then with a complete shift in tone, Guy said, "Okay. Enough of this crap. I want to talk about something else instead." And he went on with his story.

*

The following afternoon is hot, with hardly a breeze. All I can think about is a drink of cool water and a nap as I stagger up the terrace steps to our cottage loaded with a large basket of potatoes, a feather headdress, and a couple of yards of beads. "Hey, guys, look what this sweet old lady gave me," I call through the doorway.

Pico watches me as I enter with my bounty.

"Oh no!" Nando slaps his forehead. "What old woman? What did you say to her?"

"Nothing. You know, the old woman with the diamond-shaped tattoo on her forehead."

"Rurlu?" Nando looks at Pico. Pico nods.

"I met her by accident along the path, and she insisted that I take this stuff from her."

"That was no accident. Did you promise her anything in return?"

"No, nothing. She just kept repeating the word *gosha*, over and over again."

Pico begins to laugh.

"It's worse than I thought." Nando buries his face in his hands.

"What? Did I do something wrong?"

"Just pile it over there in the corner." Nando sighs.

"What did I do?"

"You just made an agreement for your juice." Nando shakes his head back and forth. "*Gosha* means juice."

"What kind of juice?" I furrow my brow. "Coconut juice? Orange juice?"

"Not that kind of juice."

Pico has a silly expression on his face. He clasps his crotch and jostles it and laughs loudly.

"No!" I hang my mouth open. "You don't mean—?"

"Yes." Nando inhales deeply. "I will take it all back tomorrow. I will explain that you have gone dry and cannot give juice. But from now on"—Nando holds his finger in the air—"when you see Rurlu, just run and hide in the forest or swim out to sea."

"But there are sharks out at sea!"

"Trust me." Nando rolls his eyes. "You are much safer with the sharks."

"Okay, okay. But I still don't understand what I did wrong."

"Don't worry." Nando reaches out and wraps me in his arms. Pico jumps over and joins in. "Tonight, there is a telling for the Planting Moon, and after you will understand better."

"Will your sister be there?" Nando has told me his sister is a very knowledgeable woman. Maybe she knows more about where the island is in relation to Cuba or some other populated place?

"The whole village will be there," Nando says enthusiastically. "The Planting Moon is a very important ceremony for both men and women."

That night, the moon is full. Nando leads me partway up the pyramid mound steps to the first platform and through a passageway to the women's side. The women's side is almost a mirror image of the men's, with a large plaza flanked by long terraced mounds with cottages on top. Like the men's village, the cottages are stucco white and painted with green-and-red bands along the walls. Instead of fish symbols like the ones painted on the walls on the men's side, oblique circular designs are painted on the walls on the woman's side.

"What do the circles mean?" I slowly trace my finger around one of the designs.

"Oh, those are potatoes. It is the symbol for vagina," Nando says.

I pull my tracing finger back sharply.

The plaza is lit with torches, and shadows jump off the walls around us. The women are already sitting in a coiled circle formation in the center of the plaza. We join the men and flop down on the back terrace facing the pyramid mound.

"Man, some of those women look strong," I whisper to Nando and jab my chin in their direction.

"Be careful. Don't point or stare. It is a sign of disrespect," he whispers back. "The women are seated in order from the strongest on the outside to the elders in the center," he continues in a low voice. "Of course, women with a child in their belly sit within the protective circle." Nando nods covertly toward a robust elderly woman with short brown hair, wearing a grass skirt and layers of wooden beads around her neck. "She is my sister, Kyle, the Big Woman of the village." For a microsecond, her eyes catch sight of him, and she smiles and winks.

"So, she is like the chief of the village?" I ask.

"I guess you could say that."

"Was she elected, or did she inherit the title?"

"No, nothing like that." Nando shakes his head. "She works very hard to prove she is always fair and just and wise. She is very well respected, and everybody agrees she is the best person to guide us in times of trouble. So she is the Big Woman of the village." Nando smiles.

"Kyle?" I say. "It sounds like an American name."

"It means Thunder Storm."

"Why do they call her that?"

"Because she sounds like a thunderstorm when she has an orgasm."

I start to giggle. Nando furrows his brow at me. I blush and try to regain my composure.

"And the small dark-haired woman holding her from behind?"

The small woman suddenly notices us looking and shoots us a venomous glare.

Nando quickly drops his head, and I follow his lead. "That's her mate, Dzil," he says out of the corner of his mouth like an amateur ventriloquist. "She does not like you because you come from the outside. Be careful of her. She is very fierce."

I shiver. Now I know how Dorothy must have felt when she met the Wicked Witch of the West.

"Why are they sitting in the center? Are they expecting a baby?"

"No, my sister is too old to have children, but she is an elder of the house of the Moon. Dzil is still without child, but she assumes a position of status because she is my sister's lover."

"I understand." I nod. "Hey, so that means you are also part of the local elite," I say half-impressed, half-teasing.

"All men belong to the houses of their mothers, not their fathers, and so a man's sister is very important."

Ahh, I think, classic matrilineal descent.

"I belong to the houses of the Moon and the Morning Star. They are good houses."

I'm just about to ask Nando why he claims he belongs to two matrilineal kin groups, when suddenly the women begin making an ear-piercing trill with their tongues oscillating back and forth. All conversation stops. Those men who are still milling around take a seat wherever they are standing. The torches are extinguished, and we sit in darkness. Then, one by one, young people dressed in white, carrying torches, appear from behind the various terraces of the pyramid mound—women from the right, men from the left—lighting it like a stage.

Kyle unwraps herself from Dzil's clutches and makes her way through the crowd to the steps of the great mound, then slowly climbs halfway up and sits down with her feet hanging over the edge of the terrace platform.

Nando leans in closer, his lips inches from my ear. "Now the great story begins."

I smell the spicy odor of his body and feel his warm breath tickle my ear. My head spins, and I begin to sweat. "I'm not sure I'll understand it very well," I say in a hush.

"Do not worry. I will make a translation for you."

The wailing women fall silent, and Kyle begins to speak. "Our island home provides us with everything we could need or want: fresh water to drink, plants to eat and make medicine, strong trees to build houses and fishing canoes, hemp to make ropes and cloth, and an abundance of fish from the sea."

Just then, I feel Lalli's familiar touch on the back of my neck as he slides in close to me and sits down. I look up and smile. Out of the corner of my eye, I catch Nando watching us with a strange expression. Aha! Maybe he's jealous of Lalli? I finally have a reaction from him.

Kyle stands and raises her arms, her voice echoing above the sound of people mumbling and shifting in their seats and babies fussing. "Nine moons after their arrival, the Daughter of the Moon and the women who had been violated by the Island people gave birth. Tara, the warrior, held out her newborn child by the foot and cried, 'Let us take our revenge upon the Island people and spill the blood of their children on our soil.'"

A low growling sound fills the plaza. Everyone around me is baring their teeth and waving their fists in the air. Kyle continues. "But the Daughter of the Moon spoke and said, 'This is how we shall take revenge for our sorrow. Our tears shall become our joy.' She took the child and placed it against her breast, where it fed. And the other women obeyed."

A baby starts to cry on the far side. Some people laugh lightly, and his mother stands up and bounces him in her arms. Kyle looks across the plaza and smiles. Suddenly Dzil lets out an enormous wail. She throws herself onto the ground as if she has been mortally wounded, and everyone's eyes turn from Kyle toward her. Women cluster around her and lift her back to her feet and hold her while she sobs loudly and flails her arms.

I lean over toward Nando. "What's wrong with her?"

He puts his lips to my ear and says, "Dzil is very skilled at expressing her ideas."

Kyle waits until Dzil has calmed down, then goes on. "Tara would not listen to the Daughter of the Moon. 'We shall take our revenge on all men,' she cried."

"No! No!" Little Lisha yells, and everyone around her joins in, yelling and pounding their feet on the ground.

With her hands spread wide, Kyle pushes against the air to signal for calm. People make hushing sounds, and the crowd quiets. In a strong, reassuring voice, Kyle says,

"The Daughter of the Moon spoke to the people, saying, 'No man shall violate woman. And women shall join with women and men with men to celebrate the gift of fertility and life.'"

The crowd breaks into wild cheers. Babies crying, woman yodeling, and men whooping and stomping their feet.

Kyle takes a burning torch, holds it in the air, and proclaims loudly above the noise, "And this is the law, as spoken by the Daughter of the Moon." She pauses. "And this is the law by which we live." Kyle turns and disappears behind the pyramid mound, and the torchbearers follow.

Everybody continues to whistle and yodel and whoop and stomp. Men embrace men and women embrace women. I stand up with Lalli and Nando. Lalli grabs me and hugs me. I pull Nando in tightly, and he buries his wet face against my neck and shoulder. My skin tingles with goose bumps.

Little by little the noise subsides, and eventually everyone falls quiet with only the crackle of burning torches and the squeals of fussing babies to disturb the stillness of the night.

I sit expectantly, waiting for something else to happen, something to break the stillness. Nothing does. After an hour or more, people rise, one by one or in little groups, and wander off. Lalli kisses my neck, and Nando immediately nudges my elbow and says, "It is time to go home." Lalli disappears through the passageway to the men's side of the village, and Nando and I follow. I feel like a child who has just been told the facts of life, and now I have more questions than answers.

The following afternoon, Pico and I are lounging on the sand patch at the bathing pool under the large breadfruit tree. Pico is sound asleep, using my thigh as his pillow, and I have an old coconut husk propped under my head. I watch as spots of sunlight poke through the canopy and tickle the surface of the water.

"C'mon, Pico." I jostle his head. "The tide should be out. Let's go and see if we can find some crabs and clams for dinner."

Before I can push myself upright, Pico is wide-awake and has sprung to his feet. I stand, stretch, and brush off the sand. Then I hold Pico by his shoulder with my one hand and brush off the sand clinging to his backside with my other. I slap his ass lightly, and we trot down the trail to the tidal pools near the cliff.

The sea is like a mirror, and the tide is almost at its lowest, exposing a world below the waterline that is usually hidden. Craggy rocks jut upward, covered with soft orange corals and green algae, glistening in the sunlight. Gurgling pools are filled with barnacles, clams, and small fish, marooned there until the sea returns. Crabs, like last-minute shoppers, scurry everywhere. As we wind our way along the patches of saturated sand, clams squirt and click.

Pico darts ahead and catches a large, blue-clawed crab. He holds it up by its claw for me to see. I throw him a thumbs-up sign. In a tidal pool just beyond, I spot something floating and go to investigate. As I draw near, I make out a tiny boat about the size of a small cradle made of woven bamboo. I carefully wade into the pool, mindful of the array of spiny black urchins along the rock walls, pull the boat toward me, and look in. I gasp and jump back. There inside, covered with flies, is the wee wizened body of a newborn boy. I scramble back to the rocks and try not to vomit.

Pico appears, wades into the pool, and retrieves the boat. Then, as I steady myself against the rocks, my head still woozy, he climbs out of the pool with the boat in his arms and carries it over to the waterline.

"Wait. Pico! What are you doing? That's a dead baby," I cry.

Pico nods, places the boat in the water, and with a gentle push sends the tiny craft outward with the receding tidal current. We stand and watch as it drifts farther and farther out to sea.

"Let's go home, Pico. I've lost my appetite."

When we arrive back at the cottage, I immediately tell Nando about the dead baby in the little boat.

"Sometimes when a baby is born," Nando says softly, "he must be returned to the Moon."

"Why? What happened to him?"

"Yabai, don't ask me. I don't know." Nando looks to the ground and shakes his head. "Try to understand. This poor baby got trapped in the tidal pools, and Pico was just sending him home."

I look at him for a moment, trying to find words. Then I say, "I'm not hungry. I'm going to the lookout to tend the signal fire." And I leave the cottage.

*

Guy stopped talking.

After a moment, Richard broke the silence. "In your story, you are always very careful to separate men from women. Do you dislike women?"

"Ha!" Guy snorted. "On the contrary, I have enormous respect for women. It's just I find their brains more interesting than their sex organs. I wish I could always say the same about men."

"Well, so far it seems that the women are in control and do all the political stuff while the men are pretty much passive."

"Apart from fishing, the men do most of the medicine and magic. But let me ask you, if it were the other way around, with the men doing all the politics and women being mostly domestic and passive, would you even question it?"

"Hmm." Richard rubbed his chin. "Probably not. I guess it just shows you how deep our gender stereotypes run."

"Well, for one thing, there are not as many men as women on the island."

"Why's that?"

"Fishing, especially when they go outside the reef, is a lot more dangerous than planting potatoes."

"Do you think they also practice some kind of male infanticide? You did say you found a dead newborn boy floating near the shore."

Guy was pensive, then spoke slowly. "Every society regards males and females differently and has different ways of regulating birth. Usually male babies are valued more than female babies, but here on the island more women are needed for farming and birth than men for fishing and insemination." He breathed in deeply. "The liver of the puffer fish is highly toxic, causing paralysis and suffocation. I don't know if unwanted newborn males were sometimes 'put to sleep and returned,' but every child I saw was loved and wanted."

"You don't know or you don't want to know?"

"Not all truth is tolerable."

Richard sat thinking for a moment. "Everyone you've told me about so far is homosexual. So where are the heterosexuals?"

"The ones that are there remain in the shadows."

"But life really isn't like that, is it?"

"No, real life is mostly the other way around. The homosexuals remain hidden in the shadows."

"Not anymore," Richard scoffed. "Gay people are more and more visible all the time."

"Think about it for a moment," Guy snapped. "In real life, if being gay were completely visible and nothing more remarkable than, say, I take sugar in my coffee, the gay movement would fade away and you wouldn't still be in the closet."

"I'm not in the closet!" Richard sounded more defensive than sincere.

"Whatever." Guy whisked his hand like he was shooing a fly. "But thankfully they still need old queers like me to hate. It's all part of their game."

"Who is *they*?"

"Family, church, society."

"And why do they need someone like you to hate?"

"Because I'm the shadowy thing that goes bump in the night and scares children." Guy grinned wickedly. "I'm the demon that sends men burdened with guilt running to the doorsteps of their churches in search of salvation." He raised his finger in the air. "I'm the destroyer of morality and the family!" Guy paused for a moment and looked directly at Richard. "But most of all, I'm the monster in the mirror that you can't look away from."

Richard made no response. His face was professional and without expression.

"Whoa." Guy rubbed his hand across his forehead and feigned flinging away the sweat from his brow. "Nothing like a little dramatic relief to get your blood going first thing in the morning." He laughed.

Richard pursed his lips and furrowed his brow.

"Pretty good, huh? What do you think?"

Richard looked as if he were trying out a phrase in his head prior to giving it voice. Then he began to speak. "Buried inside your humor I hear a lot of pain and anger." Richard paused. "I think you need to consider why you feel so persecuted."

Guy curled his lip but said nothing.

Richard checked his watch. "Oh, it's past time. Next week, I want to talk more about your feelings of hostility toward heterosexuals."

As Guy stood up, a gentle tap came on the glass of the office door. Richard swiveled around in his chair and said, "Come in."

Armando carefully opened the door. "I hope I'm not interrupting."

"No, we ran a few minutes late this morning. Come in," Richard said.

"I have the file for your next appointment, Doctor."

"Oh, thank you. I was looking for it earlier."

Richard held out his hand and Armando handed him the file. He was no longer wearing his Padre Pio medallion.

Guy walked over to the door and paused. "How's your mom doing?"

Armando looked at Guy and smiled. "Better now, thanks. We were a little worried a week ago."

Richard furrowed his brow. "Your mom's not well?"

"She had pneumonia. That's why I took a few days off. Remember?"

"I'm sorry. I guess I forgot. If I can do anything, Armando, just let me know."

As Guy stepped out and quietly closed the door behind him, he heard Armando say, "Thanks, Doctor. I appreciate it. Should I send your next patient in?"

Chapter Ten

Luca Returns

Guy entered the studio without knocking. Richard was sitting at his desk reading his screen, freshly showered, hair blown dry, and the usual odor of chlorine in the room.

"How was your swim this morning?"

"Good, thanks," Richard said casually.

"You know, Doc," Guy said as he handed Richard his coffee and took his usual place on the sofa, "I have trouble understanding people. I feel like everyone mumbles."

"Have you had your hearing checked?"

"Yes, yes. My hearing's fine." Guy fumbled in his pocket, produced a crumpled Kleenex, and blew his nose. "I can hear what people are saying, but I can't gauge their sincerity or intent."

Richard came over and sat down on the swivel chair. "Are you really listening, or are you trying to read something else into what they are saying?"

Guy slouched back in the sofa. "It's like speaking to someone in one of those glass service-boxes with the microphones. You can see them, but you only ever get part of what they're saying and the rest you guess at—'put your ticket and your money in the sliding drawer.' The glass box people always have to point in order for you to understand what they really want you to do."

Richard nodded. "When you search too hard for hidden meaning and intent in everything people say, you miss the direct message."

"How can I connect with anybody if they only want to communicate superficially?"

"It takes time to develop trust and intimacy with someone." Richard paused. Then with a slight tone of suspicion, he said, "Are you referring to anyone in particular?"

"Yes. No, I mean people in general. Look at us, for instance. According to Bion, we are supposed to link minds. We are supposed to have intimacy and trust. But your words are insincere."

"We have a professional relationship with different roles. You're the one who is supposed to reveal his emotions to me." Richard shook his head. "It's not supposed to be reciprocal."

"But Doc, it already is." Guy spoke in a low tone. "I already know a lot about what you feel. Take that young nurse Armando, for example."

Richard's expression became flat, and he slowly sat back in his chair. "What about him?"

"Black wavy hair that touches his cheekbones, bright laughing brown eyes, and a waist that's long and lean. When he turns quickly, he exposes a small patch of dark hair just below his navel."

Richard had the expression of a man who had been caught peeking. He interlocked his fingers and drew his hands in close to his waist. His foot rocked ever so slightly.

"It's obvious you're attracted to him," Guy challenged.

Richard's face flushed, and he stiffened. "Now you have gone well beyond the boundaries of our professional relationship, Mr. Palmer."

"But I'm trying to explain something," Guy said, almost scolding. "Your words tell me one thing, but your body has already told me something else."

"Enough!" Richard clenched his hands as if he were trying to contain his anger. "Why are you so intent on probing into my sexuality?"

"Because…." Guy stopped. He wrinkled his brow, looked to the floor, and mumbled, "You're right, Doc. This is not about you." For a moment, he was silent. Then he looked up and, with a tone of renewed enthusiasm, said, "Let's talk about me instead."

*

It's late in the afternoon. I'm sitting, tending the signal fire when I finally spot Luca and Kizo in the distance beyond the bay. I sigh with relief. For more than an hour I watch them as they stumble along the rocky shore. When they reach the sand, they part, and Kizo heads along the trail that leads into the village. Luca looks to where I'm perched on the cliff and without a wave, continues up the rocky path toward me.

"Good to see you back in one piece," I say as he approaches, trying my best to restrain my joy even though

I'm having trouble taming my smile. "I was getting a little worried that I'd been abandoned in paradise or something."

"Relax, Mother." He meets my beaming face with a sneer. "I was only gone a moon."

I feel like he's just rammed a fist in my stomach, and the delight drains from my face. After a moment of silence, I try not to show my hurt feelings and say casually, "Did you see anything that might give us a clue?"

"Nope, no luck at all." He wipes his forehead with his forearm and flicks the drips of sweat over the edge of the cliff. "At least we know it's an island for sure—one big fucking round island. No other villages, no other inhabitants, just jungle and shoreline."

He throws down the bundle he has slung over his shoulder and collapses onto his flat rock, directly opposite mine. He's smeared with dirt and covered with numerous cuts, scratches, and bug bites. His shoulders are raw and scabby from sunburn, and he has definitely lost weight.

"The south side looks the same as this, only a bit rougher. From what I could make out, the smaller island over there to the west is similar to this one." He pauses and swallows; his lips are swollen and cracked. "There's not a single sign of anyone over there."

"Nando did say we are on one of three islands, called the Islands of the Stars. Did you find any garbage on the shore, anything that would tell us that at least there is someone out there?"

"Like what? A sign saying Cuba fifty miles this way?"

My stomach churns, and I taste acid in the back of my throat.

He looks at me for a moment and then softens his tone. "Nothing but jungle, rocks, sand, bush, and eelgrass." He falls silent and stares out at the darkening horizon.

"Well, that doesn't make sense, does it?" My voice becomes somewhat alto, and my hands are animated in a manner I always try to suppress. "I don't think there's any place on Earth that's not on a map. They must have some kind of contact with the outside world. I mean, it's not like we're living in the eighteenth century or we've dropped off the planet."

Luca continues staring out to sea. "Kizo tells me there's a far island out beyond the reef." He turns back toward me. His Adam's apple bobs as he swallows hard. "But he also says it's really dry and desolate and nobody goes there. Funny, it was like he didn't want to talk about it."

"Well, Nando speaks English," I say, using my most encouraging tone. "American English, and so do some of the others. Some of them speak Spanish too. They must have learned it somewhere from someone."

Luca's eyes become hard. "We're either missing something or we're not being told."

"Why do you keep saying they're hiding something from us?" I scowl.

Luca reaches into a fold in his waistcloth. He leans over onto one elbow and flicks something shiny toward me.

I catch it. "More gold?"

"Yeah, Spanish doubloon. Found it on one of the beaches."

I examine the coin. "I don't give a shit if they do have gold. I'm not about to steal from them." I place the coin on the rock beside me and pull a burning stick out of the signal fire. I fling the stick off the edge and watch it plummet down, end over end into the sea below.

"Calm down. Look, all I'm saying is there must be something more to this place than fishing and fucking. And we need to know."

"I guess you're right." I slump forward and rest my chin on my hands. "Nando said his father was American. I'm going to grill him a bit more and find out how his father got here and how he left."

Luca looks at me and bites the corner of his lip. "I can tell from your smoldering signal fire you didn't see anything." Then regaining a little of his usual vigor in his voice, he says, "Shit, sooner or later a ship's got to pass close enough, and we'll be ready."

His resilience touches me, and I shiver. How can I be angry with him? He needs me.

"I'm going to rest for a few days, then head up the volcano where I can get a better view." Luca points to the volcano looming overhead.

"Go ahead. Leave me again," I say with sarcasm and a stupid grin. "Don't worry. I'll be right here tending the fire!"

Luca springs to his haunches and pounces on top of me. I topple flat onto my back. Straddling me, he pins my arms to the ground. I gasp and flinch, not sure if he's playing or wants to hurt me. But he just hovers over me, holding me there and staring into my face. Then after a moment, he flops the full weight of his hot, sticky body on top of me and buries his face in my hair.

I feel a warm tear trickle down my ear, and I pull my arms free from his grip and wrap them around him. "I won't abandon you," I promise.

We lie there like that for a few moments, and I feel him growing hard against my belly. Then, as I, too, become hard, Luca sniffs loudly and pushes himself upright until he's standing straddled above me.

I sit up quickly and adjust the bib of my loincloth, hoping to conceal my boner. "You know, you could use a bath. You smell like a dead animal," I say as I brush his sweaty grime off my chest and stomach.

"Right now, I got a volcano right here that's ready to erupt." He cups his groin and jiggles it. "And I wouldn't mind a couple of those things they pass off as beer, as well."

I roll my eyes. "If it smells like a pig and acts like a pig, it's probably a pig!"

Luca laughs and starts for the path.

"Hey," I call after him, "aren't you forgetting something?" I pick the coin off the rock and hold it up.

"Keep it." He winks. "I'll bet we can find lots more." And he continues down the path. Once he's on the beach, he calls back up to me. "Hey, Kiddo! You know what that coin means?"

"No, what?"

"It means you really are a whore now," he jeers.

I grab some stones and throw them at him.

Laughing loudly, he trots up the trail toward the village.

I tell myself there's nothing to worry about. Luca's all right. He's still his old, boy scout self. I know we can't stay here forever, and sooner or later we will have to leave. For me, being marooned on this island feels like my salvation, but maybe for Luca it's a prison.

The next day, all is back to normal with Kizo, Luca, Pico, and me in the canoe well before dawn. We paddle out to the reef as usual, and Kizo and Luca set our nets. For now, we doze in the sun and wait for fish. Pico is in the bow with his head hanging over the side watching the marine life below and lazily playing in the water with his hand as he sings one of his many happy little songs. Kizo, as always, is sitting in the stern, fishtailing his broad paddle to maintain our position along the reef as we gently bob in the surf. Luca is asleep between Kizo's legs, and I'm sitting in the middle, one hand firmly on my basket sombrero, the other gripping the gunwale.

"Rufus, Rufus!" Pico shouts, jolting us from our sun-induced trance. He points toward the reef. Luca wakes up with a start as Kizo digs his paddle in deep and heads our canoe directly toward our nets. I squint into the blinding glare and see a great black tail and dorsal fin flip out of the water. Rufus is shredding our nets and taking whatever he wants of our catch for his breakfast. I wish I could say that Rufus is a man-eating great white shark, except he's not nearly so grand. He's just a big, old, bad-tempered, fish-stealing, hammerhead shark. All the same, you can never really conceptualize how large a seven-foot shark is until he swims directly under your keel and you realize he is half the size of the fragile little craft you are sitting in. As for the man-eating part, hammerheads are normally opportunists, and I suppose he is too lazy to prey on people when fish are so readily available.

Luca stands in the bow with his spear poised, ready to stick Rufus.

"You'll never catch him that way." Kizo laughs. "If you want to kill Rufus, we will need to bring my heavy net and my longest spear."

By the time we reach our net, Rufus has, with a flip of his great tail, already swum off into deeper water. Kizo and Luca haul in what's left of our nets, and Pico and I salvage what we can of our catch. Thanks to Rufus, we'll spend the rest of the day mending our nets with barely a fish to show for our effort.

"I guess it's coconut soup for dinner tonight," I say to Pico as we head back to shore.

Pico rolls his eyes.

That evening, as usual, Luca and I climb the cliff to lounge on the flat rocks at the signal fire and watch the sun sink into the sea.

"I wonder if I tried a more formal approach, maybe Nando would get the idea," I say, poking the fire with a stick.

"Why don't you just ask him to have sex with you?"

"What if he says no? Then what would I do?"

"You're a big old chicken, aren't you?" Luca makes a sound like a squawking chicken.

"Stop it! I'm not like you. I'm not as brave as you are. Maybe I could bring him a bunch of flowers or something. They love flowers. Like these ones here. They're pretty." I examine a little patch of flowers growing out of a crag. "They sort of look like lilies."

"Oh, that's a brilliant idea. They practically worship sex. Why not give him a bunch of severed plant genitals? That ought to make him fall in love with you." Luca flops over on his back and laughs uncontrollably.

"Oh shit, I never thought about it that way." I start to giggle along with him. "I can just see him running in horror as I arrive with my bouquet of mutilated sex organs in hand."

"I thought you said you were supposed to be an anthropologist?"

"I am, but we never studied native techniques on how to get lucky."

"Too bad. That might be something useful." Luca grins at me. "Hey, when we get back home, I should go to university and become a professor or something."

"Oh please." I roll over flat on my back. "What would you teach, Sex 101?"

Luca's expression droops, and he speaks in a low, serious tone. "If I have to go to prison, I might as well spend my time studying, right?"

I swallow and look over at him. "Oops. I kind of forgot about that. Hey, would it be so terrible if we just stayed here?"

"No!" Luca sits upright. "You don't understand. I have to go back."

"But why?"

"The accident wasn't my fault." Luca turns away and looks out to sea. Then he says in a low voice, "They gave me away when I was born. I've never counted for anything. And if I stay here it's like I never existed at all. I want another chance to prove I'm somebody important—a real man."

I raise my fist to my mouth and bite my knuckle. Then I place my hand on his shoulder. "You have nothing to prove to me."

Luca remains rigid.

"I'm sure it's just a matter of time before we are rescued," I say in my most reassuring tone, but I feel like a liar. I dread the thought of going back, and more and more, with each passing day, I want to stay.

*

Guy stopped talking and looked at Richard.

"Why was the shark called Rufus?"

"Good question." Guy chuckled. "Well, when I was a child, our neighbors had a nasty black mutt by the name of Rufus, who stole shoes and newspapers from the steps or laundry off the lines and shredded whatever he got hold of. He terrorized the neighborhood children with his particular habit of lying out of sight under a bush or behind a corner, then bounding out snarling and snapping his jaws. More than one child bore a scar where Rufus had ambushed them. It felt right to name that nasty black beast after that old mutt."

"Ah, so Rufus represents a childhood fear." Richard leaned to one side and rested his chin on the back of his hand. "Didn't you say Nando was the one man on the island who wouldn't have sex with you?"

"Well, that's the way it was! Every time I made a pass at him, he evaded it."

Richard rubbed the back of his head. "But didn't you also say that Luca wasn't sexually interested in you either?"

Guy didn't respond.

Richard slid himself into a more upright position. "Sex without intimacy—intimacy without sex. It would appear that in your erotic paradise you have trouble putting the two pieces of the equation together."

"And what do sharks have to do with any of this?" Guy scoffed.

"Nothing really. It's just that between the island and home is a vast unknown stretch of sea full of dangers, like sharks. But there's also the lure of gold and the chance of going home rich. You appear to be torn between fear and desire. Do you remain within the pleasure and safety of your fantasy, or do you take the risk and return to reality?"

Guy dropped his head and held his hands together in front of his lips as if he were praying. "But here I don't have to worry about sharks or anything else, and I have all the money I need. What could I possibly fear or desire?"

"That depends on what you're looking for, doesn't it?"

"What am I looking for? That's the big question, isn't it? I don't know. What is anyone looking for?"

Richard glanced down at his watch. "Let's pick up on that next week. Okay?"

Guy got up and walked toward the door but stopped and stared at the corner between Richard's desk and the wall. "You know, the problem is we want it all."

Richard swiveled around in his chair and looked toward the corner, where he had left his gym bag wide open. Clearly visible on top of his damp towel and swim trunks was his bottle of Minoxidil hair growth tonic. Richard clenched his teeth and jerked his head back toward Guy, who was hovering in the doorway.

"But no matter how hard we try, time always creeps up on us." Guy strolled out of the room, leaving Richard with a scowl on his face.

Chapter Eleven

The Juice Market

"Doc, did you study evolution?" Guy walked into the office at exactly nine o'clock with two cups of coffee. He was wearing a faded green T-shirt with a large fish design that resembled a born-again Christian bumper sticker, but Guy's fish had feet with the name *Darwin* printed below it.

Richard quickly closed his computer file before Guy was close enough to read it. He turned. "Oh good, coffee." Richard smothered a yawn with his fist. "I could really use a second cup this morning." As he reached out for the cup, Guy glanced at the back of Richard's hand. The distinctive red wings stamp from the door of the Fly gay disco was still visible.

Guy took his seat on the sofa. Richard followed him over and sat in the swivel chair.

"Doc, where do you stand on the nature versus nurture argument? You know, are we born gay or do we become gay? By the way, new glasses, eh? Very trendy."

"I had to get reading glasses. As you pointed out, time creeps up on all of us."

"You're still young." Guy studied Richard's face. "They make your head look like a square block."

Richard frowned and sucked in air through his teeth. "The elusive gay gene, eh? Well, I doubt they'll ever find such a thing."

"There are a lot of wankers out there who want to cure us. Why not screw with the genes of unborn children?"

"You can be sure they're going to try." Richard nodded and took a sip of his coffee.

"Good machine. Bad machine." Guy moved his arms alternatively up and down and rocked back and forth like a windup toy robot.

"Do you feel like a machine?"

"No." Guy raised his arm and forefinger in the air like a crazed evangelist. "I'm an abomination of nature!"

"Unfortunately, there are still some people who think like that." Richard's eyes watered, and he clenched his teeth as he fought back another yawn.

"Breast implants. Now there's an abomination of nature." Guy cupped and jiggled his chest with both hands. "But if you really want to talk about nature, look at the American buffalo." Guy spread his arms in an arch and hollowed his chest as if he was measuring the girth of a buffalo's shoulders or posing like a bodybuilder. "Those big hairy boys are the biggest homos in nature."

Joining in the farce, Richard raised his flat hand to the side of his mouth. "I've heard some scandalous rumors going around about penguins too."

Guy snorted a laugh. "Buffalo, penguins, and people. We're social animals. And same-sex bonding leads to cooperation. It's all just part of the game of survival."

Richard stretched back in his chair. "I guess with both psychology and anthropology, it's often easier to demonstrate what tears us apart rather than what binds us together." The yawn Richard was holding back burst forth. He waved his hand as he rapidly blinked his tearing eyes. "'Scuse me, didn't get enough sleep last night."

"Late night, eh?" Guy laughed. "You still have a piece of glitter stuck on your left eyebrow."

Richard flinched, licked his fingertip, and rubbed his eyebrow vigorously.

"That's it. You got it."

Richard looked at Guy as if he expected him to make some comment or say something invasive. Instead, Guy smiled innocently, stared at the wall, and began to tell his story.

*

Tonight is the festival of the Fall Equinox. The sun has just set, and Nando and I are standing on the patio watching the men gather in the main plaza and on the lower steps of the great pyramid mound. As usual, the torches are lit, the drums and flutes are playing, and the smell of fish roasting on the spit fills the air. All along the steps, elaborate feather decorations, woven loincloths, and capes are carefully spread out in distinct clusters between baskets of corn, potatoes, and squash.

"What's all that for? Is it some kind of market?"

"Yes, it's the most important kind." Nando beams. "These are all the things the women have grown and made."

"Why are they all laid out like that?"

"For the men to see! When a man accepts a bundle of gifts, he signals he wants to enter an arrangement with a woman and her mate to make a child and to raise that child together. It is one of the most sacred rituals."

"Then what happens?"

"The woman can accept or refuse him. Women, of course, only want men who are good fishermen, affectionate and diligent fathers, and beautiful, so it's important for a man to stay in good shape and look his best." Nando laughs. "That's why Kizo and Lalli are such good fish to catch." Nando reaches over and adjusts the green feather-decorated belt I'm wearing. "My sister and Dzil have made an arrangement with Lalli for his juice."

"Who's supposed to get pregnant?"

Nando laughs. "My sister is too old, and Lalli and her are both from my mother's lineage, but Dzil's mother's lineage is different and she is still young. It's a very good match. I helped arrange it."

"You're a good brother."

"Yes, I am." Nando smiles.

"So Dzil and Kyle will be the child's mothers, and Lalli will be the father?"

"Yes, that's how it works. There are usually two fathers, but not always. Do not worry, even if you are a bad fisherman, there are still many women who will want a baby with green eyes and skin as pink as a seashell, Yabai," Nando says as he fluffs my green feather armband. For some time now, Nando and everyone else have been calling me Yabai, which means seashell. Luca, of course, still calls me Kiddo.

"I'm not making a baby with anyone." I playfully bat Nando's hand away.

"Remember, be very careful about accepting gifts." Nando taps the side of his head with his finger. "Especially from Rurlu. She is very tricky, you know, and she would give anything for her partner to give birth to a pink baby."

"I'm not pink anymore! I'm a rosy, light-brown color."

Nando smirks.

"Okay, so parts of me are pink, but I still don't want a pink baby."

We both laugh.

"Nando, there's something else I want to know." I pause for a moment, trying to think of how to phrase my question. "What happens when a man is not made, well, you know, quite right?"

At first, Nando looks at me as if he doesn't understand. Then he smiles and says, "Oh, you mean like when a baby boy is born but she is really a girl—like Rurlu. That's simple—she did the rituals with the other girls and was initiated as a woman. It happens all the time. The other way around too. Some girls are born with a penis. Some boys are born with a vagina."

"You mean Rurlu's not really a woman?"

Nando chuckles. "Of course, she is. She was born with a penis. That is all."

I'm quiet for a moment while I think. Then I screw up my face. "Well, if Rurlu has a penis, why doesn't she impregnate her partner herself?"

Nando looks at me suspiciously, then bursts out laughing. "Oh, Yabai, you say some very strange things."

I shrug and hold out my palms. Then I shake my head. "Actually, I had another question in mind. I want to know what happens to the men who, well, you know, who don't love men, if you know what I mean?"

Nando looks to the ground as if he is deeply embarrassed, clears his throat, and speaks in a hushed voice. "There are some men who cannot help that they are made wrong. It is very sad, and they do not want to bring shame upon their families. Sometimes they try to keep it secret, but those who cannot go to live on the Far Island."

"You mean the other island over there?" I bob my head sideways in the direction of the island.

"No, that is the Near Island. The Far Island is out beyond the reef. You can only see it from high up the volcano." Nando looks from side to side, checking to see if anyone else is close enough to hear. "Sometimes there are bad men who try to have sex with children. They are also sent away to the Far Island."

"And what about the women?"

"Shh." Nando signals me with his flat hand to keep my voice low. He continues in an even softer voice. "As I said, I do not know for sure, but they say on the Far Island there are both men and women who live together like animals and follow the rule of Tara the Deceiver. But I cannot believe this is true. I think it's a story they tell to frighten children. Please, no more questions about such shameful things. It is time to celebrate."

It's obvious I've made Nando very uncomfortable, so I decide it's best to leave the topic alone for now. "You're right." I smile. "Let's celebrate." I look out across the plaza and spot Mazu sauntering along, his long skinny body draped in flowing red scarves. Jab, who's shorter and somewhat chubby, is likewise wrapped in red scarves. I throw them a wave, and Mazu stops abruptly, props his bent wrist on his hip, posing like a model from the pages of *Vogue*, then whispers something into Jab's waiting ear. The two sneer, look away, and continue toward the steps of the pyramid mound.

"I think we were just snubbed," I say to Nando, who is looking at the ground.

"Mazu and Jab think they are better because they belong to the Red brotherhood."

"Kizo is a Red, and it doesn't seem to matter to him."

"Yes, but Kizo is beautiful and a good fisherman, so he does what he likes."

"Never mind, neither Mazu nor Jab are very beautiful, and they aren't very good fishermen either."

"It is not you they do not like. It is me," Nando says sorrowfully. "They call me a copa fish."

"What's a copa fish?"

"It is an ugly fish that feeds off the bottom, and nobody eats it because it tastes bad. Some of the women use it to fertilize their potato patch."

I shrug and shake my head. "Well, you are a lot more beautiful, and I'll bet you taste a lot better than those two sour parrots." Calling someone a parrot is like saying they are only feathers with no brains.

Nando forces a smile.

A few moments later, Kizo and Luca enter the plaza with their arms slung over each other's shoulders. Luca is gripping a grog gourd, and they are both staggering. Kizo, as usual, is dressed in his conquistador's helmet and gold-and-silver breastplate. Luca is wearing a red loincloth. His body is intricately painted—head to toe—with a red-and-black, geometric, snake design. Numerous red feathers are tied in his hair. He makes a whooping cry and waves the grog gourd high in the air, and Nando and I wave back. I glance down at my little bunch of green feathers attached to the belt around my waist that keeps going askew. How can Kizo and Luca be so damn sexy while I look like a big green chicken?

"Hey, Kiddo," Luca calls up to me. "Let's get this party started."

"Yes." Nando looks at me and smiles. "It is time for a celebration."

I nod. Then I notice that Nando is still wearing only his plain white loincloth and grass sandals. "Well, hurry up. Get dressed for the party!"

Suddenly there is an earsplitting cry from directly overhead, and Nando and I, along with everyone in the plaza, look toward our rooftop. There, painted entirely black, standing on the edge of the roof with both arms extended in the air, is Pico. The men in the plaza cheer, and Pico waves his arms back and forth as he makes loud monkey cries.

"Pico's going to kill himself up there."

"He is not Pico." Nando shrugs. "He is now the Monkey King."

"And I suppose you're the one who painted him black?"

Nando smiles and nods.

"All the same, he's going to be a dead Monkey King if he falls." I signal for Pico to climb down. "Pico!"

He scurries along the roof with the agility of a real monkey and swings onto the patio from an exposed roof beam, then leaps into my arms, wrapping his legs around my waist, almost sending both of us toppling over the edge. I grab his bum and hold him tightly.

"Now come on." I turn to Nando. "Pico and I are ready. Get dressed."

A look of panic shoots across Nando's face. "I do not... I mean, I cannot...." Then he stares at his feet. "Please do not ask me why." He turns and hurries inside our cottage.

Pico unwraps his legs and stands.

"Wait!" I turn to follow him, but Pico holds my arm firmly. He waves his free hand back and forth in front of my face and pulls me toward the steps. I reluctantly follow Pico down into the plaza and join the festivities, without Nando.

Throughout the night, I eat, drink, dance, and play along with the men. During a pause while we are lounging together in a sweaty pile on the pyramid mound, someone on the step below grabs my leg and strokes it. I look down and see Mazu, his eyes seductively at half-mast and his lips fully pursed, and my stomach churns. Stretching my arm up over my head to the fruit basket on the step above me, I grab a large slice of papaya. As Mazu slithers upward, ready to run his tongue along my inner thigh, I shove the piece of papaya into his open mouth. "Why not suck on this, Mazu?"

He jerks his head up in surprise and glares at me, the papaya hanging out of his mouth, while I slide away from his clutches.

It's almost dawn when Lalli, who is lying on his back resting his head on my thigh, hands me a large, polished stone dildo and grins. I take the dildo, reach down between his legs, and slowly insert it into him while he moans with pleasure. Then I shift forward and engulf his cock. Just as his balls and leg muscles tense, he pushes my head away and reaches for a gourd. With a roar, he shoots into it. Suddenly, a young man appears from nowhere, grabs the gourd, and runs off.

Lalli rolls over, grips my thighs, and buries his face in my crotch. I lean back and stare up at the mango-colored horizon, and it's not long before I climax in his mouth. Instantly, a gourd appears, and Lalli spits into it. As before, whoever is holding the gourd disappears with it, but I'm too far gone to care about what's going on with the cum. Lalli worms his way up and lies on top of me. Among the heap of warm, slippery bodies, I float in my afterglow.

*

"How was that?" Guy said to Richard.

"Fine, but I still don't understand why they're collecting sperm in gourds."

"Primitive artificial insemination!" Guy blurted out. "Kyle and Dzil and the other women are practicing seeding rituals on the other side of the pyramid mound."

"Ahhh!" Richard held his mouth open. "I didn't get that part. I was beginning to wonder when and how men and women have sex."

"They don't!" Guy bobbed his hands emphatically. "Man, for a smart person you can be a little slow sometimes. They must have loved you during story time in kindergarten."

"And what do the heterosexuals do, then?" Richard asked, ignoring the jab.

"As I told you, the few that are hopelessly hetero live in the shadows, much like it is for us queers here." Guy flicked his hand as if he were shooing a fly.

"And so on the island, the tables are turned? Homosexuals occupy center stage while the heteros are pushed out?"

"Exactly!" Guy said.

"Interesting. Even though you express a lot of antagonism toward heterosexuals, you covet the same stereotypical model of the hetero lifestyle: stable partnership, babies, and family."

"Look, I don't hate heteros. I hate their privilege. They run around and pop out unwanted kids all the time with little more concern than a poke and a squirt."

"I think most children are wanted, don't you?"

"Doc, if every child was wanted, you wouldn't have a client base."

"Sad but true." Richard took a slow breath. His expression was compassionate. "Did you feel unwanted?"

"I was an accident," Guy said, shaking his head. "I was mostly ignored." Guy paused for a moment and bit the corner of his lip. "But Luca was abandoned—just thrown away like trash. All he wanted was to be wanted by someone, by anyone." Guy looked at the floor. "But the damage had already been done, and he could never let anyone in."

"So who are you really angry at?"

"Good question, Doc." Guy tapped his fingers on the arm of the sofa. "I guess the answer is myself." He cocked his head to one side. "Your turn. So who are you really angry at?"

"You don't miss a beat, do you?" Richard tossed his head and shrugged. "Same answer as you." He glanced at his watch. "Our time is up."

Guy stood.

"Mr. Palmer, before you leave." Richard's face was stern. "As I'm sure you've already surmised, I've decided to follow your advice."

Guy paused and raised one eyebrow but didn't respond.

"My ex-girlfriend is a good person. She deserves passion, and so do I," Richard said with a cockeyed smile. "It's time I close the textbooks and figure out what I really want and need."

Guy bowed his head graciously. "And so your adventure begins."

Chapter Twelve

Pico's World

Guy walked up to the nurses' station with the cups of coffee balanced in one hand. In his other hand, he held a yellow plastic net bag filled with coin-shaped chocolates covered in gold foil. Armando and his colleague, Linda, were standing behind the counter reading the computer screen.

Armando looked up and smiled. "Good morning, Mr. Palmer."

Guy didn't respond. He reached over the counter and handed the bag to Armando.

"Are these for us?"

Guy nodded.

"Ohh," Linda squealed, "I love these little chocolate coins."

"Thank you." Armando looked surprised. "What's the occasion?"

"Nothing." Guy smiled. "Just something to brighten up your day."

"Who needs an occasion for chocolate?" Linda took one, peeled off the gold foil, and popped it into her mouth. "Oh well, there goes my diet," she said through chocolate-covered teeth.

"Don't worry." Guy nodded sincerely. "In many societies, your big rump would be considered very sexually attractive."

Armando sputtered out a laugh. Linda stopped chewing and glared at Guy. Just as she was about to speak, Armando patted her forearm and rolled his eyes. She scowled.

Armando turned back to Guy and smiled. "Thank you, Mr. Palmer. That was very thoughtful."

Guy grinned, turned, and walked down the hall humming a little tune. He entered the studio without knocking, placed Richard's coffee on the desk, and sat down on the sofa.

"Thanks." Richard got up, picked up his coffee, and moved over to the swivel chair. "Why don't you tell me a bit more about growing up?"

Guy made a low growl in the back of his throat. "Okay, we're back to playing 'The Shrink and the Looney' this morning." He blew out a breath of air. "There's not much more to tell." Guy shifted in his seat uncomfortably. "As I told you, my parents were always in the store." Guy popped off his coffee lid and took a sip. "Yuck, forgot the sugar. I either hung out there after school, helping with this and that, or stayed up in my room, pretending to study." Guy cocked his head.

Richard looked at Guy with an expression that seemed to say, "Go on."

Guy inhaled slowly and continued in a low, serious voice, "There were times I felt like I was part of the inventory in my parents' store." Guy reached into his pocket and pulled out a packet of sugar, tore it open, and poured it into his coffee. "Same old story, I guess. My dad never taught me to throw a ball, and my mom was only concerned that I did well in school."

Richard's left eye twitched.

Guy smiled coyly. "I see we do share some common experiences after all."

Richard shifted backward automatically and cleared his throat. "Did you have any childhood friends?"

Guy pulled a bent swizzle stick out of his pocket, stirred his coffee, then licked the swizzle stick and put it back into his pocket. "Not many." He took a large gulp of coffee. "That's better. I was mostly a loner. Like I told you, sometimes I was bullied, but mostly I was ignored."

Richard sat motionless, listening.

"When I was little, there was Jennifer," Guy continued. "Her mother was a teacher, so my mother held her in high esteem. She'd had German measles or something when she was pregnant with Jennifer, and well, let's just say Jennifer was a 'slow child.' Or at least that was the polite term at the time. Folks in my town acted like she was dirty and contagious. Anyways, Jennifer lived next door for a number of years, and so on Saturdays while my mom was in the store, Jennifer's mom minded me."

Guy paused for a moment. "Jennifer was older than me, but she had been held back in school. We hung out together in an obscure corner of the schoolyard during recess—the 'faggot' and the 'retard.' We certainly got called that often enough, long before either one of us knew what those names really meant."

Guy pushed himself up with his hands from where he had sunk into the sofa, resettling in a more upright position. Then he stared at the far wall like he was looking off into the distance and began to talk slowly.

*

It's dark, and we are lazing on the benches and pillows in the cottage, watching the torchlight make strange shadows along the walls.

"See, it's a dog," I say as I clasp my hands together and hold them up to the light, casting a shadow on the far wall.

"A dog?" Nando says, and I remember there are no dogs on the island.

"Well, it's an animal, anyways."

Nando holds his hands up into the light and makes a shadow. "What's this?"

"A parrot."

"A parrot? It's a jaguar," Nando says. "See his eye and ears?"

"Looks like a parrot to me." I wink at Pico. "What do you think, Pico? Is it a parrot?"

Pico nods.

Nando lowers his hands. "You two have no imagination."

"Sure we do." I snort. "We see a parrot."

Pico giggles.

"Listen, I have a story you have not heard yet," Nando says. "This story is Pico's favorite, but I will tell it to you in English."

"How will Pico understand?"

"Oh, do not worry. He has heard it so many times it does not matter what language I tell it in. He understands." Nando leans back, props a pillow under his head, and begins to tell his tale.

"A long, long time ago there existed a great jaguar. His coat was spotted brown and gold on a shiny black mat. His body was muscular and lean. His movements were flowing and seductive. He was an animal of such exquisite beauty that everyone called him Lord Jaguar. Everyday Lord Jaguar patrolled the jungle, allowing all to see and enjoy his magnificence. But Lord Jaguar was not content.

"'Oh, poor me.'" Nando switches to a low, comical voice, elongating his vowels, and Pico squeals with delight. "'I am so superb that no other animal in the forest can compare to me. I give such pleasure, but who is worthy to please me? Who? No one.'"

Returning to his narrative voice, Nando continues. "One day while Lord Jaguar was patrolling his jungle, carefully allowing the light and shadow to flow along his splendid coat, he became hungry. In a banana tree, Lord Jaguar saw a little monkey. The monkey had a big head and long skinny arms and legs. Parts of the monkey's skinny body, his back and tail, were covered with tufts of black fur, while other parts, his face and belly, were almost bare. His movements, like his chatter, were nervous and jerky. Lord Jaguar, with a grand sweeping gesture, snatched the little monkey from the banana tree and pinned him to the ground.

"'Ugly little monkey,' Nando says in a commanding voice. 'You are most fortunate, for I have chosen to eat you today.'

"'Oh'—Nando changes to a high squeaky voice—'it is a great honor for a pitiful beast like me to be eaten by such an exquisite creature like you. But first, before you eat me, allow me to show my gratitude.'

"'I am Lord Jaguar. What could such a miserable beast like you do to show me gratitude?'

"'It is true, I am an ugly monkey, but as all the animals in the forest know, monkeys are very clever at making sex.'"

Pico makes a long, squealing laugh.

"'Ha, ha, ha,' roared Lord Jaguar. 'You wish to make sex with me, little monkey? Oh, you amuse me so much that I will almost regret eating you, but I am hungry.'"

Pico bursts into a loud, hollow laugh, the way he does when he's anticipating something fun, and as laughter is contagious, I begin to laugh along with him. Nando grins widely, obviously pleased, and continues speaking in the voices of his characters.

"'Oh please, please, Lord Jaguar, please eat me, but first let me show you how monkeys make sex.'

"Lord Jaguar continued to laugh. 'Yes, my ridiculous little monkey, you can show me. Then I will eat you.'

"'Oh, thank you, Lord Jaguar. You are truly superb. Now please face the other way.'

"'Okay, but I will hold your tail so you cannot escape.'

"And Lord Jaguar, holding tightly on to the monkey's tail, turned his backside to him. First the little monkey licked his finger and slowly inserted it into Lord Jaguar's ass and began moving it in and out slowly.

"'How is this?' asked the little monkey.

"'It is pleasant enough, but a superb beast like me expects much more pleasure than this.'

"Then the little monkey removed his finger and mounted Lord Jaguar. He inserted his long, skinny penis into Lord Jaguar's ass and began to move in and out a little faster.

"'How is this?' asked the little monkey.

"'Oh, it is pleasant enough, but a superb beast like me wants much more pleasure than this.'

"So the little monkey removed his penis from Lord Jaguar's ass. He reached up to the nearby banana tree and ripped off the largest green banana he could find. He inserted it into Lord Jaguar's ass and began moving it in and out very quickly.

"'How is this?' asked the little monkey.

"'Oh, it is very pleasant. A superb beast like me demands pleasure like this. Harder, harder, do not stop.'"

Nando makes a fist and gyrates his arm back and forth vigorously. Pico jumps to his feet, thrusts his hips back and forth, and makes monkey noises.

"The little monkey pumped Lord Jaguar with the banana with all his force until Lord Jaguar came with an enormous roar, releasing his hold on the monkey's tail, and the monkey escaped."

Pico's accompanying monkey chatters become a high-pitched squeal. He leaps on top of me, and we fall off the platform bench to the floor, tossing and rolling.

Nando, barely able to continue for laughing, rises to his feet and spreads his arms wide. "And from that day on, the Jaguar always keeps to the shadows, careful not to show too much of his beauty, while the clever little monkeys sit up in the trees and laugh."

Pico climbs off me and screeches wildly, hopping and leaping around the room like a monkey. With a loud monkey cry, he bounds out the door and disappears. I sit upright, and Nando reaches out his hand and pulls me to my feet. I spring up into his waiting arms, and he embraces me. Then he gently pushes me backward onto the platform bench. I let myself fall, expecting him to fall with me. Instead, he releases his embrace, reaches down, grabs my ankles, and pulls them up over my head. Next, he smoothly slides onto the bench on his knees and presses his chest against my upturned bum, pinning me on my back like a turtle. He holds me fast, his beaming face hovering inches above mine.

With a screech, Pico reappears at the door, and Nando quickly shifts off me, slapping my bum loudly with his hand before releasing my ankles. I glance over at his boner straining against his loincloth. If he's really interested, and not just toying with me, why does he always pull away? I'm about to ask him when Pico bounds over and slides in next to me, curling up like a puppy in my arms. I carefully shift my pelvis and aching boner away from Pico's backside. Now is not the right moment, but as soon as we are alone, I resolve to muster my courage and ask Nando why he won't let me touch him.

"Did you like my little story?" Nando asks.

"I love all your stories."

Nando's face beams.

"Nando, do the women tell the same stories?"

"The really important stories are the same for everyone," he says. "But the women change some of the other stories a little."

"Like how?"

"Like this story. The women tell the same story, except she is the Monkey Queen and she uses a papaya, not a banana."

"A papaya? Why a papaya?" I see a disgusted look on Nando's face.

"Oh, wait a minute. I just figured it out. Yuck!" And we giggle wickedly, like a couple of schoolboys.

The following afternoon, like most afternoons, the sun is high. The women are up in the hills. The men, having returned from fishing, take advantage of this quiet time to be with their partners and babies. Luca and Kizo, as usual, go off to drink grog and nap. For a pasty-skinned northern boy like me, it's too hot and sunny down at the beach, but the dappled light under the green canopy at the bathing pool is my little piece of heaven. And that's where Pico and I go.

We often pretend to be returning to our cottage for a nap but take long, elaborate pathways and circle back through the jungle, just to lose any hangers-on so we will have the bathing pool to ourselves. For me, just being with Pico is my return to the haunted playground with Jennifer. But this time there is nobody throwing insults or stones.

I flop down on the sandy patch near the water's edge and watch Pico as he climbs the breadfruit tree. Like everything else about Pico, his beauty is unique. He's half mime, half dancer. I continue to watch as he wraps his lean, muscular legs around one branch and hangs upside down, his large mat of wiry, untamed black hair dangling from his slightly oversized head. Then he swings, reaches out, catches another branch, and hangs by his long, spidery arms, mimicking a monkey with a commitment that goes well beyond pretend games and playacting.

"Come on, Pico," I say as I stand up and brush the sand off my butt. "Let's go swimming. I'm hot." I dive in the clear fresh water. Pico jumps down from the tree and dives in after me. Once in the water he transforms into a frog, and as far as I can tell, he truly believes he is a frog. He swims under me toward the center of the pool where the water is deepest. I follow him with the overhand stroke I learned during the summer at my parents' cottage. Although I can't begin to match his agility, I'm faster than he is.

Pico comes up for air, then in an evasive maneuver dips under again, but I anticipate his plan and grab hold of his foot as he tries to slip away. I pull him to the surface, and we gasp for air between sputters of laughter. Finally, with both hands around his waist, I drag him wriggling and struggling back toward the shallows. I hoist him over my shoulder, carry him out of the water, and flop him down on the sandy ground. He does his best to slip away, but I pin him on his back. He tries a couple of times to struggle free, but it's obvious that the game is over and Pico is mine. I relax my hold and allow him to topple me over and pin me.

I lie on my back breathing heavily while Pico sits on my torso holding my arms above my head. He relaxes, flopping his full weight on top of me. Our breathing synchronizes, and the sweat and water from our bodies mix together. I feel Pico's hard cock against my belly. I smile and kiss him on his head. I, in a complete state of relaxation, start to drift off. Suddenly, I wake with a start. Pico has taken hold of my cock and is now slowly and rhythmically stroking and sucking me.

"Pico, c'mon, you're going too far. Game's over, time to get off me."

But Pico continues, and the more I try to push him away the harder he struggles to suck my cock. "Pico! I said stop!" I shove him hard, and he rolls over backward on the sand. I stand up.

Pico looks up at me, startled and confused.

"Sorry, Pico. Did I hurt you?" As I attempt to approach him, he backs away from me like a frightened child or animal.

"Pico," I plead. "I didn't push you that hard." And again, I try to approach him. Pico recoils, bounces to his feet, and bounds off through the forest.

"Shit!"

I decide to return to the cottage now that the afternoon is spoiled.

When I reach the cottage, Nando is waiting for me, and from the look on his face I can tell he is not happy.

"What did you do to Pico?" he demands.

"Nothing," I say, feigning innocence. "We were just playing, and he got upset and ran off." I'm too embarrassed to explain.

"Well, Pico says you attacked him and that you hate him."

"I didn't attack him, and I don't hate him. That's ridiculous. He got a little carried away, and I pushed him. That's all."

"You pushed him!"

"Yes, I just pushed him off me. He was getting too excited."

"So you pushed him?"

"It was just a little push. It wasn't hard enough to hurt him."

"Pico may live in the world of dreams but he certainly knows what he wants and what he doesn't. He's a man not a child! I thought you understood that."

"I tried to tell him I was sorry, but he wouldn't listen. He ran off."

"Then you didn't say sorry the right way."

"What am I supposed to do now?"

"Go and find him and show him you do not hate him. Now go!"

I'm taken aback. Nando has never asked anything of me, let alone made a demand. I turn and hurry off back to the bathing pool, where I suspect I might find Pico.

As I walk along the pathway, I tell myself I'm the one who should not have allowed things to get out of control.

Up ahead in the bushes I hear a familiar slap, slap of torso against buttock and the grunt and groan of Luca and Kizo. By the time I reach their little hobbit bed amongst the vegetation, they have climaxed and are lying on the ground catching their breath.

"Hey, Kiddo, don't just walk on by like you don't know we're here."

"Sorry, I didn't want to interrupt you." I blush a little. Strange, even though Luca and I have shared many sexual adventures, I'm always a little shy around him. Maybe it's because we both come from a world with different sensibilities. Maybe it's because I have feelings for him beyond brotherhood. "Did you see Pico?"

"How could we have missed him? He was screaming and jumping around like a crazy man. What's up with him? Something set him off." Luca reaches behind his head, grabs a gourd, and takes a big swig.

I scrunch up my face. "We had a little misunderstanding. He tried to have sex with me down at the pool," I say, assuming that Luca, of course, will immediately understand my moral dilemma.

"What happened?"

"What do you mean what happened? I refused."

"Hey listen, little buddy, if you're having a few problems getting it up, this stuff works wonders." He reaches out and hands me the gourd. "It'll make you hard as a bamboo."

"I'm not having problems getting it up." I shake my head. "I just don't think it's right for me to take advantage of him."

"Since when did you get so judgmental, Mr. I-am-an-anthropologist?" Luca rocks his head back and forth, taunting me.

"I'm not being judgmental. Even if he is a man on the outside. Well, you know?"

"Oh, you're right, you're not judgmental. You're patronizing. Let me see. Only smart people, like you, are allowed to fuck. Hey, big guy, what's your IQ?" Luca rolls over halfway on top of Kizo. "I want to know if you're smart enough to take it up the ass." Kizo just growls at Luca and gnaws on his nipple. "Good doggy, that-a-boy, chew your daddy."

I clench my teeth. "So I'm a piece of shit just 'cause I don't think it's right to have sex with a retarded boy?" I startle myself as I say the word 'retarded'—the same word I had defended Jennifer against, I'm now using as a weapon.

"Let me see if us retards can explain it to you smart people. In case you hadn't noticed, we are not in Kansas anymore, Dorothy." Luca maneuvers himself between Kizo's legs and lifts Kizo's backside up against his groin. "Ready for round two, big boy? Ride the pony."

I turn and storm off toward the bathing pool. Behind me I can hear their grunts and moans. As I suspect, I find Pico at the pool, up a tree, clinging to a branch. I call out to him, but he ignores me and hugs the branch tighter.

"Pico," I plead, "come down. I said I was sorry. We can go swimming together. Let's play fish and frog."

Pico doesn't move from his branch. He buries his face in his arm and begins making monkey sounds.

"Monkey King, tell Pico I am sorry and I want him to come and play."

Pico continues to make monkey sounds.

"If you won't come down, then I will have to come up there with you." I reach for the lowest branch and place my foot on a gnarl of the tree trunk, ready to climb up. As

I do so, Pico screeches wildly and shows his teeth menacingly. Then he bounces up and down on the branch. I immediately withdraw, and Pico is quiet again.

"Well, that's obviously not going to work."

Not knowing what else to do, I look around the pool to where there is a small cluster of banana trees. I walk over, rip a few ripe ones from the stalk, and return to the tree where Pico is. Without saying anything more I sit down and play with the bananas.

Suddenly, with an earsplitting screech Pico jumps down out of the tree, bounces up and down on the ground twice, and climbs on top of me. Then, Pico grabs one of the bananas, peels it with his teeth and pushes it into my mouth, smearing it all over my face. Sliding off me, he falls to the ground on his back, and I flop on top of him, kissing his mouth and covering his face with banana slime. At some point, I look up briefly and catch a glimpse of a figure in the shadows on the far side of the pool, watching us. Maybe it's Nando?

After a swim to wash off the banana, we lie together in the sun, drying. When the sun sinks low, we return to the cottage, me giving Pico a piggyback ride most of the way home.

Nando is waiting in the doorway with a coy grin on his face. I climb the steep steps with Pico on my back chirping his monkey language in my ear and me huffing and puffing.

"You found Pico?"

"Nope, I found the Monkey King."

"Do you want something to eat, perhaps a banana, or are you full?" Nando says with a smirk.

"Quite full, thanks," I say, picking some banana residue from my hair.

*

Guy repositioned himself, making the vinyl sofa groan. "Well?"

Richard closed his eyes in a slow-motion blink. "Jennifer and Pico—you identify with people who are mentally challenged in some way, don't you?"

"Is it wrong to care about other people?"

"No, of course not, but you seem to have a sense of victimization."

"Pico is certainly not a victim!"

"No, in fact he's one of the happiest, most well-adjusted characters in your story so far. I'm referring to you. Do you feel like a victim?"

"It's hard to be gay and not to feel victimized, isn't it?"

"Maybe, but is that sufficient to build your identity upon?"

Guy sat pensively for a few minutes, chewing on his lower lip. "An interesting thought just occurred to me." Guy wrinkled his forehead. "I wonder if Jennifer understood the meaning of the word 'retard' before I understood the meaning of the word 'faggot.'" Guy tensed his jaw.

"Many children who are different—not just gay kids—suffer from name-calling and bullying. You can't change that experience. But you need to realize that was in the past and you are no longer being persecuted or bullied."

Guy began to speak slowly. "By middle school, Jennifer was bussed to another school and put in an occupational program for mentally disabled kids. The truth is, by then I didn't want to hang out with her anymore. I had developed enough skills to mask my secret—an advantage Jennifer, of course, never had. I don't need to tell you lying to yourself and hiding from others is more like an addiction that little by little takes control of you and robs you of all that you are."

Richard grimaced. "You're right. You don't need to tell me. So what happened to Jennifer?"

"Years later, my mom told me she had found a boyfriend and she had become more and more 'unmanageable.' They—meaning her mother and some doctors—put her on the pill or some other medicine, but that didn't really solve the 'problem.'"

"Do you know where she is now?"

"Inside the machine, I guess." Guy swallowed hard.

"Do you mean in an institution?"

"Maybe, I don't know." Guy glanced up at the clock.

"Isn't it rather narcissistic of you to think you are responsible for Jennifer?" Richard said.

"But I abandoned her." Guy got up from the sofa. "Like I've done with everyone else in my life."

Guy left.

Chapter Thirteen

New Babies

Guy tapped twice on the glass, then opened the door to the office.

Richard was bent over with his back to the door, haphazardly stuffing his gym bag into the space between his desk and the wall. His chair was still pushed up against his desk and his computer off.

Guy stood in the doorway, watching.

"Come in," Richard said. "It's not like you to wait outside. Is there something wrong?"

"No." Guy walked in slowly. Richard's hair was heavily gelled, and instead of the usual faint odor of chlorine, cologne dominated the room. "Didn't make it to the pool this morning, eh?"

"No, I was running late. I'll go during lunch." Richard's tone was flat.

"So how was your weekend with your folks?" Guy went over and claimed his usual spot on the sofa.

"It was fine." Richard's expression was suspicious. "But I don't recall telling you I was spending the weekend with my parents."

"You didn't."

"Why did you assume that, then?"

Guy shrugged. "I didn't assume anything."

"How do you know I spent the weekend with my parents?" Richard's tone was now defensive.

"Simple," Guy said. "On the Monday mornings after you visit your folks, you are always late getting to the office."

"Your keen powers of observation are quite unnerving." Richard frowned and sat down on the swivel chair.

"Nothing brings back childhood garbage quite like a visit home, does it?" Guy waved his hand dismissively. "But enough about your story line. Mine is much more interesting."

Richard rubbed his temples as Guy stared at the far wall and began.

*

"It's strange," I say as I haul Lisha out of the central pool and wrap a cloth over her shoulders, patting her back dry.

"What is strange?" Nando says.

"Oh nothing, I was just thinking out loud—hold still, honey. Let me dry your hair—I mean it's strange. Everyone seems to eat, sleep, and breathe babies."

"What! Nobody eats babies! Do they eat babies in Kanada?"

"No, nobody eats babies in Canada. It's just a stupid expression."

"Oh, I do not like that expression."

"What I mean is every day seems to revolve around babies and children."

"And so, what else is there?"

"Well, I don't know."

"We fish. We plant. We make sex. We have wonderful festivals. What else should we do?"

"Fishing, planting, fucking, playing, and raising babies: hmm, I guess you're right. What else should we do?" I smile. "I guess it's just me who's strange."

"Yes, you are very strange...." Nando pauses, then breathes his words. "And interesting and wonderful and...."

I turn my head away from Lisha and toward Nando, who is barely inches from my face. I breathe in slowly, expecting our lips to touch. Lisha squeals and swats my hand away. "Sorry, darling, was I rubbing too hard?" I kiss her head, and she grabs my neck and kisses me back. Then she darts off, trailing the cloth hung half over her bare backside.

"I think you are her favorite today. You will make a good daddy someday. That is the highest honor any man can hope for. It is the final step in becoming complete."

"Somehow, I don't think fatherhood is my destiny."

"How can you know your destiny? It does not exist yet. You cannot know what does not exist."

"True, but where I come from it's almost impossible for a..." They have no specific word for homosexual, so it's difficult to explain the unlikelihood of becoming a gay father. "It would be impossible for me to raise a child alone. That's just the way things are where I come from. And there is nothing I can do about that."

"Then you must find a man here and become a daddy," Nando says in a way that's both hopeful and forlorn.

"Sooner or later, we will be rescued."

"Rescued? From what?"

"I mean, sooner or later I may have to return to Canada. Luca needs to go back."

"But you must stay. This is your home now." Nando's voice becomes a little panicked. "All I want is happiness for you. Just don't leave!"

I'm confused. Nando seems to desperately want me to stay, but at the same time he still won't let me touch him. "Relax," I say. "I'm not going anywhere for a while."

Nando furrows his brow. Then with renewed enthusiasm, he says, "I am certain you will make a fine daddy. With your permission, I will talk to my sister."

"No, don't do that. I am not ready." I rapidly wave my hands back and forth. "I don't even know if I am fertile."

"Oh, you are fertile." Nando holds his elbow high in the air the way people on the island do to make the sign for a big erection. "Do not worry about that."

"Hey, just 'cause I can squirt juice does not mean that I can make a baby."

"Everyone knows that. But you are fertile." He can barely restrain the smirk on his face.

"You can't tell. Nobody can really tell until you actually make a baby."

"Everybody knows you are fertile." Nando looks perplexed, as if he's telling me something I should have already known.

"Oh, c'mon. How can you—" And I stop, afraid of what his answer might be.

"There are many women who wish to have a baby with skin as pink as a seashell, hair like gold, and eyes the color of the sea."

I freeze with my mouth hanging open at the sudden realization that the game I've been playing for the past months is more than a game.

"Nando, are you telling me I am going to be a father?"

"No, Yabai, do not be ridiculous."

"Oh, thank goodness. You scared me." I lie back on the edge of the pool.

"You cannot be a daddy until you have first made an arrangement with a woman."

I sit back up. "I can't even imagine looking at a baby who has my eyes and face."

"Oh, do not worry about that. Tuss and many of the woman have already seeded themselves with your juice, and in a few moons, we will see how many new pink babies we have."

My mouth falls open, but I'm silent. Have I been deceived? No one has hidden anything or lied to me. I feel sick.

"Yabai, you do not appear well. Perhaps you should return to the cottage to sleep."

I stagger off toward the cliff, my window between two worlds, or maybe it's just a spot with a nice view and a pleasant breeze. Part of me is horrified that a woman might be carrying my child. Part of me is ecstatic at the prospect of seeing a new life that came from me—something I never allowed myself to dream about.

A couple of hours later, Nando finds me there staring out to sea. He sits next to me and puts his arm around me without saying a word.

"Nando," I start slowly, "I have decided to accept my responsibility. I will try to be a good father."

"Wonderful. I will talk with my sister tomorrow."

"That's not what I mean. I mean if any of the new babies are mine, I will accept I am their father."

"You cannot!" Nando withdraws his arm and bumps me with his shoulder in one sudden sharp movement.

"What do you mean, I can't? It should be easy enough to tell if a baby is mine or not."

"All the new babies already have daddies. The arrangements have been made. You cannot steal someone's baby. Oh, that would be very bad, very bad indeed."

"But if the baby is obviously mine?"

"You do not understand. Juice does not make you a daddy. It only makes a baby. You must make an arrangement if you want to grow up a baby. A baby is not a possession."

Nando stares out to sea with me for a moment. Then with a forlorn expression on his face, he turns and says slowly, "If you wish to be a daddy, it is best that you choose a mate. There are many men who would love to be your mate and grow up a baby with you."

"And what about you? Why are you not a daddy?" I challenge.

"I cannot be a daddy. I will never be complete." Nando looks wounded. He stands up, his eyes cast downward. "Don't make me talk about this, Yabai. It is too shameful."

"I thought you said we can't know our destiny because it doesn't exist yet."

He walks away without further words. I let him go. If he won't tell me, I can't force him. I'll just have to wait.

*

Guy stopped talking, leaned back, and stretched his arms like a bodybuilder about to do bench presses. His tattooed biceps bulged beyond the sleeves of his plain blue T-shirt.

Richard studied him. "Let's continue talking about your feelings of being pushed into the shadows. Would it be so terrible to try to fit in?"

"You mean lie so I can fit in?" Guy barked.

"Why would you assume you have to lie or hide?" Richard's tone was professional.

"Doc, we all hide the truth." Guy cocked his head. "Have you told your parents yet?"

Richard frowned and crossed his arms. "Yes, as a matter of fact I just did. But this is not about me!" Richard punched out the words.

"Oh? And I'm willing to bet after your visit to your folks you linked up with a fuck buddy on Grindr on your way home. What's that called? Oh yeah, acting out."

Richard clamped his fists and scowled. "Your comments on my personal life are quite invasive, you know?"

"Hmm." Guy poked himself in the chest three times. Then he slid forward, reached over, and touched Richard lightly on the shoulder. Richard moved back into his chair.

"What are you doing?"

"Just checking to see if you're real or part of my fantasy."

Richard said nothing.

"'Truth is the nutrient of the mind and lies are poison.'" Guy shrugged. "Wasn't it Bion who said that?"

"And what's your point?"

"Nothing. It's just I remember two people in this room agreeing to tell the truth."

Guy stuck his finger in his ear and wiggled it, then continued. "Beautiful, smart, and athletic. Excellent grades in school, volleyball, and swim team, right? Oh, and popular. Yes, I'll bet you are the almost perfect son."

"Why are you still focusing on me?" Richard barked.

Guy inflated his broad chest and half grunted, half yawned. "Because I was the other boy—the boy who wasn't quite good enough, teased in gym class, arms like a chicken, and a chest like a sparrow—the boy nobody wanted to be friends with."

"But all that's changed now. You're well educated, successful, and from the size of your biceps and pecs now, you can hardly feel like a sparrow anymore."

Guy continued, "As a child, I ate cakes to fill my loneliness." He paused and looked directly at Richard.

Richard breathed in and out slowly, as if he were contemplating something. Then he held up his hands in surrender. "Haagen-Dazs Cookie Dough ice cream. I have a tub waiting for me in the freezer at home."

"Hostess Twinkies." Guy laughed.

The harshness drained from Richard's face, and he laughed too. "I guess it goes to show you that even headshrinkers can be human."

"Just don't let anyone else find out."

"No, I promise." Richard lowered his head in mock submission.

Guy stood up and moved toward the door. "By the way, nothing quite like too much borrowed cologne and hair gel in the morning to let everyone know you didn't shower at home."

Richard turned his head to his shoulder and took a quick sniff.

"How do you know my cologne is borrowed?" Richard challenged.

Guy grinned. "CK One. Not really your style, is it?" He stepped through the doorway, leaving Richard shaking his head.

Chapter Fourteen

Short Penis

"Doc, you can suck a stranger's dick without so much as a how do you do, but the minute you become friends, sex is a no-go zone," Guy announced as he entered the studio.

"Intimacy and relationships have different forms, and sex can complicate a friendship," Richard said while he continued to stare at his computer screen.

"Why?" Guy challenged.

"I wish I knew." Richard closed the file, looked up, and shrugged.

"Still haven't sorted that one out either—the lines between love, friendship, and sex. Do they really exist, or are they just another way we partition our emotions?" Guy sat down on the sofa. "Maybe sex is a currency we use, continually trying to trade up. If you only have sex with people who are young, beautiful, popular, and rich, that means you must be important and valuable too."

"Must friendship always involve sex?" Richard clicked on the tape recorder sitting on the corner of his desk and moved over and sat down in the swivel chair.

"Good question." Guy paused for a moment. "Doc, did you know they have two different ways of saying 'I love you' in Italian? One is for a lover. The other is for love between friends and family. It kind of translates as 'I want goodness for you.'"

"*Ti voglio bene.*" Richard's eyes twinkled.

"Doc, I didn't know you could speak Italian."

"I can't. I did three weeks in Tuscany last summer." He grinned and shifted comfortably into his chair.

"I have a little theory," Guy said.

"And I'm sure you're going to tell me about it."

"Well, it goes like this. Men mostly make friends based on shared activities. Men need to do something together in order to become and stay friends."

"Like what?" Richard leaned back and folded his arms.

"Like anything..." Guy squirmed. "I don't know, like fishing, for example. And when that something is over, the connection is broken." Guy mindlessly caressed the tattoo of a fish on his forearm.

"It's common for many older men to feel lonely."

"Especially old gay men." Guy stopped caressing the fish and sat up straight. "We have no place, no shared activities, and so we end up either recluses or silly old faggots chasing after twinkies who largely regard us as pathetic or invisible."

"That's pretty harsh, don't you think?" Richard absently swept his hand over the traces of salt and pepper along his temples.

Guy scoffed. "Ha! You're still young, but soon you're going to find out that nobody pushes their way to the front of the line to buy old fish and potatoes."

"Have you ever tried the Queer Seniors group at the 519 Community Center?"

"If I wanted to spend time with some selfish, self-involved, self-absorbed old prune, I can spend time with myself." Guy curled his lip.

"Not everyone is an old prune. How can you meet people if you don't try?" Richard said in an exasperated tone.

Guy didn't respond. He rested his forehead in his palm and shook his head. "Every time I've gotten mixed up with someone, I've done something to screw it up."

"Friendships are often temporary. People grow and change along with friendships. It doesn't necessarily mean you screwed it up." Richard's voice was once again patient. "Come on. You must have had some friends in high school."

Guy sighed. "Here we go again with the lab rat stuff. Okay, there was this one boy named Larry. Yeah, I guess Larry was my friend. We didn't really have that much in common. In fact, he was pretty much everything I was not. He was tall, muscular, and handsome. He had a big group of friends, so we didn't hang out together at school. After school and on Saturdays, he started to come by while my folks were in the store. His mom was always at her church, and his dad drank. We didn't talk much, mostly just hung out in front of the TV. To be honest with you, I never really knew why he wasted his time on me at all. Maybe it was because his folks didn't have a TV. You know there were still families who didn't have TVs back then. But even after his dad finally broke down and bought one, he still came around."

"Maybe it was because he liked you?"

Guy flinched, as if Richard had just made an absurd suggestion. "Like I said, he was handsome and he turned me on. I guess I had a crush on him."

"Was there something more to it than just physical attraction?"

"I felt safe with him. The other boys left me alone. No one gave me too much trouble 'cause Larry said I was okay."

"One summer when we were both sixteen, Larry and I spent a week back at my parents' cottage, just the two of us. That's when it first happened. Of course, we had talked a lot about sex before, adolescent boy stuff, but we had never found the courage to do anything. Then one afternoon we were lounging on some sunny secluded rocks down by the shore, Larry in his orange Speedo, me in my baggy, stretched-out, brown boxers. We had found my dad's secret stash and had stolen his mickey of whisky. Halfway through, we started to talk about sex and gave ourselves boners. The next thing I knew Larry had his hands down my trunks, and it wasn't long before I had my face down his Speedos. For the rest of that short vacation, we wanked and sucked each other raw. I remember one day going for a record. Larry came six times, and I came eight."

"Eight times?"

"I was young and horny. It was the only time I ever beat Larry at anything. Ha, you know I still have fantasies about Larry."

"Did sex change anything between the two of you?"

"Yeah, when school started again, he joined the football team. Shortly afterwards, I came around the hall corner, and Larry was there with a group of his new football buddies and his arm around a girl with big tits. They were laughing and joking about some kid they said was a faggot. They had shoved this poor kid's head down the toilet in the boys' washroom. I looked at Larry, but he just looked past me as if I weren't there. Then he leaned over and kissed the girl on her mouth. From then on, Larry never came over or spoke to me again."

"How did that make you feel?"

"Like he had stabbed a jagged spike into my chest." Guy bit his lip. "Later I realized how absurd it was for a loser like me to assume I could be friends with a guy as cool as Larry."

"What did you do after that?"

"I became invisible. I hid for most of high school, and in the summer, I spent as much time as I could alone at my parents' cottage. In our final term, Larry got his girlfriend pregnant. They were going to get married after graduation. One night, right before his wedding, he showed up at the cottage in his pickup truck. He was drunk and wanted to do it."

"And?"

"We did it, and I never saw him again. Heard he got fat, had a couple of kids, and bought a house overlooking the high school football field."

"But I still don't see why you blame yourself because Larry obviously had unresolved sexual issues."

Guy shook his head and continued shaking it slower and slower until he finally became still. "I guess you're right. I felt so... I don't know, worthless, guilty." Guy lifted his head and stared at the wall as if his gaze had the power to change time and events.

*

It's just before dawn, and Pico as usual is perched in the bow of the canoe. I'm fidgeting, trying to make myself comfortable, while Kizo and Luca are knee-deep in the surf. Molap pushes his canoe into the water beside us and barks orders at Den, his partner, to hold the boat steady. Then he yells up to his son, Tiki, to bring him his net. A shy, skinny boy appears carrying a bundle so large he can barely see over it as he staggers down the beach to the water's edge.

"Watch what you're doing, boy. You're trailing my net!" Molap grabs the bundle from him. Tiki stands motionless, his small feet sinking into the wet sand as Molap wades back to the canoe.

"Molap," Den says carefully. "Don't be so harsh with him. He is still only a boy."

"Well, it is time he grew up and started to act like a man," Molap growls.

"I'm his father too, you know!"

"If you don't stay quiet, I will leave you both on shore." Molap throws the bundle of net into the bottom of the canoe and turns to retrieve some spears from the shore.

Den curls his lip at Molap, then looks over to Tiki, who is still standing somberly at the water's edge. Holding his closed fist to his mouth, Den makes a couple of loud kissing noises and launches them toward Tiki. Tiki smiles and catches the kisses, then pounds his chest twice. Den winks and climbs into the canoe but says nothing more.

Suddenly Kizo gets a strange expression on his face. "Hey, Molap," he calls. "Lend me one of your spears?"

Molap sneers. "Why do you want my spear?"

"Kizo..." I point to the two spears lying along the gunwale beside me. Kizo shoots me a look.

"We are four, and there is only you and Den. Come on," Kizo pleads. "We are almost brothers. Our mothers come from the same house. Don't be a short penis with me and give me your extra spear."

Molap scrunches up his face and growls as he tosses the spear over to Kizo. Den leaps into the canoe with his back to Molap, drops his head, and laughs. Molap grunts, pushes his canoe out, climbs in the stern, and paddles off toward the reef. I can see Den still shaking, holding in his laughter as he waves good-bye.

"Why did you call Molap a short penis?" I ask Kizo as he paddles us out.

"Oh, I was just having a bit of fun with him." Kizo grins.

Pico jumps up and down in the bow, repeating, "Short penis, short penis."

"Hey, don't worry, little buddy," Luca says. "Your penis is not that short." He punches me on the shoulder, almost sending me toppling overboard.

"Thank you, Long-Dong Silver." I grab the back of his loincloth to steady myself and give it a sharp tug. Luca yelps.

Kizo laughs. "No, a short penis is someone who does not want to share. Old Molap is the shortest penis on the island, so we play games by borrowing everything we can from him."

"Can't he just say no?"

"Oh no, no. That would be very bad." Kizo shakes his head. "Borrowing is how we show we are friends. If he said no, it would mean he no longer wants to be friends with us." Kizo's face becomes serious. "And then he would be all alone."

For the rest of the morning, I try to think of something I might have that Kizo and Pico could borrow. But I have nothing.

That afternoon back at the beach, it's especially hot, and while Kizo and Luca head off to their hut for some grog and a nap, Pico and I set out along the jungle path to the bathing pool. By the time we arrive, we are dripping with sweat. After a swim in the cool fresh water, we settle down on a sandy patch to laze in the shade of the large breadfruit tree. I pick up a piece of charcoal and a dried banana leaf and begin to draw. Pico watches intently as I sketch a simple fish and a snail. After I finish, I toss the charcoal away, place the banana leaf on the ground next to me, and lie back. Pico reaches over and picks up the leaf. He inspects the drawing, smiles, and sets it on the ground next to him. I smile back. Pico has borrowed something from me, and now we're officially friends.

The following day, while we are out on the boat, Kizo, standing in the stern, leans over and slaps his butt. "A big shark!"

Luca and I jump and look around, nervously checking for a dorsal fin in the water. Nothing. I look back at Kizo, mystified. "Where's the shark?"

"No. I want you to make a tattoo of a big shark chasing a school of fish right here, and Pico wants a monkey climbing a banana tree."

Pico is patting his left shoulder and nodding.

"Oh, oh. You're in trouble now." Luca laughs.

"But I don't know how to do a tattoo!"

"I told you." Luca holds up his thumb and forefinger to Kizo. "Short penis."

I swat his hand away. "Stop it. I'm not a short penis. It's just I've never made a tattoo before."

"Short penis." Luca nods.

"You're not helping."

That afternoon when we return to the beach, Luca announces he's dying of thirst, and he goes off to find some grog, leaving us to hang out the nets and clean the fish. After we're done, Pico and I linger, waiting for Kizo, who is by the beached boat splicing some pieces of old rope together.

"C'mon, Kizo, let's go to the bathing pool." I moan. "It's hot as hell, and Pico stinks like fish."

Pico lifts his arm and smells his pit.

"Yes, you, Pico. You smell like dead fish!"

Pico flexes his bicep and makes a monkey cry. Meanwhile, Kizo takes a small bundle from the canoe and walks up to the shady patch under the coconut tree where I'm hiding from the scorching sun. He hands me the bundle, and I unwrap it: some long, spiny thorns and a little ceramic pot with a cork lid, filled with an inky black substance.

"I want it right here." He twists around and rubs his left buttock.

"Okay, but for starters, I'm only going to do a simple tattoo on your leg."

Kizo lies down on the sand, and I trace out a starfish design in black ink. My hand is shaking, and I'm running with sweat as I begin to jab him with the spines along the black lines. At first I don't sink the spines in deep enough and the black ink doesn't penetrate the skin. Then I jab the spine in deeper. Kizo yelps, and a small amount of blood appears.

"Sorry." I sit back and wipe the sweat from my brow. "I'm not sure I can do this."

Pico is bent over Kizo's leg, closely inspecting the fine lines I've already made.

"Go on, go on," Kizo encourages.

"Okay, give me space, Pico." I press him back and hunch over Kizo's leg. "Kizo, I'm worried about Luca," I say as I stretch his skin with my thumb and forefinger. "He's drinking grog all the time." I insert a spine into his skin.

Kizo flinches. "He says he drinks because he is unhappy and cannot stay here."

"I know he wants to leave, but we have to wait until we're rescued." I make sharp little jabs on Kizo's leg with the ink-covered spine.

"He says he cannot wait anymore, and he will leave as soon as the calm season arrives."

I shiver. It's obvious that Luca is more desperate than I thought, and time is running out for both of us. "When is the calm season?"

"In about three moons. I will leave with him."

I say nothing more and continue to jab Kizo with the spine, but all the while I'm thinking about what to do. Could I really abandon Luca and stay here on the island like a native, or should I leave with Luca and return to the outside world? Whatever choice I make, it will be forever.

After about an hour, I'm finished. Kizo gets up and goes down to the water to rinse off the extra black ink smeared all over his leg. Pico lies down in his place, and I trace a snail design on his shoulder.

"Let me see it before I start on Pico."

Kizo strolls up, and I closely inspect my work. The star on his leg is red and swollen, but he's not bleeding, and the black lines are more or less even.

"Okay, victim number two."

Having determined the correct depth to jab in the spines, I'm much less nervous now as I work on Pico. And before the sun has set below the aquamarine horizon, Pico and Kizo have their tattoos.

A few days later, I'm down at the beach with Kizo for his second tattoo. He's bent over a fallen coconut tree, and I'm kneeling in the sand, my face inches away from his left buttock. I delicately grip a long spine with my right hand while holding the pot of ink with my left.

"Did you give that tattoo to Luca—the one on his arm?" Kizo asks, his hands firmly clasped to the tree trunk.

"Hold still, big boy." I steady his trembling butt cheek as I carefully put the finishing touches on. "Oh, Luca's anchor? No, he's a sailor. Sailors do that in the outside world."

"Ouch!" Kizo jumps.

"Sorry. Did that last one hurt?" I dab away a drop of blood. "I'm almost finished."

"His daddy or some special boy must have given it to him," Kizo says and sniffles a little.

I dip my spines into the inkpot again. "Luca doesn't have a father. No, I'm sure it was just a tattoo artist, no one special to him."

"Well, it must have been someone special to him, or why else would he wear his sign?"

"I don't know." I sit back and examine my work. "Kizo, do you get jealous about Luca sometimes?"

"What do you mean?" Kizo twists his head to look past his hip at me.

"Well, I'm sure you know he'll fuck anything on the island."

"I know." Kizo smiles. "It makes me so proud to be in love with a man that so many other men desire."

"How do you separate love and sex without jealousy?" I now lean sideways to look at Kizo's face.

"Sex is like talking. You can't tell someone you love not to talk to anyone else."

"And jealousy?" I ask.

"Jealousy is always a problem. Big problem," Kizo says, shaking his head.

I sit back and examine my work. "Kizo, who gave Nando the butterfly tattoo on his chest?" I say, trying to mask my curiosity.

"Ah, Tukuman, of course. Nando is very devoted to him." Kizo nods.

"Tukuman!" I feel a sudden pang of jealousy. "Have I met him already?"

"Yes," Kizo says. "When you were out of your head. It was Tukuman who cured you."

"Well, maybe I should thank him," I say, probing for a casual way to meet and size up my competition.

"No. That would not be a good idea." Kizo shakes his head vigorously. "He does not want to meet you." Kizo is so definite it's obvious our discussion of Tukuman has been terminated. I sneer and continue with the tattoo. Kizo is right, jealousy leads to problems. At least now I know there is someone else in Nando's life.

"There. All finished." I slap Kizo's ass. "Go wash off the extra ink and let me see."

"Okay." Kizo grins. "Then we can make sex."

It's not long after I've finished the shark chasing the school of fish on Kizo's buttocks and the monkey in a banana tree on Pico's shoulder that word spreads. Suddenly I've become the most popular tattoo artist on the island, and I now have a long list of men who all want to wear my mark of friendship.

Shortly after, I meet Luca at our spot up on the cliff. He's agitated, and he smells of grog, as usual. "Have you found out anything new from Nando?" he barks.

I know if I tell him about the myths Nando told me, he'll only get angry. "Nothing that would help," I say.

"Damn, they gotta know something. We haven't seen a passing ship or even a plane, not even a little smoke on the horizon the whole time we've been here."

"It hasn't been that long, only about six moons or so."

"Try ten."

"Ten?"

"Yes, muffin head. Let's face it, we're stuck here, and we're never gonna get out of this hellhole and back to civilization." Luca points toward the flat, empty horizon. He still hasn't mentioned his plans to leave in our lifeboat as soon as the calm season comes, so I play along like I don't know anything.

"It's hardly a hellhole, and I'm sure it's just a matter of time until we see a passing ship. We just have to be patient." I feel no sense of urgency or even melancholy. Truthfully, I dread the day we'll be rescued.

"Fine for you. You have Nando."

"You have Kizo."

"It's not the same thing. We're just fuck buddies."

I sit upright and look sternly at him. "Well, Kizo's certainly in love with you."

"Love." Luca practically spits the word. "I'm not like you. I don't want to spend the rest of my life with a man. It's not natural! It's all these queers on this island. They're turning us into faggots."

Suddenly I remember one of my mother's favorite sayings, "You can take the boy out of the religion, but you can't take the religion out of the boy." Luca may have escaped St. Mike's, but not before they'd poisoned his mind and heart.

"Nobody's turning *me* into anything," I snarl back at him. "You just want someone to blame."

"I don't want to be a faggot!" he yells, but it's as if he's yelling at himself, not me.

"You mean a faggot like me," I yell back.

Luca rises to his feet. "You need to make up your mind if you want to return home with me or spend the rest of your life rotting here with these queers." Then he grabs himself. "This is my dick, and I'll do what I want with it."

I shake my head in disgust. "Why are you being such a jerk?"

Luca throws me his middle finger and stomps down the path.

I stare out to sea, but I'm shaking with anger. I've spent my whole life searching for a place where I belong. Everything I've ever fantasized about is right here on the island, and Luca is doing his best to ruin it. I know I have to help him leave. I owe him that much. But I don't know if I want to leave with him. Once I've made my decision to either stay or go, there will be no turning back.

As I sit there contemplating my options, I spy a lone canoe in the moonlight. I'm not sure, but it appears to be Dzil. The canoe silently traverses the bay, heads out toward the reef in the direction of the Far Island, and disappears into the cover of darkness. I shiver. I have the ominous feeling trouble is coming, and I don't know why.

*

Guy stopped speaking and folded his hands on his lap with satisfaction.

"And so your characters, Guy and Luca, learn to fish, and have lots of friends and lots of sex." Richard rubbed the back of his head. "But Luca rejects his homosexuality and any suggestion of love with Kizo. Whereas Guy embraces his homosexuality but is unable to find intimacy with Nando."

"You got it, Doc." Guy nods.

Richard scratches his chin. "One struggles to escape the fantasy while the other is drawn deeper into it. To me, these two characters represent your own internal struggle."

"Ha. Doc, I got a question for you," Guy said with a challenging tone. "What do you think of bisexuals?"

Richard contemplates for a moment. "I'm sure I don't have to tell you, sexuality is not that specific, especially when we're young."

"Now you're blowing smoke up my ass. I know what the literature says. I'm asking you. What do you think about bisexuals?" Guy barked.

"The answer is, I think many people are bisexual." Richard sounded irritated.

"I think a lot of bisexuals are like Larry and Luca—full of shit. They're just repressed fags who can get it up with pretty much anyone. They lie and hide to get all the privileges and advantages of being straight, but the minute nobody's looking, they're out playing the boys. The only thing a bisexual ever thinks about is himself."

"That's pretty harsh." Richard had a sour expression.

"You tell me then, have you ever met a bisexual you could trust?" Guy tossed out his words.

Richard rolled his head and crossed his arms. "I have a number of bisexual patients and friends."

"I didn't ask you if you had friends. I asked you if you could trust them." Guy waved his hand dismissively. "I'll take that as a no."

Richard uncrossed his arms and gripped the arms of the chair. "I can see that our discussion has awakened a lot of angry feelings. Are we really talking about bisexuals, or are we talking about something specific?"

"We're talking about me, Doc." Guy forced a bitter smile. "It's always about me." Guy paused and clenched his teeth.

"Are you saying that you are bisexual?" Richard spoke with a clinical tone.

"No, I'm saying I once tried to be." Guy clenched his fists. "Just like I tried to be heterosexual before that. And I think you already know what that's all about, don't you?"

Richard nodded. "I guess I do."

"Oh, by the way, that kid whose head Larry and the others shoved down the toilet dropped out of school." Guy stood up. "They found him frozen to death in a snowbank in Toronto the following spring." Guy looked to the floor as he slowly walked out of the room.

Chapter Fifteen

Boyhood Forever

"Good morning, Armando. You look nice today," Guy said as he walked up to the nurses' station.

"Oh, hi, Mr. Palmer. Thanks, I just got my hair cut. Thought I'd try something a little different." Armando grinned self-consciously. "Heaven knows the old style wasn't working, so why not change the bait?"

"Oh, so you're a fisherman?" Guy smiled. "If you're just looking to hook whatever fish comes your way then any old bait will do, but if you have a specific catch in mind, you'll need the right lure." Guy flexed his eyebrows. "Speaking of fishing." Guy placed the cups of coffee on the counter and dug in his pocket. "I have something that might help." He reached across the counter and held out his closed fist to Armando.

Armando blushed. "Oh no, Mr. Palmer, we can't accept money."

Guy chuckled. "No, no, it's not money. It's my lucky fishing lure."

Armando cautiously held out his hand, and Guy placed something cold and heavy in his palm, a gold medallion and chain. Armando turned it over and examined it. A double-headed eagle was embossed into the face of the medallion. It was slightly irregular, as if it had been made by hand, and it appeared very old.

"A fishing buddy gave it to me a long time ago. Don't worry, Kiddo. It's just a stupid little trinket, and I have plenty more where that came from." Guy waved his hand. "It just might attract the attention of the right fish." Guy nodded in the direction of Richard's office.

Armando bit his lower lip. "Thanks, Mr. Palmer, but he barely even notices me." His face was now bright red. "I guess I'm only dreaming. He's way out of my league."

"Nobody's out of your league, Kiddo. Wear it and see what happens." Guy grabbed a coffee in each hand, winked, turned, and headed down the corridor. He walked into the office humming.

Richard looked up from his screen. "You're certainly bright today."

"Was just talking to a young fishing buddy of mine this morning. That always lifts me up."

"So you've made a friend?"

"Hey, who knows?" Guy shrugged. "Maybe our sessions are helping."

"Well, it must be doing something, or you wouldn't keep bringing me coffee." Richard peeled back the plastic top and took a careful sip.

"I'm sure I'm not the first self-absorbed old fag to take advantage of a captive audience."

Richard smiled. "Everyone needs someone they can talk to."

"I like talking to you youngsters. I like your energy and naiveté."

"Well, I'm hardly a youngster," Richard said.

"You know, I think I'd make a good grandfather. I'd take my grandson fishing, teach him to belch and make armpit farts, tell him stories about the war, and show him the battle scar on my leg."

"You were in the war?"

"No, don't be ridiculous." Guy flipped his hand.

"Why don't you try volunteering with the Gay Youth Outreach Program?"

"Too dangerous. When it comes to children, an accusation is a condemnation, proof or not, and gay men are sitting ducks. Do I really care if someone else's kid grows up lonely, unhappy, and self-destructive?"

"I think you do."

Guy turned and gazed out the window for a moment, then began to speak again. "When I was young, I knew I was different, but I had no one I could talk to. My puberty was an event largely ignored by my parents in Presbyterian silence. Back then, discoveries about the changes to my body and mind were solitary and frightening, based on bits of information I got or overheard from the other boys at school, most of which was incomplete or wrong. So I decided if I tried hard enough I would magically begin to act and feel like the other boys. I would become a real boy."

"You mean like Pinocchio?"

"Exactly! Pinocchio. A boy with a heart of wood who tells lies." Guy exhaled loudly. "I tried so hard to become a real heterosexual boy."

"And how did that make you feel?"

Guy said nothing. He held both arms up limply, as if they were suspended by strings. Then he placed them back on his lap and began to tell his tale.

*

Even though I live with Nando and we spend a lot of time together, nobody seems to regard us as a couple the way they do Luca and Kizo. Nando continues to skillfully divert any attempts on my part to consummate our relationship, which only frustrates me more. I want to tell him how I feel, but I'm afraid if I push him, I will mess up what we already have. And then there is Tukuman. Maybe Nando is in a committed relationship with him and is only interested in me as a friend. For now, all I can do is gaze at him with starry eyes but not touch him.

It's almost dark by the time I return from the signal fire and Nando from one of his usual visits to Tukuman. After a light dinner of fruit and cold fish, we sit outside on the platform terrace listening to the rhythmic sound of frogs and watching the shadows made by flickering torches leap along the steps of the pyramid mound and the plaza. I lie back with my head resting on my hands, breathe in the aroma of salt air and jungle mixed with smoke from smoldering fires, and stare up into the night sky. Nando looks at me, and I smile. "Yabai, you look as if you have eaten the moon."

"What does that mean?" I lift my head.

"Oh, it is an expression we use when someone has everything they desire. We say they have eaten the moon."

"Not the entire moon. I don't have everything I desire." I rest my head back on my hands.

Nando lies down next to me, and we both stare skyward. Then he begins to tell me a story. "The Shark Beast went to the sky to be with the Daughter of the Moon. See that? That's the Shark there, those three stars." Nando extends his arm and points the way Luca did when we were on board the ship that fatal night.

"But there was nothing to eat in the sky," Nando continues. "So the Daughter of the Moon told the Shark Beast to eat the moon. Every night the Shark Beast takes a bite out of the moon until it is completely gone. Then three nights later, the moon begins to reappear little by little until it is whole again."

"Nando, you don't really believe these myths, do you?"

"Of course, I do. We count everything by the bites of the moon," Nando says flatly.

"You know back home they have flown to the moon?"

"We have been telling stories about sailing to the moon for generations," Nando says with no tone of surprise. "Probably, you have some of the same stories as we do."

Nando reaches over and starts to play with a strand of my hair. "Yabai, do you not believe my stories?"

"I want to believe more than you know, but I'm not sure I can." I roll my head to the side and lightly kiss the back of his hand. He rests it for a moment then pulls his hand away.

"Oh, I can help you." His eyes sparkle.

"How?"

"Tomorrow, you will come with me to put the children down for their afternoon sleep. And you will discover that none of them will settle down until you have played the shark eats the moon with them. After that, when you finally have them all in their hammocks asleep, you will say 'Nando, I believe, I believe.'"

The next afternoon after fishing, while Lalli and I are relaxing together at the beach, I catch a glimpse of someone in the shadows watching us. For some time now, I've had the omnipresent feeling that I'm being watched—a sensation more than anything I see or hear. I hope it's Nando who has followed me, and I'm encouraged, flattered, even excited by what I think is his voyeuristic attention. You know what they say; voyeurism is participation. Just as I'm about to turn around and see who it is, Lalli grabs my head and slides his dick in my mouth. By the time we shift our positions to where I can see over his backside, the figure is gone.

An hour later, when I return to the village, I find Nando and Pico sitting cross-legged in the central plaza surrounded by children.

"It's a little late in the afternoon to start pottery class, isn't it?"

Nando casually looks up from a coil pot he's making with Lisha. Like Pico and the children, he has dried chalky clay smears on his face and chest. He smiles brightly. "How was fishing, Yabai?"

"Not so good," I say. "We came back early."

"Were you out with Kizo?"

"No, Kizo and Luca went off together. I was out with Lalli."

"Ahh," Nando says and looks to the ground.

After a moment of uncomfortable silence, I ask, "What have you been doing all day?"

"Pico and I have been very busy with the children. We have been making pots all day." He gestures over to the row of tiny irregular-shaped bowls drying in the sun along the lower step.

I think about the mysterious figure who's been watching me. I now know it's not Nando. But who could it be? The figure has a form and manner that is familiar. I can't say with certainty, but the figure has the feel of Luca. For the life of me, I have no idea why Luca should be so interested in my activities.

I sit down, grab a lump of clay, and start kneading it. Tiki moves in close to me, and I turn and smile. The other boys Tiki's age are all off learning to spear fish or make nets, their voices squeaking and cracking uncontrollably, their baby fat and smooth skin transforming into muscle and body hair. The dark shadow of peach fuzz on Tiki's upper lip says his manhood will soon overtake his lingering childhood, but for the time being, he remains with Nando and the younger children.

The following afternoon, Nando is teaching the children how to make baskets. Since the old basket I've been using as a fishing hat is starting to fray badly, and without it my Irish nose will be bare against the scorching sun, basketmaking is a skill I need to learn.

I sit with Nando and a cluster of children on the bottom steps of the pyramid mound. Piles of dried hemp and bamboo strips lie at our feet. Nando smiles. "It is simple. Make a sun shape on the ground with the strips of bamboo. Secure the center with a hemp knot. Holding the center with your foot, bend the bamboo upward to create the ribs of the basket and tie them at the other end. Now start at the bottom and weave hemp in and out of the ribs to form the body. To finish off the basket, bend over each bamboo rib at the top and weave it into the hemp body. You have a basket!"

In thirty minutes, Nando has a basket. Soon after, most of the children are finishing off their baskets. With a hand from Nando, even little Lisha has a basket. But after numerous tries and great effort, I still do not have anything that might resemble a basket. By now, the children are getting impatient, so Nando sings with them while I labor on until eventually, I have what you might call a basket. Unsuccessfully, I try to push the bottom of my basket flat and force it to sit upright. Lisha and some of the children giggle. Obviously, it will be a while before I have mastered the skill well enough to produce a serviceable hat.

As I inspect my basket, I glance over at Tiki. The center of his bamboo ribs have come untied, and all his weaving is about to unravel. I lean over and hold the center together while he grabs another piece of hemp and reties it. He smiles nervously and finishes weaving the body of his basket. He ties off his final bamboo rib and holds it up for me to see. I throw him a thumbs-up.

Nando comes to the end of his song and looks over at me helping Tiki. "I think you made a friend."

I give Nando a covert wink.

"Some of the children, like Lisha, want to spend all their time in the men's village." Nando speaks in English so the children can't understand him. "Others—" Nando lightly jerks his head in the direction of Tiki. "—are very timid and don't want to leave their mothers."

I nod gently and raise one eyebrow, signaling to Nando that I understand.

Basketmaking is over for the day, and as usual it's time for a story before a nap. Nando and I sit cross-legged in a circle with the children around and on top of us. Lisha is resting in Nando's lap.

"Today I am going to tell you the story of Ichti the Fish Boy," Nando says. "Ichti was a very beautiful boy. The most beautiful boy who ever was. His eyes were blue-green like the sea." Nando turns, looks into my eyes, and smiles. "His hair was red like the sky at sunset. His skin was as smooth and as perfect as the water of the bathing pool. His legs, strong and slender, grew like the giant ceiba tree. His penis hung like a banana in flower. Ichti's chest was as broad and flat as the washing rocks at the mouth of the river. He truly was a gift of nature, and every boy competed to be close to him."

One of the little boys in the circle squirms over and hugs a red-haired boy from behind. Nando pauses a moment, looks at them, and grins.

"In fact," Nando continues, "his beauty was so strong that Ichti rarely spoke to anyone. He spent long hours staring into the water at his own reflection. The people laughed and said, 'Ichti has fallen in love with himself.'"

"Wait a minute," I said. "This story sounds familiar. I've heard it before."

"Maybe you heard this story when you were a baby?"

"I must have heard it somewhere, I'm sure," I half mumble, embarrassed that I'm interrupting story time.

Nando ignores me and continues on. "Ichti said, 'I am trying to see through my beauty to find out who is inside.'

"Later some of the men found Ichti lying facedown in the water, floating motionless. At first they thought he had drowned, but then they realized he was holding his breath.

"The men laughed and said, 'Ichti has fallen in love with fish.'

"Ichti said, 'Fish do not care about my beauty because all fish are beautiful.'

"Then one day, Ichti did not return from his swim. The men took their canoes and went to find the lost boy, but after searching day and night all they found was his loincloth and a patch of red hair floating in the sea. They cried, 'A shark has taken our beautiful boy and eaten him.'"

Nando makes an exaggerated gesture with his arms like a shark's jaw, and the children squeal.

"Seven full moons later, the men came across a marvelous school of rainbow fish and filled their nets. As always, the beautiful colors of the fish drained to gray as they flapped and gasped for air on the bottom of the canoes. Just as the men were about to return to shore and share their good fortune with their sisters, one fish called to them. 'Do you not know me? I am Ichti, the lost boy from the village. I beg you to set me and my brother fish free.' And that's when the men realized that this fish was truly their lost boy, Ichti."

"What happened to Ichti and his brothers?" the red-haired boy, who is still being held in the arms of the other boy, calls out.

"Well," Nando says in a serious and exaggerated tone. "The men took him and his brother fish back to the village and cooked them and ate them... just like I am going to do to you!" Nando scoops up Lisha and one of the other children in his arms and buries his face in their soft bellies, making growls and gnawing sounds. The other children instantly join in, and quiet story time dissolves into a wrestle and tickle session. Nando and I are buried in children.

I've never been so happy in my life. I want this moment to last forever. Then a sudden dread flows through me as I think about Luca and his plans to leave. I hold my breath and look at Nando with an expression of panic.

"What's wrong, Yabai?"

I want to yell. *I can't leave! Not now. I just got here.* Instead I exhale loudly and say, "Oh, nothing, nothing really. I'm just being stupid."

Nando looks at me sweetly and smiles back. "You could never be stupid."

I try to force a smile, but the muscles in my neck are rigid.

A few afternoons later, Pico and I return home from fishing to find a large basket of potatoes and yams in the center of the room. "Where did all of this come from?"

Pico sits down in front of the basket, inspecting the tubers and making little grunts of approval as he turns each spud over in his hands.

"Tuss brought them for you," Nando says.

"Me." I grit my teeth. "I thought I wasn't supposed to accept gifts from women. I'm not going to give her my juice!"

"She did not give you these potatoes in exchange for juice. She gave them to you to thank you for being Tiki's friend."

I drop my shoulders. "I didn't do anything. I just helped him with his baskets and clay pots."

Nando smiles. "Every boy needs a hero."

I blush.

Later on after dinner, Nando and I sit outside on the lower terrace step and watch the night sky.

"See that star over there and the group of stars below?" Nando points. "That is the Monkey King. The bright star is his eye, and those three stars in a row make his tail."

"Wait a minute, right there?" I point to where Nando was pointing. "Yeah, I see him. There he is." I drop my arm and turn toward Nando. "Tell me more about Tiki. Isn't he too old for the group?"

Nando sighs and sits back against his outstretched arms. "Yes, he is too old. His one mother died in childbirth and left Tuss alone with him. The women say that Tuss is now with child in her belly, but she still does not have a mate. It will be very difficult for her to look after Tiki all alone once the new baby arrives. His older father, Molap, pushes him too hard and wants him to become a man and move to the men's village, but Tiki is not ready yet. And his younger father, Den, is not strong enough to oppose Molap and protect him."

"Sometimes things like this happen where I'm from too."

"The problem is, Tiki is a boy who refuses to grow up."

"I'm sure he'll grow up when he's ready."

Nando looks to the ground and speaks. "Sometimes a boy gets stuck and never becomes a real man. He stays a boy forever."

"It sounds like the story of Peter Pan," I say and tell him the story the best I can remember it. When I finish, Nando sits silently, still looking at the ground.

"Did you like the story?"

"Oh yes." He looks up and forces a smile. "It is very frightening."

"Frightening?"

"Yes, the evil spirit, the Tinker Bell, who tricked Peter Pan into remaining a boy, and the bad man, the Captain Hook, who wants to have sex with him even though he is still a boy. Very frightening."

"Maybe I didn't tell it quite right."

"No, no. You told it very well." Nando drops his voice. "A man must never have sex with a boy until that boy is initiated and becomes a true man."

I realize we are no longer talking about children's stories.

Nando looks directly at me with pleading eyes. "When a boy is not properly initiated, he remains a boy forever. He can never be a true man." Nando's face is sad, and I don't know why. He gets up and says, "I am tired now. I must go to bed." He leaves me alone on the step.

*

Guy's head sank, and he began to sob.

"It's okay." Richard handed him a Kleenex.

Guy sniffed loudly, coughed, then blew his nose into the Kleenex and tossed it into the paper bin.

"Take your time."

Still sniffling, Guy shook his head.

"Can you tell me why you are crying?"

"Peter Pan, I guess." Guy took two deep breaths. "I know it's stupid, but why can't I be a boy again? Maybe I could get it right the second time around."

"We've all had that wish at one time or another," Richard said in a slow, delicate tone as he rubbed his brow.

"Or maybe I would just repeat the same old mistakes." Guy dragged his forearm across his eyes and sniffled.

"Guy, do you have anyone you really care for—that you love?" Richard said with a continued delicacy in his voice.

"Yes, an entire village." Guy shook his head. "Man, I miss my boys." He wiped his eyes again, cleared his throat, and pushed himself forward in the sofa. "I think that's enough for today."

Richard looked at his watch. "Are you okay?"

"Fine, Doc. I just get a little sentimental at times."

As Guy rose to his feet, the silhouette of a figure knocked on the frosted glass of the office door.

Richard swiveled around in his chair. "Come in."

Armando entered cautiously, wearing the nervous smile of someone who has accidentally intruded on a private conversation. "Sorry to interrupt."

"No, we went past time again. I wasn't watching the clock."

"Here are the clinical files you asked for." Armando leaned forward and handed the files to Richard. The V-neck collar of his scrub top hung low, exposing the upper part of his dark hairy chest like a view onto a Mediterranean landscape. The medallion dangling from his neck gleamed in the light as it turned.

"That's nice." Richard reached up and took it in his fingertips. "It looks like an old Spanish doubloon." Then he quickly retracted his hand and shifted back in his chair.

Armando stood slowly upright and took the coin in his own fingers, rubbing it slowly. "A friend gave it to me." Armando glanced quickly over his shoulder at Guy, who was still lingering in the doorway. Guy winked and disappeared.

Chapter Sixteen

Fugi Birds

It was unseasonably warm. The air conditioning in the outpatient department, which had been blasting cold all through the summer regardless of the temperature outside, was now barely emitting a whiff of fresh air. Richard was already sitting in the swivel chair. He had removed his tie and unbuttoned the collar of his white Egyptian cotton shirt. He watched as Guy walked into the studio carrying a small paper bag. He was wearing a pair of oversized khaki Bermuda shorts and a white undershirt. The array of tattoos, which had been partially hidden under the T-shirts he usually wore, were now visible: a jaguar on his left shoulder, a shark on his right, a monkey peeking out on his pectoral, and a school of fish swimming around the base of his neck and disappearing down his back.

"Good morning," Richard said. "You look cooler than me this morning."

"I wasn't sure if hot coffee would be right, so I also brought you one of those frozen coffee things."

"Oh, that was very thoughtful. It's like an oven in here today."

Guy took a clear plastic cup with a dome lid out of the bag and handed it to Richard. He took a foam coffee cup out for himself and placed the bag in the waste bin.

"You're not having one of these?" Richard sucked on the straw that was wedged through the dome lid.

"No, I'll stick to my regular coffee and leave the milkshakes to you kids."

Richard stopped sucking on the straw, removed the lid, and took a small drink from the cup before setting it on the desk.

Guy walked over to the sofa and sat down slowly, grunting slightly as he did so. "I'm a little stiff today. I'm getting too old for this nonsense."

"Why? Have you been working out a little too much?"

"Well, you might say that. Actually, I went on a little trip to Cobourg."

"Did you drive?"

"Oh no. Last week I gave my car to a chubby little chap I met at Sailors."

"You gave it or lent it to him?"

"No, I gave it to him."

Richard scrunched up his face. "Was he a good friend?"

"Nope. Actually, the other evening was the first time I talked with him. His name is Joel or Joey—one of those soap opera names—usually comes in with his tall skinny friend, but he was alone the other night. He's the young chap I had sex with in the dark room at the Black Eagle a few weeks ago, remember?"

Richard nodded.

"Anyway, it seems like his tall skinny friend had abandoned him to head off to Provincetown for a week with the cool crowd." Guy yawned and stretched. "And this kid wanted to drive down there on his own."

"You know people don't usually give their car away to people they've just met in a bar, don't you?" Richard held out his hands. "Was it an old car?"

"Brand-new Kompressor. Just bought it last year, but I don't use it much. Don't really get a whole lot of pleasure out of it sitting in the garage collecting dust."

"Yeah, but—"

"Look," Guy said as if he were about to explain something so obvious even a child could understand. "For me it was just a stupid toy. For that poor kid, it might be the defining moment in his life. Who knows? But I do know this. His nasty friend is going to shit himself when that kid shows up in P-town driving a sixty-thousand-dollar Mercedes."

Richard covered his eyes with his hands and laughed, shaking his head. "Umm, so how did you get to Cobourg? Did you take the bus or the train?"

Guy stretched both arms over his head and groaned. "No, actually I swam down the lake."

"What! Swam? Cobourg must be a hundred and fifty kilometers away."

"Yeah, I know," Guy said. "Pretty silly, huh?"

"Wait a minute. Are you trying to tell me you swam all the way to Cobourg?" Richard crossed his arms and straightened up in his chair.

"No. I realized that Cobourg was a lot farther than I had anticipated, so I only swam as far as Scarborough."

"Scarborough must be—what?—at least thirty kilometers down the lake." Richard's mouth hung open.

"Well, I had my flippers and a float board. All the same, it took me about fifteen hours. But don't worry. I was wearing my swim trunks this time."

Richard shook his head. "What did you do when you reached Scarborough?" He cocked one eyebrow.

"Slept on a beach that night and continued by foot Sunday morning."

"So you're telling me you walked to Cobourg?"

"Nope, only got as far as Port of Newcastle. Then decided I had to come back. Didn't want to be late for our Monday-morning session."

"When did you get back?"

"'Bout four this morning."

Richard breathed in deeply. He propped his chin on his hand. "Were you searching for something, or were you running away from something?"

"Good question." Guy took a slow sip of his coffee. "Both, I guess."

*

Kizo is standing near the canoe holding up the remains of our net as Pico and I walk across the sand toward him.

"What happened?"

Pico wades over to the boat and picks up two broken spears.

"I should not have left our net and spears here at the beach overnight where they could find them."

"Who would do such a thing?"

"Tara," Pico growls as he carries the broken spears back.

"Tara?" I furrow my brow. "But why would the Tara people come all the way from the Far Island just to destroy our fishing gear?"

"It's a warning to stay away. Swordfish season is coming, and the big fish run in the deep water between the reef and their Island. The Tara say the swordfish are theirs, and they do not want us fishing them."

"Well, what can we do now without a net or spears?"

"I will go back to my cottage and get my other net. Pico, ask Lalli for his extra spear." Kizo throws the ruined net onto the sand and walks back toward the village.

A short while later, Kizo returns. We push the canoe into the water, and Pico and I climb in. Luca has still not appeared. "Is Luca coming?"

Just then Luca steps out from the trees and staggers down the beach with a grog gourd in his hand. "Hey, Kizo," he calls out. "You weren't going to leave me behind, were you?"

"C'mon," I yell. "Get in."

Luca stumbles knee-deep into the water and up to the boat. He braces himself on the gunwales with one hand, carefully holding his gourd high in the air with the other.

Then, as if in slow motion, he sits down in the water. "Oops!" He laughs. "I seem to have wet my pants."

I laugh nervously as Kizo lifts him to his feet. "Are you sure you're in any condition to come out with us this morning?"

"I'm fine. Just lost my sea legs, that's all," he slurs and falls forward, but Kizo catches him. "Okay. I'm just going to lie down over there under that big old coconut tree for a while." His outstretched arm wavers as he points. "You boys go. I'll be fine. Just fine."

Kizo picks him up and carries him over to the coconut tree. He seats him in the sand and kisses his forehead. Luca tries to swat him away but only connects with air. "I'm gonna stay here and take a little nap." Luca takes a swig from the gourd and falls backward onto the sand. Kizo stands there looking like he doesn't know what to do.

"C'mon, Kizo," I call. "He's fine. We'll pick him up when we get back."

"Go, go, go, go," Luca mumbles and waves his hand spastically.

Kizo hesitantly returns to the boat and shoves us out. He jumps in the stern and paddles toward the reef, all the while looking over his shoulder to where Luca is stretched out on the beach.

Kizo is completely devoted to Luca and looks after him as if he were a child. All the same, it's been moons since I've seen Luca without a grog gourd in his hand. I don't think he's bathing anymore, and he's even started to smell like grog when he sweats. I'm growing more worried about him each day.

That night, the Reds have organized a kind of singsong competition between the brotherhoods. As I head toward the great bonfire at the beach, I pass Mazu and Jab. Mazu leans his bony elbow on Jab's head, flicks the bib of his loincloth, and throws out his hip in one smooth gesture. I glance at his exposed butt and try not to grimace. "Is Nando at home with the other children tonight?" he says in a mocking tone, and both he and Jab snicker.

I cringe.

"Oh, don't look like that," he says. "I'm only having a bit of fun with you. I'm sure it's just a matter of time before you will want to have some fun with me too." He licks his lips and rolls his eyes seductively.

I'm just about to say something nasty to Mazu for the way he treats Nando when Pico appears and growls at them. They both jump back. Pico grabs my arm and pulls me away. We walk over to the bonfire and greet everyone at the gathering, and all the while I look around nervously for Luca. No sign of him or Kizo. Lalli wraps his arms around me and hands me a grog gourd. I kiss his neck and take a swig. The drumbeats begin, and we all sway to the rhythm. Suddenly, an ear-piercing birdcall catches everyone's attention. We look up at Luca and Kizo, who are standing on the cliff waving torches. Pico and I make silly birdcalls back at them. Luca bends his arms behind his back and flaps them as he struts around like a chicken. Then he lets out a whoop and comes bounding down the trail with Kizo following. Once on the beach, he bounces around, hugging and kissing everybody. Luca darts over to Den, who is sitting shyly by himself, throws him over his shoulder, and carries him toward the bonfire while Kizo slaps out a rhythm on Den's butt.

I breathe a sigh of relief.

"Okay, let's get this party started," Luca calls out. "Who's first?"

Lalli, who is a Blue brother, begins by singing a raucous song about riding a fish as he dances like a rodeo rider. The crowd cheers, laughs, and dances along with him, and the grog flows freely.

"C'mon, Kiddo." Luca jumps up behind me and gives me a hug. "It's time for the Green brothers." Luca holds the grog gourd up and pours some in my mouth. I start to choke and spit half of it out onto my chest.

"Careful, Kiddo. This stuff burns a little on the way down." He takes a large swig. "Okay, you're on." He gives me a little shove toward the bonfire. I'm surrounded by flickering silhouettes of men. Luca waves his hands up and down. "Shh, shh, everybody. Listen up." He takes another big gulp of grog.

When I was young, I often made up little songs to sing to myself, so it's not too difficult for me to create a song about the sea. Kizo hands me the grog gourd, I take another swig, clear my throat, and begin to sing a melancholy tune as I swerve and sway with the rhythm of the sea.

"Oh little squid, you swim alone,

The coral reef, you call your home.

You have no tail, you have no fin,

With your arms, is how you swim.

Up and down, you float and sink,

Oh little squid, you shoot your ink."

And I throw my arms into the air to signal the end of my song. But instead of cheers, I hear a low groan from the crowd while Mazu and Jab titter in the background like a couple of hyenas. Pico covers his head with his arms. Suddenly Luca bursts in, laughing hysterically and dancing around the bonfire.

I make a quick retreat to where Kizo is standing. "I need a drink, big boy." Kizo pours some grog into my mouth then folds me into his giant arms and rocks me. I bury my face in his hairy chest.

Luca is still laughing as he bounds over to us. "That was so brave. Not everyone has the courage to admit they have a small dick and like to wank."

I lift my face from Kizo's chest. "Small dick? What are you talking about?"

"Kiddo! The songs are not supposed to be bucolic images of the sea! Watch and learn how the Reds do it." Luca takes an enormous drink of grog, leaps to the center of the ring, and begins to sing loudly off-key.

"Big fish, little fish,

Red fish, green,

I've had all the fish,

In the deep blue sea.

Of all the fish,

That I have ever seen.

Kizo has the biggest.

Yes, he's the fish for me."

Luca points to Kizo with both hands, and the crowd goes wild. They sweep Kizo into the center as they dance and sing, "Big fish, little fish...." Kizo lifts Luca up and dances with him on his shoulders. I stand aside and sulk. Then I think, if I'm ever going to live down my reputation as a squid, I'd better join in the fun. Later, I partially redeem myself with a badly rhyming song about a surfacing dolphin spurting in my face.

We sing and dance and drink around the bonfire, the silliness continuing on into the night. With each song, Luca dances faster and harder, coming dangerously close to the flames and only pausing to take great gulps from the gourd. Suddenly he stops and stares into the fire as if he's catching his breath. Pico and I form a conga line and dance. Mazu immediately runs up and grabs hold of my butt, his hands creeping farther toward my crotch with every bounce. Kizo grabs hold of Luca's butt and tries to steer him toward us, but Luca is frozen and refuses to budge, his eyes still fixed on the flames.

Suddenly he yells, "Fire!"

I think he's starting a new song or just yelling out nonsense for the fun of it. I yell back, "Yeah. Burn, man, burn!"

"Fire!" he yells again with panic in his voice. "It's burning. She's gonna blow. Abandon ship. She's going to blow!"

He runs in circles, frantically pushing people away from the bonfire. Kizo trips and falls on top of Mazu, and I trip over Pico. Some of the men continue to dance and laugh while others stand and look confused.

"Oh shit," I say to Kizo. "Something's wrong."

By the time we get to our feet, Luca has run down the beach, screaming in terror. "Fire, abandon ship!"

When we catch up with him, he's curled in a tight ball, wedged into a nook in the cliff at the end of the beach. "We are all going to burn," he repeats over and over. "We're all going to burn."

I remembered my mother saying, "Guilt leaves a stain that never washes out."

Kizo lifts him into his arms, and we take him back to the village. Shortly after we have gotten him settled in Kizo's hut, a strange, fierce-looking old man arrives. His tanned and leathery frame is straight and tall, a dirty loincloth is loosely strung around his waist, and he's covered in tattoos and piercings from head to toe.

"He is Tukuman, the Seer," Kizo says. "He will know what to do."

I'm immediately taken aback. So this is the great Tukuman, the man Nando is so dedicated to—my competition? I cringe at the sight of him. Although it's common for an older man to pair with a younger man, like Den and Molap, I wonder how Nando could be in love with a freaky old man like Tukuman? Then I feel guilty, and my thoughts return to Luca.

Tukuman turns and looks at me, roars something incomprehensible, and points to the doorway.

"I'm not leaving him alone with this guy." But Kizo and Pico grab me and pull me outside the hut. For the next hour or so, we sit huddled together waiting for Tukuman's diagnosis. Suddenly, Tukuman appears in the doorway. He speaks so fast that I can't understand him. He grunts and spits, then stomps off into the darkness.

"What did he say? What did he say?"

"The grog has captured Luca and carried him into the world of dreams. The spirits are too strong for him there. He must not drink grog or they will consume him." Kizo shakes his head. "It's my fault."

"It's no one's fault." I hug Kizo. "What do we do now?"

"He will be fine in a few days, but for now he must rest." Kizo looks to the ground.

A few days later, while I'm sitting at the signal fire, I spot Luca plodding up the trail. He looks weak and jittery and is soaked with sweat.

"It's good to see you out and about, Boy Scout. I missed you," I say in a cheery voice, doing my best to mask my concern. "How are you feeling?"

"I missed you too, Kiddo. I'm fine now, really." He sits beside me and puts his arm around me. "I guess I'm on the wagon for a while."

I snort. "Luca, you're on the wagon permanently." My words sound as if they've come from my father, not me.

"Probably right. I'm a teetotaler now. Listen, I've decided to move up to high ground."

"What? What are you talking about?"

"Kizo and I are going to build a camp in the hills. There's a good spot about there." Luca points to an outcropping part way up the volcano. "I'll have a bird's-eye view of the reef and any ships that come close."

"But you'll be all alone up there. What if something happens?" Now my words sound as though my mother has spoken them.

"Hey, relax, Kiddo. Kizo is staying with me, and it's only an hour's walk up and twenty minutes down.

Besides, as you said, I need to stay away from the grog, and it's too hard living right here in the village."

"Don't you think you'll get lonely up there?" The truth is I don't want to be without him, but I can't quite find the words to tell him.

The next day, Kizo and Luca move to the hills, and for the following couple of weeks, Kizo comes down every morning before dawn to go fishing with Pico and me while Luca remains at their camp. Then one morning, Luca reappears on the beach looking rested and ready, and we head out in the canoe together as if nothing happened. All morning long he and Pico invent songs, which they sing off-key together. Luca splashes Pico with water and grabs the back of my loincloth and hoists it up the crack of my butt.

That afternoon on the beach, he ties a live fish to the back of Molap's loincloth. When Molap realizes there's something wriggling behind him, he jumps around frantically trying to free himself while everyone laughs. Then Luca chases Den down the beach with a sea cucumber. "C'mon, Den. I've got a big green penis just for you!"

When Lalli falls asleep under a tree while mending his net, Luca draws enormous eyebrows on him with a piece of charcoal. Lalli walks around for about twenty minutes before Molap tells him why everyone is laughing. At the bathing pool, Luca and Pico build a swing, and we dive into the water making Tarzan calls.

For the next half moon, Luca continues to arrive with Kizo before dawn, and we all go out fishing together the way we used to. I'm still Kiddo, and now he calls Kizo Tin

Man. It feels like the old Luca is back—the Luca without grog.

In the evenings, although Luca comes to most of the parties, he doesn't drink any grog and usually leaves early with Kizo and one or two friends, but never with me. Nevertheless, we resume our little ritual of watching the sunset up at the signal fire, and it feels like everything is back to the way it once was. I thank the stars Luca has beaten the grog, but I'm also hurt that he is not interested in me. I know he will never be mine, but all the same, I can't seem to let him go.

"Why don't you come back and live in the village?"

"What? And leave Luca Land so you and the others can keep an eye on me?" He gives me a sour grin.

"No, not to spy on you. I just want to make sure you're all right."

"I'm fine, Kiddo. I've got a few ghosts to wrestle with, and I need to be alone. Besides, Tin Man is always nearby." He smiles. "I'm okay... really."

"I know you are. It's just..." I drop my head and bite my lip. Then, half speaking, half mumbling, I say, "You're my best friend—the best friend I've ever had—and I don't know what I'd do if something were to happen to you." I look up at him with longing.

He grins widely at me and leaps on top of me and begins to playfully bat my shoulders. "Kisses, kisses," he calls out and presses his lips to my chest, making loud, slobbering fart noises.

"Stop. Stop it!" I protest through my laughter, but I want him to go on and on.

About a half a moon after that, Luca leaves Kizo behind and sets off in a canoe on his own to explore Far Island outside the reef. I tell myself he's a sailor and a great swimmer, so he'll be fine. All the same, I'm relieved a few days later when he tramps up the stone trail to our lookout spot on the cliff, where I'm tending the fire before bed.

I want to grab him and hug him, but I'm nervous about showing him how much I missed him. Instead, I feign ambivalence and make a little joke. "I hope you brought back a few fish and souvenirs from your holiday."

"Good to see you too, Kiddo. Get buggered by the savages while I was gone?" His words burn like acid.

"Wow, what has you in such a pleasant mood?"

"I'm sick of this shithole: fish, coconuts, and faggots."

"I guess that would include me." I swallow and push back the rising lump in my throat.

Luca doesn't reply. He steps around me and sits on his favorite rock. I continue to poke the burning embers while Luca stares out to sea.

Then he drops his head and clasps it in his hands. Without turning to look at me, he begins to speak. "The Far Island is pretty desolate and a lot dryer than this one. I paddled around it to the other side. There wasn't even a place to beach my canoe, so I dragged it up on some rocks out of sight and hiked up the hill to where I saw some crappy little huts—you could hardly even call it a village." He scratches his head. "I took my fishing spear with me just in case, and it was a good thing too." Luca pauses and rocks like he's trying to calm himself. "When I got there, I stood in the center of the huts near a smoldering fire pit, spread my arms out to show I didn't want to cause trouble, and called out." Luca pauses again and sucks air in through his teeth. "At first, everything was real quiet, and then I heard something like that noise the women make with their tongues coming from the bushes and trees all around me."

"The one they make during the ceremonies?"

"That's it. Anyway, I kept my arms spread out wide and called again, really friendly like." Luca pauses again and scratches his butt.

"And what happened?"

"All of a sudden sticks and rocks and who knows what started raining down on me. I decided it was time to hightail it out of there, but not before I took a couple of blows to the head." He clasps his head, spreads his hair, and leans over for me to look. He has a big bump on the side of his head, and the hair around is crusted with blood.

"Shit!" I reach up to touch his head, but Luca pulls back. "Well, did you see who they were?"

"I didn't get a good look at anyone. As I said, they were hiding in the bushes. But one thing's for sure—whoever lives there doesn't want visitors."

Luca is agitated, and I don't want to stir the pot anymore, so I don't tell him what Nando told me about Tara people living on the Far Island.

"I'm beat." Luca rises. "And I need to be alone and think about some stuff."

"There's a lovesick Tin Man looking for you."

"Don't say that."

"Why not? It's the truth."

"I'm not worth it." Luca starts down the trail. Then he stops and calls back, "Tell him I'm under a tree somewhere with a gourd of grog." And he disappears into the shadows.

I clench my fists. "Damn." Luca is my hero. He's my Superman, and the grog is his kryptonite. I remember how it was with Larry's father back in my village, Dr. Jekyll and Mr. Hyde. When he wasn't drinking, it was stupid jokes and fishing trips for Larry. And when he was, which was most of the time, Larry bore blackened eyes and swollen lips.

I sit there playing with the fire for a while more, then turn and look out to sea. It's a purple void. I listen to the waves crashing against the barrier reef beyond the island and feel safe and protected. I think about all the stories and things Nando has told me—the thoughtful way he pronounces each word, the way he animates each character, and the sincerity of his gentle smile at the end of each tale. Automatically, I raise my forearm to my nose and sniff. I can even smell him on my skin. Why do I always fall for men who are unobtainable?

As I sit there staring out to sea, in the sliver of moonlight I catch sight of the mysterious canoe as it traverses the reef coming from the direction of the Far Island. It silently approaches the cliff at the far end of the bay, and I am able to make out the figure of a small woman paddling. This time I'm sure the woman is Kyle's partner, Dzil, the warrior, the social climber, the one to watch out for. "What's Dzil doing alone in the open sea at night?" I ask. I close my eyes and think. Whatever it is, I hope it doesn't involve Luca. I have a strange feeling—a premonition—Luca hasn't told me everything he discovered on the Far Island. I strain to follow the silvery craft as it glides across the purple surface and is swallowed by the night.

After about twenty minutes, I get up and go home to bed.

"Nando," I say as we lie there in our hammocks in the darkness. "You must know something more about how to get off the island—an old story or a myth or something. If we don't get rescued soon, I'm afraid of what might happen to Luca."

Nando pushes himself up, causing his hammock to swing. The cords grunt against the beams. "Um, well, there is an old story about leaving the island we tell the children."

"Tell me anything that might give us a clue."

"Okay, but I do not think it will help." Nando sounds very unsure as he speaks. "You see, a long time ago, before people came here, there were only animals. The animals had lots of food and were very content. One day after a big storm, a flock of fugi birds arrived on the island. Fugi birds have very big beaks, and they eat bananas, but they cannot swim. There were plenty of bananas on the island for the fugi birds to eat, but soon they became tired of eating bananas and complained they wanted other things to eat.

"The lizards suggested they eat insects, but the fugi birds did not want to eat insects. The jaguar suggested they eat monkeys, but the fugi birds did not want to eat monkeys. The monkeys suggested they eat bananas, and the fugi birds became angry."

"So what did the fugi birds do?" I grab the edge of Nando's hammock and give it a tug to start my hammock swinging.

"The fugi birds said the island was too small, and they wanted to leave. So they gathered up all the bananas they could carry."

"And what happened?" I sit up in my hammock.

"Well—" Nando pauses as if he is searching for the right words or trying to remember the ending. "The fugi birds flew out toward the open sea with their beaks full, but they had gathered too many bananas and they could not fly very far. The other animals sat on the cliff and watched the fugi birds, one by one, grow tired and fall into the sea."

"And?"

"And they all drowned," Nando says quickly.

I say nothing as I rock back and forth in my hammock, thinking about what message this story could have: the futility of trying to leave, the folly of discontentment and greed. Maybe both, maybe neither. "That's a terrible story," I blurt out.

"Well, it's the only one I know. Besides, I have never seen a fugi bird, so something must have happened to them."

"That's not proof that fugi birds ever existed." As soon as the words leave my mouth, I know I'm in trouble.

"Of course, they existed." Nando's voice is agitated. "I have a plate with a picture of a fugi bird on it, and the story is very old, so there must have been fugi birds. Why would anyone make up the story?"

All of a sudden, I start to suspect that's exactly what he's done—made up the story for my benefit. I look over at his big brown eyes shining in the darkness, and at that moment, he can tell me anything and I will believe it. The only words I long to hear are, *love me and stay with me.*

The sound of frogs takes over as we lie quietly swinging in our hammocks.

Then just as I'm drifting to sleep, Nando whispers, "You will leave with Luca?"

Maybe it's not only his devotion to Tukuman that keeps us apart. Maybe Nando is afraid to love me, knowing I will leave him someday. "Yes, probably." I choke out the words. *If only you would give me a reason to stay*, I think. I bite my lip and fight back my tears in silence.

*

Richard swayed the swivel chair back and forth. Then he stopped. "So Guy on the island is faced with a dilemma. He realizes he will never have Luca. Nando, it would appear, belongs to someone else and won't reciprocate his advances. At the same time, more cracks are beginning to show with the Tara people, who are obviously antagonistic and want to disrupt the peace and harmony of this little paradise."

Guy nodded vigorously. "And don't forget the moral of the story." Guy held up his finger. "Nobody ever leaves the island!"

Richard interlaced his fingers. "Yes, but you are with me here and now—in this studio, in Toronto. What concerns me is, can you leave the fantasy?"

Guy grabbed the front of his undershirt and pulled it up, exposing his body mural. "This." He pointed to a large glyph-like tattoo on his belly. "This is a fugi bird."

Richard squinted and leaned forward to take a closer look. "And do fugi birds really exist?"

"Of course they do!" Guy let go of his shirt and thumped his chest with his fist. "Me!" He stood up suddenly. "I'm a fugi bird. Too self-centered and greedy to know what I had." Guy stomped out of the office.

Chapter Seventeen

All for Nando

Guy's cowboy boots made a clopping sound as he walked down the corridor toward Richard's office. He entered and placed both cups of coffee on Richard's desk. "Got to take a piss," he said and darted out of the room.

Five minutes later, Guy clopped down the hallway again. He walked in, took his coffee from the desk, and sat down on the sofa. "Life, growing up, getting old, it's all a comedy. It's the long, lonely pauses between punch lines that are hard to take."

"Guy, you live in the center of Canada's largest city and teach at the largest university, yet you do your best to avoid human contact."

Guy scrunched up his face. "I like to keep people at arm's length. It's safer and less complicated that way."

"Why is that?"

"Hmm," Guy said flatly. "I don't trust people."

"Have you ever thought about getting a pet?" Richard delicately scratched his nape without ruffling his hair.

"Owning a pet could give you something to care for and keep you company—something to love."

"I could never do that."

"You mean take the responsibility?" Richard's foot was jiggling. "It might do you good."

"I mean take ownership over another living thing," Guy challenged. "What about you? Do you have a dog or cat?"

"Well, I had a cat."

"What happened to it?"

"I had to give her to my sister. I didn't want her to claw my new sofa."

Guy nodded. "Yes, a new sofa is a big responsibility."

Richard rolled his eyes. "Didn't you have a dog or cat growing up?"

Guy smiled. "I kind of had a bull calf. Well, he wasn't really mine, but almost every afternoon when I was about eleven, I'd go over to Stover's farm on the edge of our village and sit in the pasture with the cows. I know, for you city kids, that sounds like a strange thing to do, but for a country boy it's perfectly natural. We have a relationship—a type of love—for our animals. We birth them, feed them, breed them, and fuss and care for them. Their lives depend on us and ours on them. It's not quite the same thing as having a pet."

Richard looked curious. "Did your bull calf have a name?"

"Sure did. Leo. I helped Mr. Stover birth him and bottle-feed him."

"That must have been fun."

"Leo was robust and muscled. He had a deep red-brown coat with a white chest, belly, and muzzle. Oh, and he had these adorable white curly locks around his face and ears. What a babe!

"What happened to Leo?"

"One day I went to see him, and he was gone. Stover had taken him to the sales barn. Never even told me."

"You felt responsible for him, didn't you?" Richard's face was compassionate.

"Of course. He was my baby."

"Go ahead." Richard nodded.

"Well, he often tried to lick my crotch through my jeans, but that's as far as we ever got, romantically speaking, if that's what you're getting at." Guy hunched his shoulders.

Richard shook his head and blew out a breath of air, as if to acknowledge he had fallen into another one of Guy's little traps.

"Now, enough of your fantasies about us simple country boys." Guy tried not to smirk. "Can we get back to my story?" Guy closed his eyes and continued with his tale.

*

It's the end of another day in paradise. After we come in from fishing, Luca and Kizo trek up the hill to their camp loaded with supplies, and Pico and I, as usual, head back to the village.

"What did you bring for dinner?" Nando says as Pico and I trudge up the steps.

"Some nice fat yellow jack," I say. "Oh, and this." I hold up a small squirrelfish.

Nando looks. "What's that? It's hardly worth cleaning."

"It's a gift from Tiki. He was at the beach fishing with some of the big boys."

"Tiki? At the beach with the big boys?" Nando opens his eyes widely.

"*Omi.*" Pico sings the word.

Nando grins. "At last."

Pico pokes me and begins to giggle.

"What's that?"

"Tiki gave you the fish so the other boys could see you are his omi." Nando's smile stretches across his face. "You are his first love."

"Me!" I gasp. "Oh no, not me."

"Yes, you. Tiki has finally started his journey toward manhood."

"But he's a kid! There is absolutely no way I'm having sex with him!" I vigorously slash both hands back and forth in front of me.

"Of course not!" Nando's smile instantly turns sour. "Omi is not that kind of love." Then his face softens again, as if he is about to explain something to a child. "It is the kind of love a boy has for a man he admires and wants to be like."

"Who would want to be like me? I don't want to be his *ommo.*"

Pico begins to laugh loudly. "Omi," he corrects and starts poking me again.

"Omi," Nando echoes and begins to giggle. "*Ommo* means the hair in your nose. Besides, the choice is not yours to make. Tiki has chosen his man."

"I don't even know what I'm supposed to do for the kid."

"Nothing." Nando hunches his shoulders and turns his hands upward. "Just be yourself. Show him how to do things: make baskets, throw a spear, shave, fish, and dance. When he is ready, you will carry him to his initiation ceremony."

Pico jumps up and wraps his arms around me. "Omi, omi."

"Who was your omi?"

Nando looks to the ground. "One of my fathers." Nando tries to swallow. "But he went away before he could prepare me for my initiation." He has a lost look in his eyes.

"Sorry." I reach out to hug him, but Pico is still holding me tight.

The next morning at sunrise, Pico and I trot down the path to where the men are gathered on the beach. And, as usual, amongst the men preparing their boats, spears, and nets, numerous boys are in attendance. I suddenly realize that this is probably what Nando is talking about. These boys are not simply helping out in the hope of receiving a fish when the men return. They're there to be close to their omi in the hope of being asked to come along.

Kizo and Luca push the boat into the water, and three boys appear and hold it steady while we climb in. "Wait, I forgot my spear on the beach." I hop out again, and I wade back toward shore. Tiki appears from nowhere and comes running into the surf carrying my spear and a water gourd. He holds them out for me.

"Thanks, Tiki."

He beams.

As I turn to go back to our boat, I catch sight of his father, Molap, in his boat nearby. He scowls at me and barks at Tiki to bring him his net and spear. Den, who is sitting in the canoe, watches Molap, then drops his head and covers the side of his face with his hand. I look over at Kizo, who rolls his eyes and shakes his head. "Come, get in. The fish are not getting any younger." I hop in the boat, and the boys push us out.

Just as I settle myself, I hear someone call me, and I look up.

"Yabai, bring home a big fat fish for me and I'll cook it up for you." Mazu is poised on a rock, waving.

I force a smile through gritted teeth and throw him a tight little wave. Then I put my hand behind my ear and pretend I can't hear him over the sound of the surf.

As we float out of the bay, I nudge Luca, who is half-asleep, leaning on me. "Hey, do you know anything about this omi stuff?"

"Sure, it's kind of like a Batman and Robin, Tarzan and Boy thing." Luca yawns.

I clasp my head in my hands. "Ahh, I'm going to be the worst omi on the whole island," I whine.

"Stop worrying. All you have to do is spend a little time with Tiki. That's all."

I force a smile. "Well, I guess it is a pretty big compliment. Yeah, I could teach him some things, like swimming and... Well I don't know, just stuff."

Luca reaches up and holds my face in his hands. He looks intensely into my eyes. "Guy, you're my hero. Would you be my omi?" He can barely finish the sentence before he bursts into gales of laughter and falls backward into the boat.

Pico sings out, "Omi, omi," as he bounces in the prow, splashing us with water. Kizo, who's sitting high in the stern, breaks into a deep roar. He digs his paddle into the water but misses the stroke and almost falls overboard. His manly roar becomes a high-pitched, girlie squeal, making us laugh all the harder.

I finally catch my breath. "Thanks. You know, with friends like you, I should just go live on the Far Island." I point.

Kizo and Pico stop laughing instantly and look at me with shock. Luca sputters some more laughs but then stops. "Oops! I think you said something wrong, Kiddo."

"Sorry, sorry. I was just making a joke. I didn't mean it."

Pico turns and stares out to sea, and Kizo resumes paddling. I hunch over and hang my head.

"Don't worry too much." Luca puts his arm over my shoulder.

"But I didn't mean it."

"They know." He pats me. "They'll get over it."

We paddle the rest of the way in silence. As I sit there sulking, I realize that although I love and admire Luca and want to be just like him, we have never been lovers, nor will we ever be. The truth is, Luca is my omi.

That afternoon back in the village, it's particularly hot and sticky. Nando, Pico, and I are doing nothing, just hanging out in our hammocks.

"Let's go to the beach for a swim." Of course, my motives are not entirely innocent since the beach is my favorite seduction spot. Nando, as usual, declines but suggests Pico and I go.

"C'mon, don't be such a sissy." From the furrow on his brow, I realize that Nando has no idea what a sissy is. "It'll be fun," I add. "Come to think of it, we've never been swimming together. You're not afraid of a little water, are you?"

Suddenly, Nando stops swinging his hammock and becomes serious.

"Yes."

"Yes? You're afraid of water?"

"Not the water, the sea."

"The sea? You live on an island. How can you be afraid of the sea?"

"Not the sea, what's in the sea!"

"Sharks? Well, I don't think sharks are a problem inside the reef." With the mention of sharks, Nando looks more anxious, almost panicked.

"No, no, no! I cannot, I cannot!"

"Relax." I touch his arm.

"But I cannot swim!" he bursts out.

"What do you mean you can't swim? Everybody here swims like a fish!"

"Not me. I cannot. I am not a fish. I will never be a fish. I will always be a—" And Nando cuts off his sentence and presses his lips tight.

"Shh, shh, relax. It's no big deal." I pat his arm. "We'll go to the bathing pool, and if you want, I'll teach you to swim."

"You cannot. I am beyond hope." Nando shakes his head vigorously. "I will never be a fish."

"Don't get so upset. I can teach you. Trust me?"

"I will disappoint you."

"Sunshine, you could never disappoint me." I lightly hold his chin and look into his eyes. "Do you trust me?"

"Yes."

"Well, now's the time to show me. C'mon, Pico. We're gonna teach Nando to swim."

Pico jumps to his feet and dances around the hammocks chanting, "Nando, Nando, Nando."

I know I've touched something delicate with Nando, and all I can do is smile.

And so, our swimming lessons commence. It takes four days to get Nando past his knees into the water. After that, we move on to theory and principles of holding your nose and ducking your head. Even though his progress is incredibly slow, I admire his commitment and persistence. At the time, I don't really understand why someone who is so terrified of the water should be so determined to learn to swim. I learn the answer soon enough.

One afternoon after we have finished our swimming lessons and are just about to leave, Mazu appears from out of nowhere and saunters across the sand toward us.

"Hello, Yabai," he says in his seductive voice as he bats his eyes at me.

Pico makes a low growling sound in the back of his throat.

"I was afraid you got the wrong idea the other night at the seeding ritual."

"I don't think I did," I say while Pico continues to growl.

Mazu makes a wide circle around Pico and walks up to me with his palms held up, as is common for a formal greeting. I reluctantly hold up my palms, but instead of pressing his in mine, he presses both his flat hands firmly against my chest and holds them there.

"You have such a lovely chest," he purrs.

I step back.

"Oh, do I make you nervous, Yabai?"

I say nothing. My skin tingles unpleasantly where he's touched me.

Then he saunters over to Nando. "Little Nando, even though you are Green and I am Red, we are still brothers, really."

"I hold nothing against you, Mazu." Nando moistens his lips. "But why do you call me a *copa* fish?" he says nervously.

"Oh that, dear little Nando." Mazu makes a false chuckle. "We were just having a bit of fun with you. That's all. Think nothing of it. And to show you I have no bad feelings toward you, I want to share this offering of friendship with you." Mazu holds out a grog gourd toward Nando.

My first instinct is to tell Nando not to drink. Then I feel guilty for being so suspicious. It's true, Mazu is nasty, but I'm certain he's only playing one of his little games to try to intimidate Nando.

Nando's hand shakes as he reaches out for the gourd. Pico growls louder and leaps forward, but I swing around, catch him, and hold him in my arms. By the time I look over at Nando again, he's handing the gourd back to Mazu.

"There, now we are friends once again. I'm sure we all feel better." Mazu looks at me. "Tonight, the Reds are having a hammock party at the beach, and I hope I have the opportunity to share some grog with you then." We watch him slink down the trail and out of sight.

"What was that all about?" I say when he's out of earshot. "I thought Pico was going to attack him." I release Pico.

Nando looks to the ground. "He is a shark, and he wants you."

"Over my dead body!" I snort. "Enough about Mazu," I say and scratch my chest, which is now beginning to itch. "I'm starving. Let's go home and eat." I start down the trail. Pico bounds over to Nando and grabs his arm, and they follow. "Well, Sunshine, I think we made some real progress today," I say, looking back over my shoulder as we walk along.

He smiles and puffs out his chest. "You and Pico are the two best teachers on the whole island." Pico squeals at the mention of his name and hugs Nando from behind.

"And the two best friends." Nando pats Pico's head.

The word I long to hear is lover, not friend. I can no longer hide my feelings. I resolve that as soon as we are alone back at the cottage, I will confess my feelings for him and ask him if I can stay on the island with him forever. I have to take the risk, even if he rejects me.

"Soon you'll be ready to swim across the strait to the Near Island," I joke.

"The Near Island!" Nando stops.

"Well, not for a while," I say, talking over my shoulder. "Besides, there's no hurry. We have all the time in the world."

"Nando, Nando!" I hear a strange panic in Pico's voice. I swing around. Nando is standing in the middle of the path, gasping for breath, pale and running with sweat. Pico is gently shaking his arm.

"What's wrong?" I dart back.

"Pico, go get help. Something is wrong with Nando."

Pico dashes off like a deer through the forest toward the village.

*

Guy leaned sideways, propped his elbow on the arm of the sofa, and rested his head on the back of his hand.

"So there is a boy on the island, Tiki, right, who wants you to be his male role model. In the meantime, you have come to the realization that your feelings toward Luca are more like hero worship than love, and you have finally decided to confront Nando and resolve the issue of intimacy between the two of you, right?"

"You got it, Doc."

"You told me earlier about your desire to be a grandfather, or a mentor to some boy, but you also talked about your fear of getting close."

"Mm-hmm." Guy nodded cautiously.

"You've expressed a great need to love and be wanted by someone, but at the same time you seem unwilling to allow anyone to love you. Why is that?"

Guy's left eye began to twitch.

"If you won't let anyone in, how can you expect them to let you in?"

He trembled and clasped his fists.

Richard wrinkled his brow. "Are you all right?"

Guy jumped up from the sofa and darted for the door. Richard stood.

Guy waved his hand vigorously for Richard not to follow. "Damn prostate."

Chapter Eighteen

Tukuman

The summer heat wave, which had been pushed north by tempests in the Caribbean, ended during the weekend with a large thunderstorm, and the cool continental air, so typical of central Canada, settled back in. Guy wore an old handmade sweater, unraveling at the sleeves, and a pair of ripped jeans and high-tops.

It was still a few seconds before nine. Guy pressed his nose against the frosted glass panel of the door. Inside he could see Richard's silhouette. He was seated in front of his computer, typing. Guy opened the door quietly and stepped in.

Richard took no notice as he continued to type.

Guy skulked up, leaned over Richard's left shoulder, and read his computer screen. "Bion: Theory and Clinical Studies Conference in Boston."

Richard jumped, turned his head toward Guy, glaring at him as if to say, do you mind?

Guy shot Richard a toothy grin, placed his coffee on the desk, and went over and sat down on the sofa.

Richard clicked his screen closed, picked up his coffee, and moved over to the swivel chair.

"Hey, Doc, did you hear the one about the postmodern anthropologist?"

"We don't hear a lot of anthropology jokes around here." Richard clicked on the tape recorder.

"Here goes. There was a postmodern anthropologist studying a group of people in PNG."

"PNG?"

"Papua New Guinea. And he was doing a very intensive interview with the village Big Man."

"Yes."

"The interview started early in the morning and went on and on for hours and hours. The anthropologist took copious quantities of notes and recordings."

"Okay."

"The interview continued with no sign of conclusion, when suddenly the Big Man spoke up and said to the anthropologist, 'Hey, it's almost nightfall. Can we stop talking about you for a moment and talk about me?'"

Richard laughed. "That's a good one. I think you've described some of my colleagues."

"I thought it might appeal to you. You could probably tell it at the Bion conference in Boston when you talk about me."

Richard squinted and shook his head.

Guy smiled innocently, then continued with his story as if no time had passed between sessions.

*

By the time I carry Nando back to our cottage and settle him in his hammock, the news has spread throughout the village. His sister, Kyle, is the first to come. She checks him all over to see if he was bitten by a scorpion or a spider. Nothing.

"Did he drink or eat anything unusual?" she asks me.

"Yes. Mazu gave him a drink from a gourd."

"Haaa!" she gasps and holds her hands to her chest.

"You don't think Mazu…"

She quickly puts a hand over my mouth. "Say no more unless you know for sure."

"I didn't actually see him drink," I groan.

"And you do not know for sure if there was anything in the drink. Words are spears, and false accusations can kill both the accused and the accuser."

"But what if Mazu did—"

Kyle shakes her head. "You must trust our ways. The truth will be revealed in time." She looks directly into my eyes. "But for now, say nothing more to anyone."

Others soon arrive, filling our small quarters and spilling out the doorway. Kyle holds Nando's head in her lap, and I hold his rigid arm. His eyes are fixed on the ceiling. He lies straight and stiff, barely breathing.

Tukuman enters our cottage with a roar, and everyone moves aside except for Kyle and me. I briefly glance up as Tukuman bows his head and says something to Kyle that I don't understand. He stands at the edge of the hammock and glares at me. Then he points toward the open door with his outstretched arm. Pico grabs my arm and pulls me away from Nando. Reluctantly, I follow him out the cottage door and sit down on the step. Pico sits down beside me, hugs my waist, and buries his face in my stomach. I feel his tears on my belly, and I hug him back. "Shh, shh, I'm sure he will be all right. Tukuman has some very powerful plants and medicines. He'll know what to do. After all, he brought me back from the dead, didn't he?" I say, trying to reassure myself as much as Pico.

From inside our cottage, I can hear Tukuman's strange, guttural chanting. Others who have remained inside wail and cry loudly, and I smell the stench of burning hair. I shiver and wish there were a real doctor we could take him to, not just a weird guy with bush medicines. Paradise does not seem so much like paradise right now.

Pico and I wait on the terrace step. The sun dips behind the pyramid mound. Suddenly Tukuman makes a loud, startling cry and bursts out of the doorway. He points directly at me and growls, then lumbers down the terrace steps and across the plaza.

Everyone stares at me with cold, hard expressions. I have no idea what I've done to make everyone so angry at me. I rise to my feet to return to Nando's side, but Kizo blocks the doorway.

"Kizo, tell me what's wrong. Did I do something wrong? Kizo, tell me."

Kizo just stares at me and does not answer. Luca appears from behind me and jostles my shoulder. Pico grabs my arm and tugs at me to follow him. All things considered, I can't make the situation any better by staying, so I follow Pico down the terrace steps. Luca moves to go with us, but Kizo makes a clicking sound with his tongue, shakes his head, wraps his arms around him, and holds him. Luca stays.

Pico leads me across the plaza, in the same direction Tukuman has gone. Once on the other side of the plaza, Pico hurries down an unfamiliar path into the jungle. I'm sure I'm being banished from the village, and all my illusions about being one of the natives vanish. As we walk along in silence, I try to think of what I've done to cause Nando's illness. How could I have made such a mess of everything? Once we're well along the forest path away from the village, I speak.

"Pico, where are you taking me? Where are we going?"

"Tukuman." Pico points ahead, increasing his pace slightly, making me more nervous.

After about twenty minutes winding along the very rugged path in semidarkness, we arrive at a cluster of small, dilapidated huts. Pico leads me to the doorway of the largest one, then slips behind me, firmly pushes me inside, and disappears.

The room is very dark and smoky. I can barely make out anything except for the large silhouette of Tukuman dressed in a hooded robe.

"What's wrong? What did—?"

Tukuman grabs the back of my head and places his hand firmly over my mouth. I shut up. He holds a drinking gourd up. Fueled by a childhood of Tarzan movies, I imagine I'm about to be drugged, then sacrificed to the volcano. He firmly presses the gourd against my lips, and I take a cautious sip. This only makes him angry, and he grips my hair, shakes my head, and tilts the gourd higher. I submit and swallow large gulps of the sour grog until I choke and sputter. He takes the gourd away from my mouth and releases his hold on me. I stand there trembling. Then I feel the grog take effect, and I begin to spin, losing my sense of orientation and footing.

Tukuman grabs me before I hit the floor. He picks me up and lays me on my back on a large wooden table. Sounds come and go like swallowed echoes. I'm unable to focus my eyes on anything long enough to see what's happening. I'm aware of Tukuman rubbing his hands all over my body, but I'm so out of it that it seems as if it's not me he's touching. I smell foul odors—burning hair and rotting vegetation. He rubs warm stinking oils on my chest and stomach. Then he rolls me over onto my belly and folds my knees up under me. I do not resist. He ties my wrists over my head and binds my knees to the table with my ass high in the air, like a pig ready for market.

Chanting loudly, he examines my eyes and ears. He pries open my mouth, looks inside, and shoves his two fingers down my throat. I gag and squirm. He slaps my ass hard. Then he moves behind me and caresses me, at first with gentle touches and massages to my buttocks, then probing fingers. I know it sounds ludicrous, but it's like he's trying to see what's inside me. Tukuman continues to probe deeper. Over and over again, I reach the point where I am about to come, but I just hang there on the edge of orgasm, never climaxing. I imagine Nando fucking me, but I know I must be hallucinating. I completely lose all sense of time and can't say how long

Tukuman works on me. By morning light, I eventually climax with such a loud moan it feels like it has come from somewhere else.

Afterward, my head begins to clear somewhat, and I realize I'm now alone. I start to worry if Tukuman is planning to leave me like this—his prisoner, his toy—and torture me. Maybe he's planning to kill me through orgasm, draining me of my fluid, strength, and will.

A short while later, Tukuman reappears from outside. His hooded robe hangs open, exposing his tattooed chest, belly, and loins. Even his face is covered with tattoos and piercings. He's truly the fiercest individual I've met so far. In his hands he carries a small calabash bowl and a large obsidian blade.

Oh God! Here it comes, death or worse!

With a lightning movement, he slashes the blade across the cords that bind me, and I pop open like a spring. My legs are sore and cramped. I rotate myself around to a sitting position with my legs dangling over the edge of the table, hunched like a defeated athlete. He shoves a bowl in my face. I look at it apprehensively, assuming he's going to drug me again for a second round. I know my legs are too wobbly to attempt a dash, and besides, where would I run to? He flicks his finger, signaling for me to drink. Resigned to my captivity, I take the bowl and raise it to my lips, my hands trembling out of exhaustion and fear.

"Coffee?" I say with surprise.

He growls and nods.

"Are you going to torture me?" My voice is shaky, and

sweat runs down my face and body.

"Torture you? Why would I want to do that?" His accent is unmistakably American—Midwestern, I think. I stare with my mouth hanging open. His bizarre facade seems to fade, and his voice and attitude are as comforting as a letter from home. "I suppose you already know, my name's Tukuman. That means Butt-Face in their language." He roars with laughter like a jolly truck driver.

"But... you're... you're not American, are you?"

"Bet your sweet ass I am, or at least was." He stands at attention and salutes me. "But all that can wait till later." He speaks in a low and serious tone. "Right now, we got one very sick boy, and you're the problem."

"But I don't know what I did!" I cry.

"Don't expect you to understand, son. Best I can do is tell you this. Sometimes a person's spirit is too strong, too attractive, and a weaker spirit kind of gets stuck to it."

I remember reading about a similar kind of thing amongst the indigenous people of Mexico. "I didn't mean to make him sick."

"Intentions don't count for too much here. But you got a piece of that boy's spirit stuck inside you. That's what I had to see for sure last night."

"Wait a minute. How can you know all this stuff?"

"Let me see if I can explain it like this," Tukuman continues. "They got them fancy shrinks in New York City who can tell what's wrong with you just by talking to you. In case you hadn't noticed, folks here don't do a lot a talking, but they fuck all the time. It's the way they say most everything they got bottled up inside. That's where I come in. It's called a 'seeing.' They say I got the gift for it."

I cringe.

"If you don't believe me, take a look on your chest. See that red patch. It looks suspiciously like the tattoo Nando's got."

I look down and rub my chest. Sure enough, there's a distinct red mark in the same place as the butterfly tattoo Nando has on his chest. It must be a trick. Tukuman must have put it there last night. But I can't see how tricking me could possibly serve any real purpose.

"Everything was fine." Tukuman waves his finger in my face. "Then you guys showed up and set the balance of things all off, and now we got us a problem. Let me assure you, Nando's in big danger."

"What can I do?"

"You'll find out soon enough." He takes the bowl from my hands.

"Right now, I'm a little freaked out and confused as shit."

He laughs. "Don't pay no mind. That grog I gave you was pretty strong. You just got your marbles scrambled a bit. It'll pass." He goes outside to the fire and comes back and hands me more coffee. "Wow! Sure been some time since I spoke American like this to anyone. Feels a little funny in my mouth, like my tongue's all out of shape or something."

"But if you're American, what are you doing here?" I feel like we're two tourists who've just connected, even if one has stayed in paradise a little too long and gone native.

"You know, I ask myself that question a lot. Answer

is, pretty much the same as you."

"Nando said his father was American too. Did you know him?" I take a sip of the burnt coffee.

Tukuman's face becomes hard. "Might have. What's it to you?"

"I want to know how he left the island."

"Nobody leaves!" Tukuman yells, and I flinch backward, spilling some of my coffee.

Then his face softens again, and he looks at me and smiles. "But you? Where in the States are you from?"

"I'm not. I'm Canadian."

"Canadian. You boys got right in there from the start, while our lame-ass government sat back on its hands and watched that little Nazi walk right across Europe. Took the sneaky Japs to bomb Pearl Harbor before we finally did something about it. Hey, you in the army?"

"Canada doesn't have much of an army, mostly peacekeeping."

"Peacekeeping, so that's what they call it. Russians behaving themselves?"

"I could update you a bit, but I'm not too good at history and politics."

"History! Now there's a laugh. No, no, son, it's not really that important to me now. Just a little curious about the outcome, that's all."

"How long have you been here, anyways?"

He grasps his chin and looks at me as if he doesn't understand the question, and then he nods. "Long time, son, if time means anything."

I sit there staring at him, not knowing what to say. My

eyes follow the endless flowing swirls of tattoos covering his body. Some resemble the glyphs and pictograms decorating the pottery and walls of the village. On his left shoulder is a pruny scar the size of my hand, and I can make out what appears to be a classic Betty Boop tattoo.

"You staring at my past?"

"Oh, no, no. Not really. Just curious, that's all."

"Well, Miss Betty here, or what's left of her, got me into some big problems with the women when I first came here. I told them she was one of our gods back home, which seemed to appease most of them, but as a matter of good taste, some of the women thought it best to set her free. Hurt like shit at the time, and now all that's left of her is this scar. Take a look at this one. Now this is a real tattoo." And he shifts his right shoulder toward me and shows me a cartoon shark tattoo. "Got this in the Philippines during the war. Gus and me got drunk and had these done. You know, the Flying Tiger Sharks, just like the ones painted on the nose cones of our planes. Man, those were the days. Booze, sex, and flying. Gus and me together, no matter what."

He stops talking, his eyes glaze over, and he stares off into the distance. "Long time no see, Gus," he says as if someone else is in the room with us.

I turn to look, but no one's there.

"You know it didn't have to be like this. You didn't have to leave us, buddy." Then he refocuses his eyes and looks at me.

"You miss it?" I say.

"Miss what?"

"Home."

"Like a case of anal warts." He howls with laughter. "Caught those one time back in Manila. Nasty things. Doctor had to burn 'em off my butthole with a red-hot blade. I'll show you the scars if you want."

"No, no, that's okay. Maybe some other time."

"This is home for me now. Ain't got nothing else left out there. A few old ghosts show up from time to time, but I made peace with them long ago. Now they're like souvenirs from a trip, nothing more, just little reminders and keepsakes. That's all." Suddenly he stops, and whatever comforting Americanisms I see in him vanish like he has been possessed by a demon. He moves his face in close to mine, and I look deep into his eyes, but they are clouded, dark, and savage.

By now the effect of the grog has worn off, and so has my patience. Anger boils up inside me. Maybe Tukuman is jealous and just trying to scare me off with all his witch-doctor crap. "Don't just stare at me," I bark. "Tell me what I'm supposed to do for Nando!"

"Do for him what he can't do for himself," he yells back.

"What does that mean?"

"Go through the rites of passage for him!" Then, with a roar and strength far beyond what I imagine for a man his age, he picks me up by the shoulders and tosses me out the door of the hut as if I weigh nothing. I lie on the ground, stunned. Then I feel Pico's familiar grasp on my arm. He pulls me to my feet and leads me away.

*

Guy paused, blinked rapidly, then held his finger in the air and said in a commanding voice, "'Ladies and gentlemen. When you're out there in the field and you have no idea what to do, just relax and follow the program. Remember, you are not the one in control.' That's what Dr. Roberts, an old professor of mine, had once told us at the end of a lecture on anthropological fieldwork. I'm sure Bion understood that too. Don't you think?"

Richard nodded. "I'm sure he did. I wish I could say the same for some of my colleagues."

"Pity, eh?" Guy said.

"Were you traumatized by your experience with Tukuman?"

"'Bout the same as I was by my last prostate exam, why?"

Richard shrugged and nodded. "Just asking."

Guy put his hands on his knees and grunted as he rose to his feet. "See you later, Doc." And he left.

Chapter Nineteen

Rite of Passage

The door was slightly ajar.

Guy stood watching as Richard read a pink flyer, unaware of Guy's presence. The light from the window shining through the paper illuminated the bold title in reverse.

"The big LGBT Achievement Awards dinner, eh?"

Richard sat up with a start and abruptly placed the flyer on his desk face down.

Guy walked in.

"Yes," Richard said with a slight tone of irritation as he swung around to look at Guy. "I decided to join the committee—you know, get involved with the community."

"So you're rubbing elbows with the pink elite now. You've really jumped into the deep end, haven't you?" Guy said as he placed Richard's coffee on the corner of the desk and moved over to the sofa.

"Well, if you're thinking of coming, you'd better get a ticket fast. They're almost gone." Richard followed Guy and sat down in the swivel chair. He popped the lip off his cappuccino and took a careful sip.

"Not a problem," Guy said as he squirmed his butt back and forth, making himself comfortable. "You know I always felt I had to be more intelligent and in better physical shape, more sophisticated and popular than everyone else just to be good enough. So I got a PhD, bought an expensive car, and went to the gym obsessively. I made all the right social connections with all the right people."

Richard fidgeted in his chair but didn't respond.

"Whatever." Guy waved his hand over his head. "But then I discovered the only people I attracted were people who were also caught up in the same superficial loop, and I drove away the people I really wanted near me."

"So you think I'm trying to validate my self-worth through the company I keep?"

Guy scrunched up his face. "No, not really. Guess you got to get out there and explore. Why not start at the top?" Guy cleared his throat. "Thing is, I've never been much for those society queens and social climbers."

"Why are you so judgmental? I see it as a way to meet people and get involved. There's more to the gay community than just bars and saunas, you know." Richard set the tape recorder on the corner of the desk, then took another sip of his cappuccino.

"Doc, have I ever shown you this?" Guy held up a shark's tooth necklace he had strung around his neck with a hemp cord.

"That's an impressive tooth. Is it from Rufus?"

Guy nodded. "I wear it to remember."

"To remember what?" Richard tilted his head.

"That life is fragile and fleeting." Guy sat quietly for a moment, then began. "As I was telling you..."

*

I follow Pico through a maze of jungle paths that until now I had no idea existed. Deep in the bush, we come to a smoky clearing with a large, thatched structure in the center. Pico stops abruptly and signals for me to lie over his shoulders in a fireman fashion. But I'm too big for him, and he staggers under my weight. Then, as if from nowhere, Luca appears. I start to speak, but Luca puts his hand over my mouth and shakes his head. He shifts me off Pico's shoulders and onto his own and carries me inside the hut. Eight young guys, who I recognize from the beach, are seated on the ground in a circle: the skinny one with blue eyes called Bright Eyes, the hairy one with a brilliant smile called Smiley, and a few emerging young muscle men. I slip off Luca's shoulders and sit next to them. No sooner am I settled than Tiki's younger father, Den, comes in carrying Tiki, with Molap following closely, barking orders. Molap looks down at me, curls his lip, and spits on the ground. An old man who is seated in the center stands up and comes toward me. He doesn't look at my face.

"Nando?" he says as he carefully examines the butterfly-shaped blotch on my chest.

I say nothing.

The old man digs his finger into my chest and yells, "*Babo!*" the name given to boys undergoing their rite of passage into manhood. Since Nando is about my age, I assumed he had already undergone the ritual to become a man years ago, but apparently, I'm here as a babo, in his place. Even though I have no idea what their actual ages are, they look old enough to me, except perhaps Tiki, but as I said he was a late bloomer. All the same, sitting on the floor amongst the group, I feel like the big kid who got held back in school too long. But whatever is in store for me, this is the only way I have of helping Nando.

Pico, Kizo, and Luca come toward me. They strip me of my loincloth and sponge me down with water and scented oils from a large ceramic pot. The old man produces an obsidian blade and carefully begins to shave me—first my face, then head, then entire body until I'm as smooth as a skinned rabbit. All around me the other babo are being washed and shaved. I look over at Tiki, and he is shivering nervously. I throw him a reassuring wink, and he forces a smile back at me. Molap glares at me and growls, then he turns Tiki, so his back is to me.

Once we are all shaved, we sit naked, cross-legged on the ground, chanting, led by the old man in the center. I do my best to follow along, trying not to cough or sneeze from the incense-choked air. After a couple of hours, some older men appear with bowls of foul-smelling gruel. We drink, then continue to chant. I'm among the first to feel the effects of the gruel. It begins with loud grumbles and snarls in my stomach and progresses to cramps and nausea. One by one we topple over, doubling up and moaning in pain.

We are carried outside to a kind of stinking bog where we proceed to vomit and shit violently. Everything comes out. I'm dripping with sweat and shivering. Even after the dry heaves have ceased, I'm unable to stand. I lie there on the dirty ground amongst the other soiled and stinking babo.

The men form a tight circle around us and begin to taunt, mock, and insult us. They laugh and jeer and spit at us. Some men flip out their dicks and wave them at us, laughing all the harder. I scramble out of the way just as Molap tries to piss on me.

I hear Mazu's and Jab's hyena laughter, and I grab a handful of mud and hurl it at Mazu. He squeals and dodges it. I spring to my feet and lurch toward him but lose my footing and fall face-first into the muck. By the time I drag myself up again, Mazu and Jab have disappeared. The babo around me are crying, and I soon join in with my own sobs of misery. I look over at Luca and feel humiliated, having him witness me like this. I want to call him to rescue me. For the first time since I have come to the island, I feel truly lost and I want to go home. I try to remember something of myself I can hang on to, but everything seems so distant and futile. I know I'm supposed to be doing this for Nando, but I don't know how this will help him. I tremble with the thought of what is yet to come.

Thankfully, the pandemonium doesn't last long, and soon drums begin to beat and conch shells are blown. Kizo moves amongst the men, telling them to calm themselves. Luca and Pico come over and lift me out of my disgusting squalor, hoisting me by my hands and feet and placing me on a raised oval stone platform along with the other babo. Each holding urns, the men surround the platform and begin to douse us with warm water, washing away our caked-on disgust. Luca and Pico climb up onto the platform and wash me, gently caressing me like mothers with a newborn baby, cleaning my mouth, nose holes, ears, wiping my butt and genitals. I lie helplessly while they carefully inspect every part of me, making certain no trace of grime or soil remains. Then they clean me again.

After I pass inspection, they hoist me from the platform and carry me like an invalid to a small dark sweathouse where they lay me, side by side, with the other babo on a bed of aromatic leaves and bark. The hot, humid air smells like cinnamon, allspice, nutmeg, lemongrass, and mahogany. After the stench of the bog pit, the perfumed vapors are a delight. Within minutes I begin to run with sweat. Luca and Pico pour cool water on my face and body, rubbing me with scented oils and holding my head delicately while I drink.

Stripped of my name, identity, and hair, then humiliated and degraded, I have been separated from my old life, and now I'm waiting to be reborn as a man. Not knowing what else is in store, I dread my reintegration back into society will be as traumatic as my separation has been.

After we lounge in the sweathouse for what feels like hours, the men carefully dry us and wrap us in mounds of white cloth. Luca throws me over his shoulder again and, with Pico holding my dangling legs, carries me back to the main lodge, where he places me next to the other babo on the floor, which has been covered with layers of broad banana leaves.

Once everyone has been positioned, we are unwrapped like fresh tamales. Pico helps me to my feet. Bowls of chalky liquid appear, and Luca and Pico proceed to paint me white head to toe, back to front. The solemn atmosphere changes, and the men sing and chant while they paint. Some of the babo giggle and squirm with the tickle of the brushes. As each babo is completed, we are inspected with smiles and laughter. All covered with chalky white, we look like ghosts or corpses, although I must say the contrast for me and my naturally pale skin is not nearly as striking nor as amusing as it is for some of the darker babo. The drying paint feels strange on my skin. I desperately want to scratch my nose. Eventually I can take it no longer. I sneeze, bringing more laughter and giggling. Pico wipes my nose and repairs my makeup. I'm ready for the next step.

We are arranged in a circle, and Tukuman appears, wearing a black robe with a hood pulled low over his face, and steps into the center. He speaks slowly and monotonously, recounting stories, many of the same stories Nando has told me, some of them word for word. I long for Nando. I worry about his deterioration and wish he was with me to share this, or at least be by my side, guiding me through, as he has done for just about everything I have experienced thus far.

As Tukuman concludes with the story of the Daughter of the Moon, the men start to chant a rhythmic grunt, slowly at first, increasing in speed and volume. Everyone joins in the measured hysteria, and the doors of the great hut are flung open. Men outside with their torches form two rows. Luca and Pico grab me by the arms. We all run through the corridor of light, down the path in a kind of military formation, torchbearers leading and following the troop, winding our way through the jungle toward the sea.

As we reach the beach, the men form a line along the water's edge, and we, the babo, caught up in the excitement, continue to run into the surf. At first, I expect, rather hope, that this is a group bath, some kind of simple baptism—the final phase of the ritual. The water around us turns cloudy white from the paint washing off our bodies. As we swim farther and farther out to sea, I keep expecting the group to turn back. Eventually, I understand that the ritual is not over yet. I look back and see the row of torchlights on the beach. There is a full moon. I strain my head up high in the water and look ahead. I can see we are swimming across the strait toward the Near Island, about two miles away. A good swim, yes, but nothing too difficult for me, especially in salt water. I shiver as I think about who or what else might also be swimming below us, but we are inside the safety of the reef, the sea is calm, and we are careful to stay close to one another.

"Let me know if you start to get tired," I say to Tiki, who is earnestly swimming beside me.

He nods and flashes me a nervous little grin.

The slow undulating sea lifts us up into the bluish light of the moon. The purplish water is filled with fluorescent plankton, creating delicate patterns of light as it swirls around our bodies, protecting us from the infinity of darkness below. I feel like we are moving through the heavens—able to change the constellations with a gentle sweep of our hands, like gods. If only I could, I would sweep my hand and Nando would awaken.

After a couple of hours, we reach the Near Island. We crawl out of the surf and flop down on the little patch of rough beach, heads on chests and limbs entwined. I'm tired but not exhausted. Everyone is breathing heavily. My head, resting upon Smiley's chest, rises and falls like the gentle surf as he breathes in and out. Tiki rests his head on my leg, and I comb my fingers through his wet hair.

This was no world record achievement, but all the same, I'm immersed in our collective heroism. It may sound strange, but for the first time in my life, here on the island, I feel like a real man on the inside, not just on the outside. Judging from the smiles of self-satisfaction and puffed-out chests of the other babo, they are experiencing a similar sense of their own awakening manliness.

After about ten minutes, the babo begin gathering dried sticks and logs, but we are naked, wet, and without matches. Bright Eyes selects a flexible stick and, using the cords he's wearing around his neck, makes a small bow. Smiley drags a large, dry log over, while others arrive with handfuls of dried plant fibers, as fine as hair, loosely rolled into little wads.

Straddling the log, Bright Eyes loops the cord of his bow around a stick and places one end on the log while Smiley holds a flat beach pebble on top of the stick. Then, oscillating his bow back and forth like a fiddle, Bright Eyes rotates the stick like a very crude drill. It takes a few practice trials to coordinate the right sawing motion with the correct pressure of the rock on top of the stick, but with a little sweat, advice, and cursing, the pair synchronize themselves. The stick begins to drill into the surface of the log, and it's not long until a tiny whiff of smoke appears. At that point, another babo delicately places a wad of fine plant fiber at the base of the drill, blowing on it ever so lightly. The wisp of smoke becomes a tiny flame that spreads through the fibers. Soon we have a roaring bonfire.

We sit arm in arm in the warmth of the blaze and congratulate ourselves. All the while, I have the uncomfortable sensation we are not alone—that we are being watched by someone or something.

Suddenly, from out of the darkness, they descend upon us wielding clubs and screaming like banshees.

I initially think this must be part of the ritual, but then two longhaired, clay-covered figures leap upon Bright Eyes, beating him and attempting to drag him off. He screams in terror and rolls on his back, struggling to protect himself with his flailing arms and legs. I jump to my feet and hurl his two attackers aside onto the sand. As I bend over him, one of them leaps onto my back and tries to strangle me. I whirl around with a sudden force and bat my assailant hard with the back of my hand, sending the savage creature flying to the ground with a thud. Without really looking, I grab Bright Eyes and half hoist, half drag him between me and the fire. We all move in close and form a tight circle. Another attacker leaps at me, flailing a club, and I cover my head. Smiley swings a burning log, setting fire to my assailant's hair and sending them off in a crazed frenzy toward the sea.

My mouth is dry, and my teeth are chattering as I stand, poised with a burning log in my hand, ready for their next attack. "Who are they?" I yell.

"Tara," Bright Eyes yells back.

Suddenly we are startled by a familiar cry coming from the darkness. That's when we realize Tiki is missing.

Without a word, each babo grabs a rock or burning log, and we run down the beach toward the cry.

We don't have to search far. A short distance behind a large outcropping of rocks, we see Tiki on his back, his arms and legs pinned to the ground by two of our clay-covered adversaries. Another one is straddling him, riding up and down on his torso.

We strike savagely, hurling burning logs, pelting them with stones, and punching and kicking. I swing my log like a baseball bat and strike the one riding Tiki on the side of their head. They fall sideways and remain motionless on the ground. I grab Tiki and hoist him over my shoulders. He clings to me, and we run back to the safety of the fire.

All accounted for back at the fire, we agree to make our escape before they have time to regroup and attack again.

Tiki was badly beaten and is in shock. It's obvious he won't be able to swim back on his own. At that point, I'm glad my father and mother sent me to those lifesaving classes during the summer at the lake. With Tiki floating on his back, Smiley and I tow him across the strait, while the others swim in a close formation around us.

Our return swim feels much farther. Smiley and I are panting for breath, and my arms and legs are aching by the time I catch sight of the torchlights in the distance. "We're almost home." I'm exhausted but jubilant. My ordeal is nearly over, and maybe I will have saved Nando.

It's only about five hundred feet to shore when I first feel an odd current, like something large has passed beneath us. I stick my face in the water and look into the abyss. Deep below us, a shadow penetrates the swirling plankton stars. The salt water stings my eyes, and I lift my head for air.

"What's wrong?" Smiley asks.

"Nothing," I sputter. "Keep swimming."

Along the shore, the men are waving their torches back and forth. Some of the babo break formation and swim toward them with renewed vigor.

"C'mon, just a little farther." As I speak, something comes up from behind us like a wave. I look over my shoulder, but I see nothing.

I shiver, firm my grip under Tiki's armpit, and pull him in closer to me. Smiley moves in tighter and begins to hum a low tune as we make slow, frog kicks in unison.

Ahead of us, babo are splashing and calling to the men who are now standing in the surf, waving and whistling. I raise my free arm and wave. As I roll onto my side and readjust my grip on Tiki, I think I see a fin break the surface behind us and disappear into the murk. Again, I feel a current of water flow underneath us.

"Rufus!"

We twist our heads around frantically but see nothing.

"We've just about reached the sand shallows," I say, trying to reassure myself and Smiley, but my heart is pounding and I'm panting like a dog. Smiley continues to hum between jittery, little gasps for air. Our strokes become tight and rapid, and we bob and jerk through the darkness toward the lights on the beach with Tiki braced closely between us.

Then Rufus strikes, slamming into Tiki and dragging the three of us under. I toss around like a cork, gasping as my nose and mouth fill with water. I kick blindly, connecting with something rough and impenetrable. I claw and flail my way to the surface and choke as I try to grasp a strangled breath of air. My arm feels like it has been wrenched out of its socket. I'm completely disoriented. Smiley bursts to the surface near me, flailing his arms and coughing up water. Terror engulfs me. "Tiki!" I cry and swing wildly in the black water, trying to spot him. All around me, panicked babo are screaming and splashing. "Tiki," I cry again. Something clamps down on to my wrist. I twist toward a large dark mass looming near me, throw my other fist as hard as I can, and kick frantically.

"Stop! It is me!" Kizo's familiar voice calls. "Are you all right?"

"Where's Tiki?" I gasp.

"Go in. I will look for Tiki." Kizo pushes me forward, and I swim toward the torches. Luca and Pico grab me and drag me from the surf onto the sand next to Smiley. I grasp him by the shoulders and cry, "Where's Tiki?" He stares at me blankly. His golden smile is gone, and his face is empty. I look up at Luca with my mouth open. I can't form words. Luca crouches on the sand and cradles us both in his arms, and we begin to sob.

*

Guy's hand trembled as he clutched his shark tooth pendant. He began to rock back and forth, cradling himself, and large tears rolled down his cheeks.

Richard rested his chin on his fists and said nothing.

"I tried." Guy dug into his pocket and pulled out a handkerchief, wiped his face, and blew his nose loudly. "Really I did. I tried."

"Let it go." Richard's voice was soft and gentle.

Guy sniffed loudly. "Our time is up."

"It's okay." Richard motioned. "Take your time."

But Guy was already up off the sofa and walking toward the door, still huffing, and holding his handkerchief to his face.

Chapter Twenty

Back to Tukuman

Guy walked up to the nurses' station. Armando wasn't there. He turned and scanned the notice board. Tacked on one side was an announcement: *Starlight boat cruise for nurses and support staff.* He removed the paper, carefully replacing the tacks on the board, then leaned over the edge of the counter and took a pen from a little collection in an old coffee cup.

On the back of the announcement, he wrote: The fish has nibbled on your bait. It's time to sink the hook.

Guy reached into his pocket and took out two tickets printed on fine stock in an elegant black scroll, embossed with a gold border: *The Annual LGBT Achievement Awards Dinner, The Royal Leeds Hotel.* He held the tickets for a moment, then wrote: *Bring your friend with the big bum but send her home when you reel your fish in.* After folding the paper twice around the tickets, he made an envelope and wrote *Armando* on the face, then replaced the pen and placed the envelope neatly next to the keyboard. He turned and continued down the corridor.

Guy glanced up at the clock on the wall as he walked into Richard's office. It was two minutes after nine. "Sorry I'm late. Had to take care of some important business this morning."

"Nothing serious, I hope?" Richard said.

"No, just one of my little investment ventures." Guy waved his hand dismissively. "Hey, you missed a good one on TV last night."

"Do you watch a lot of TV?"

"Huh. If I ever calculated all the time I wasted in front of the tube, it would scare me. Sometimes I think, why am I watching this shit? With all the extra time, I could write a book or prepare a lecture or do something productive. And then I say to myself, I'll definitely think about that, but right now my show's on."

"What were you watching last night?"

"*Strange Phenomena of the Paranormal.* It was about the Bermuda Triangle. They were talking about the disappearance of this training flight mission at the end of World War II. Of course, the theory is they disappeared into another dimension or something."

"Of course." Richard snorted a grimace and nodded.

"The cool part is that they had old photos of the guys. Baby faces. And they interviewed friends, family members, and military people who were there. It was like they were talking about someone I knew."

"I thought you didn't believe in the paranormal."

"I didn't say I believed the stuff." Guy yawned and scratched his head. "Besides, who would watch a show called *Ordinary Phenomena of the Completely Normal*?"

"Well, you're a scientist and a sailor." Richard shrugged casually. "What's your opinion on the mysterious disappearances?"

"I do have a theory."

"I thought you might." Richard's smile widened.

"My theory is this." Guy held up his forefinger. "When a plane falls from the sky into the ocean, it sinks."

"That's quite a theory." Richard chuckled.

"Yes, I call it the Guy Palmer Theory of Things That Sink."

"Your theory sounds a little easier to swallow than paranormal disappearances."

"Of course, there's one way to prove the planes actually did disappear into some kind of different dimension, you know?"

"And what's that?" Richard leaned back and stretched his shoulders.

"Go there and come back," Guy said flatly.

"And for proof?"

Guy gave Richard a dreary-eyed glare. "That's a little harder. Most people would think you've crossed the line between reality and fantasy."

"Isn't that what we're talking about here?" Richard sat forward.

"It is." Guy continued with his story.

*

With the return of the babo, the rites of passage are finally over and the babo have become men. Tiki's death has left me confused and frightened and the village in turmoil. Luca wraps his arm over my shoulder and leads me to our spot at the signal fire, where we sit and stare out to sea. The swoosh of the gentle waves washing back and forth along the sand below us seem to say *hush, hush*, and my breathing and heartbeat slow. In the background, the low, deep grumble of the surf, breaking against the outer reef, warns of a world outside filled with danger.

After a long silence, I speak. "I was his omi. I was supposed to protect him. I've made a mess with Nando, and now Tiki is…"

Luca stares at me, saying nothing. Then he begins speaking in a low tone. "There was a new boy named Sasha who came to St. Mike's when we were about fifteen. He was very pretty, maybe a little girly, and very innocent. At first, the older boys bullied him, but I kind of took him under my wing and they left him alone. I told him, when the priests come to get you in the night, do what they want and you'll be okay. Most of the time they just want to touch you or play with you, maybe a blow job. That's all." Luca tossed a stone over the edge of the cliff. "We had a code name for it. We called it making confession if the priest touched you and taking communion if you serviced him."

Luca runs his fingertip back and forth in the sandy dirt. Then he stops. "But there was one priest, Father Segars, we called him Father Cigarette, because he always smoked. He was big and looked like a soldier or a policeman. We were all frightened of him. He could be pretty nasty too. Here, look." Luca pulls the skin of his inner thigh and shows me four round burn scars. "These are from Father Cigarette." Luca pauses and lies down on his side with his head leaning on his bent arm.

"Anyway, Father Cigarette decided he liked Sasha, and almost every night he would come to take him. In the morning, Sasha would be covered with bruises or burn marks. Sometimes he was bleeding from his ass. The other boys started calling Sasha his whore." Luca stops, swallows, then tosses a piece of root into the fire.

"This went on for six months or so. Sasha stopped talking altogether. There was nothing I could do." Luca rolls over and looks out to sea.

"What happened to Sasha in the end?"

Luca continues to stare out to sea as he speaks. "We came back to the dorm after a game of football one afternoon, me and some of the other boys." Luca pauses, rolls back, and faces me. "We found Sasha hanging from the rafters by the neck—dead." Luca drops his eyes and begins making lines in the dirt again. "I couldn't protect him," he mumbles.

Tears roll down my cheeks. Luca slides over, cradles me in his arms, and rocks me gently.

Hours later, Pico comes and brings us back to Kizo's hut.

As I lie in my hammock in the dark, questions roll over in my mind like waves washing on the beach. Why did the Tara people attack us? Why had I seen Dzil going to the Far Island the week before? What could I have done to save Tiki?

I still don't understand what I did to make Nando sick, and even after going through the rites of passage for him, I haven't set things right at all. I'm desperate, unable to sleep. It's not quite dawn yet, and while the others are still asleep, I get up and go to see Tukuman. I hope I find the sympathetic American and not the freaky savage.

By the time I arrive at Tukuman's hut, the sky has become pink and orange.

"Why are you here?" he growls.

"I need to know what's going to happen to Nando."

"Go away. Or are you just looking to get your ass licked again?" He bursts out into strange, hysterical laughter, and if I was not convinced he's truly mad before, I am now.

"I've done everything I could. Everything," I yell over his laughter. "And he's still sick!"

He stops laughing and stares at me so intensely I start to back away. Then with a slow and careful voice, as if he were talking to a child, he says, "Ah, yes, for every action, there is a reaction of equal force. Son, I can still remember the laws of cause and effect. Well, I hate to break it to you, but where people are concerned, it's slightly more complicated than that."

"But you told me since I caused Nando's sickness, I had to fix it."

"No, I told you if you care for Nando, you must do for him what he can't do for himself. That's different. You think if you do certain things you can control the outcome? Nobody can control the future. Who do you think you are, some kind of god?" And he breaks into laughter again.

"So what am I supposed to do now?" I bark at him.

"Nothing," he says flatly.

"Nothing?"

"When you decided to interfere and help him, you also accepted responsibility for him. That's the way it works around here. So when things went wrong, you had to go through the rites of passage for him."

"But I didn't mean to cause problems."

"Then you should have stayed away and minded your own damn business." Tukuman clears his throat loudly and spits a large glob over his shoulder onto a nearby plant. "So now, my Nando is finally a man."

I try to swallow. I've been humiliated, attacked, and I swam across shark-infested water for Nando, and now it's confirmed—he belongs to Tukuman. "I-I don't understand. Nando is yours?" I croak.

"Yes, coconut head, my Nando! Who the fuck do you think his daddy is?"

"His father?" I stand there with my mouth hanging open.

"Well, I'm sure as shit not one of his mothers. Nando is my boy, so you watch yourself with him. See here, you still have his sign." He leans over and pokes the butterfly stain on my chest.

"Will it fade away?"

"Yes. Now go back, get drunk, and have sex, and well..."

"Well, what?" I say.

"Wait!"

It takes more than a few minutes for it to sink in, but then I put together the pieces. The reason Nando refused my advances was because he hadn't gone through his initiation, and so, socially, he was still a child, not yet a man. It's so obvious! I was forbidden to have sex with him. He was protecting me. I smile, then quiver at my next thought. I've had his father's face literally shoved up my ass!

"Hey." Tukuman jolts me from my thoughts. "You wouldn't by chance have a stick of Beech-Nut, would you?"

"Chewing gum? No, sorry." I try to think of a way to diplomatically take my leave.

"Didn't think so."

"I guess there must be some things you still miss?"

His face changes suddenly, losing all expression. It's as if he is someplace else. "December 5, 1945, Flight 19, we were scheduled to do an over-water training flight out of Fort Lauderdale. Just dog fucking, really. The instructor, Lieutenant Taylor, had been in the Pacific Theater and had a lot of combat flying time. Now, with everything over—you know, after the bomb—he had been mothballed, doing defense training in Florida."

"Hey, why did you ask me who had won the war if you already knew?"

"I just wanted to know if you knew." He rolls his head, reaches into a small pouch, and produces a corncob pipe. He sits cross-legged on the ground. "Fetch me a light from the fire, son, would you?"

I go over to the smoldering fire pit, find a small stick, and light the end. I return, carefully shielding the burning end, hand it to him, and sit facing him.

He lights the pipe, puffs three times, and offers it to me. I take a draw and cough.

"See, the game had changed from military action to peacekeeping and political negotiation." He takes the pipe back and inhales deeply. "Dividing the spoils of war, negotiating with the Russians, stabilizing Germany, Japan, and Italy, and generally trying to clean up the mess after years of war. Some of the big boys at the top, like Marshall, had made the transition from war to politics. Lower down the ladder, anyone with a rank was desperately scrambling to make a place for themselves in the new military. With the war over, the combat boys, the grunts who were no longer needed, came home by the thousands. Most of the boys were more than happy to catch the first transport ship or plane back to their families, wives, and girlfriends. The whole of America was caught up with white gowns and wedding bouquets, baby booties and picket fences. America was back in business, raising families, building homes and careers, and buying four-door sedans."

He draws on his pipe and offers it to me again. I say nothing, just wave a light refusal. He shrugs, puffs a couple of times, and continues.

"Well, that's how most people saw it, anyway. Some of us have a bit of a different take on it. We called it shell-shocked, but the government shrinks call it Post Combat Trauma. That's the way they do things, you know—give it a scientific-sounding label and a file number, nice and neat, and nobody ever has to mention the real reason why so many boys came home, broke down, and killed themselves."

He stops and looks past me as if someone has just arrived behind me. I turn to see who it is, but no one is there. He nods in acknowledgment, but it's not directed toward me. Then he continues.

"For the boys like me, the end of the war meant everything changed overnight, and the world was a far more frightening place than it had been with those crazy Japs and Krauts running around. Being shot down, blown up, or even left for dead was peanuts compared to what me and some of the other boys had to look forward to back home. After we had won the war for peace and democracy and all that red, white, and blue, we lost everything."

He makes a couple of darting glances past me, breathes in deeply, and half sighs, half grunts.

"I remember the night the news spread through the base that it was all over, the mad euphoria, the tears of joy, the deep embraces. We had made it through alive, and many of us were still in one piece. Not everyone's tears were tears of joy. Not everyone embraced to say congratulations. Many of us knew this was good-bye forever. Those fucking bastards hadn't got me. They had cheated me. God, how I wanted to die."

His eyes are filled with pain. "Oh, I'm not telling you anything the military didn't know already. Of course, they knew. Everybody knew! How can you live, eat, sleep, and die together and not know? There were official policies forbidding anything of the sort with court marshals and jail. Hey, but during combat many of the boys were going to die anyways, so who really gave a shit who they fucked. Unofficially, beatings, murders, and accidents went on all the time. For the most part, with a little discretion and common sense, one could carry on and nobody gave you too much trouble. As long as it wasn't talked about, it didn't exist, not officially anyway. Just let the problem take care of itself."

His expression of pain turns to anger. "So there it was. I had three choices: swallow my pistol and come home in a box, go back and pretend like nothing ever happened and die inside, or stay in the military and try to hang on to the remnants of my life. I, like some of the others who had a little rank, took the third option. There was still an army and a need for defense." Then he stops and glares at me. "Think about it. Where would you go if suddenly your whole world collapsed?"

I say nothing.

"I think you already know the answer to that, don't you?" He puffs on his pipe. "Anyway, the new military was a very different place. It was all about building a career, having security, maybe a nice desk job or training assignment in someplace warm and sunny and getting a pension. Since I had done pretty well during the war, I was able to land a sweet post in Florida doing training missions. But what might have been overlooked and even at times tolerated during combat had no place in the new military. Little groups of self-appointed cleanup boys started to take out the trash by either official or unofficial means. I had kept my head low and my cards close to my chest, but of course there were those who knew about me, and I was getting more and more jittery all the time. The clocks should have tipped me off."

"The clocks?"

"Yeah, the clocks. There were fourteen of us in all, five TBM Avengers. We were supposed to fly out to sea due east fifty-six miles and drop our load over the practice target at Hen and Chicken shoals, continue for another sixty-seven miles, turn a course 346 degrees for seventy-three miles, flying over the Grand Bahamas, then finally turn a course of 241 degrees for one hundred and twenty miles, bringing us back to base at Fort Lauderdale. I knew our commander, Lieutenant Taylor, as well as most of the other boys who were assigned to that training flight. All our paths had crossed before, at one time or another, if you know what I mean. At first, I didn't think too much about it. Nice coincidence, I thought. Routine flight, clear weather, friendly squadron, no problem, except for one curious little hitch. All the clocks in all our planes had been ripped out. You know, you saw stupid shit like that all the time in the military, and you just made do. Besides, most of us had watches, so it was no big deal."

I study Tukuman doing my best to picture him as a young man—short hair, freshly shaved, and in uniform.

"Just after takeoff, however, it was obvious our compasses were also not up to scratch. We radioed back for further instructions and were told to navigate by the sun and the seat of our pants. The first leg was a breeze. We dropped our load on target. The second leg required more guesswork. Lieutenant Taylor had a lot of air time and a great reputation for flying by the seat of his pants, so we continued on, confident we would soon see the Grand Bahamas below us." He cast a faraway gaze as if he were scanning the horizon.

"Pretty soon it was obvious that something was very wrong. Our fuel gauge should have read three-quarters full by now, but the needle still showed full. Some of the other planes read half-empty. Taylor radioed back for instructions and was ordered to complete the mission. And that's when we should have figured it out. We had been set up by the cleanup squad." Tukuman's face becomes hard.

"Taylor kept us in close formation and instructed us with the first plane to run out of fuel, we all ditch and wait for a sea rescue. By now the weather was closing in and visibility was poor. Taylor spotted a group of islands that were too small for the Grand Bahamas. He thought we must have flown off course and were now over the Florida Keys. It would have been simple enough, if they were in fact the Keys, to turn north and hug the coastline back to base. He radioed for instructions. None came. The fog had completely closed in on us, and with no instruments we could trust, no sun, and no visible land below us, we were truly flying blind. Taylor radioed for the squadron to stay in tight formation, but his radio was breaking up. Somewhere in the fog off the Florida coast, he lost sight of the others. Up ahead, he thought he saw a patch of blue sky, so that's where he headed until his engines, with fuel gauges still reading three-quarters full, cut out. The sea was a lot closer than he had calculated, and when he ditched, he ditched her hard, shearing off both wings and the tail. The copilot, Lieutenant Gus McKenzie, was strapped in with a huge gash to his head, and the plane was taking on water fast. Taylor had only enough time to pop the release and drag Gus out through the smashed cockpit windscreen before the plane went down like a rock, nose first."

He pauses, taps his pipe on the ground, and breathes in deeply. "It's the oddest feeling. One moment you are flying through the clouds, your best buddy so close you can almost feel his breath, and suddenly you're in the middle of the sea, trying to hold his head above water while fighting for your own life."

He freezes. Not moving. Not breathing. Then his eyes return to focus, as if he has only just realized I'm there in front of him.

"That's it. That's all. That's how I ended up here. Is that what you wanted to know?"

I squint at him, surveying his face, trying to see through the tanned, pierced, and tattooed savage before me. I imagine the face of a young air pilot in his early twenties.

"You're Lieutenant Taylor, aren't you?"

"Taylor's dead!" he roars. He hurls his pipe past my head toward whoever it is he thinks he sees. "Go away!"

I get up and leave. As I hurry back down the jungle trail, I can hear him laughing hysterically and chanting.

*

Guy turned his head toward Richard and blinked rapidly, as if he had suddenly awoken and was trying to remember where he was. Then he pushed himself up from the sofa and stepped past Richard. "Madness is its own country, isn't it?" he said as he left the room.

Guy walked down the corridor past the nurses' station. Armando wasn't there, and neither was the envelope with the tickets. He smiled.

Chapter Twenty-One

Molap's Finding

"Where's your Audi? I didn't see it in your space this morning. I was worried you had canceled our appointment," Guy said as he burst through the door.

"No, I'm here." Richard swung around in his chair. "Took the subway this morning. Had a little fender bender over the weekend. Nothing at all really, but it was enough to blow the airbags. So now it's in the shop."

"Safety glass, seat belts, and now airbags." Guy paused. "Was a time when none of the cars had that stuff."

"Were you worried about me?" Richard furrowed his brow.

"Yes," Guy said, trying to catch his breath.

"Why?" Richard tilted his head to one side.

"Because you promised me you would listen, and my story is not finished yet," Guy said sternly.

"I'm here and I'm listening, just as I promised you," Richard said in a reassuring tone.

Guy flopped down onto the sofa. His breathing slowed and he resumed his tale.

*

The next day, the men find Tiki's body floating peacefully facedown near the reef, missing a leg. Rufus had only been looking for a light snack, not a meal. Even though Tiki is officially a man now, Tuss begs to have him returned to her, and the women prepare him for burial, washing his body in oil and wrapping him in cloth, then interring him inside a giant terra-cotta urn. Once all is ready, the entire village, both women and men, form a procession at sunset. Molap takes the lead. Den, his head cast low, follows. I'm overwhelmed with shame and guilt for not having saved Tiki, but no one seems angry with me or appears to hold me responsible. Smiley and I are among the men chosen to carry Tiki's urn, I guess because we're the ones who had contact with him last. All the same, I'm careful to steer clear of Molap. With Tiki's burial urn on our shoulders, we somberly march to the men's burial cave in the cliff near the sea.

We enter the burial cave with the urn while the others wait outside in silence. The passageway is small and deep with barely enough room for all of us. We have to stoop and slide the urn along the sandy floor. After about fifty meters, we reach a grotto where we can stand up straight. The torchlight flickers wildly, casting shadows and filling the air with smoke. It's difficult to see through my tears. The grotto was probably a natural cave that had been chiseled and shaped more or less rectangular. The walls and ceiling are painted with life-size murals, figures of men, ancestors, loved ones, and heroes, I suppose, although this is hardly the occasion for me to examine the murals more closely. Along the walls, there are numerous urns, and some appear quite ancient. We rest Tiki's urn in the corner alongside the others and leave in silence.

As we emerge from the cave, other men enter, a few at a time, carrying small offerings and simple grave goods. Pico has a painted ceramic plate, Kizo some wooden beads, Lalli a few carved seashells, and others offer bowls of corn, tobacco, and coffee. The burial is a brief affair. Hardly anyone speaks. Nobody gives kind words of condolence. Once all the offerings have been deposited, everyone turns and leaves.

As we near the village, the silent procession splits into two groups, men and women, and I assume it's finished. Suddenly Tuss bursts into a hysterical rage. I freeze with fear, thinking it's directed toward me. She lashes and flails her arms and screeches words I can't understand, and I suspect they are not real words at all. She lunges at Molap and throws him to the ground, beating his face and chest. The other men stand back in shock, and a group of women haul her off him and carry her back home, wailing and sobbing. The rest of the women storm off, leaving the men with their heads hung low.

Kizo hugs me from behind. "This is not finished yet," he mutters.

"What happens now, Kizo?" I'm still shaking.

"Tuss holds Molap responsible for Tiki's death."

"But it was Rufus," Luca bursts in. "Everyone saw that! We need to kill Rufus!"

"Whatever for?" Kizo has a look of bewilderment on his face.

"What's wrong with you people!" Luca throws his arms in the air. "Rufus killed Tiki!" he yells, then storms off.

Kizo looks at the ground, then looks up. "Yes, this is true." He clasps my face in his big hands. "But you cannot punish a tree for being a tree or a bird for being a bird. And you cannot punish Rufus for being a shark."

"What if he does it again?"

Kizo nods. "Then we will be ready for him. The sea is full of sharks, and you cannot kill them all. A death cannot be paid for with another death. Tiki was not ready to become a man. It was Molap, his father, who, out of pride and vanity, pushed him too early."

"Tiki was awfully immature," I said.

"Now we must have a finding." Kizo nods.

"What's a finding?" I grit my teeth.

"It will be argued in front of all, and responsibility determined."

"When?" Considering the mess I got myself into with Nando, I worry that I might be blamed as well.

"That is for the women to decide."

A few days following the funeral, the finding is announced. That night the moon is full as we gather in the women's plaza. Kyle, who presides over the finding, is seated on the upper platform of the great pyramid mound, while Tuss and Molap stand in the plaza below, facing her. The men and women of the village sit in two separate groups on the steps.

I sit with Pico and Lalli. A few minutes later, Kizo appears, looking quite agitated.

"Where's Luca?" I ask.

Kizo looks to the ground. "He said he had something important to do. He took my boat at dawn."

"Maybe he wanted to go out fishing?"

"Yes, but he also took my heavy net and my longest spear."

I think of how agitated he was at the funeral, and I hope he is not up to something stupid, like trying to kill Rufus. Ever since Luca started hitting the grog again, his behavior has become more unpredictable. "I'm sure he just wants to be alone. He'll be fine." I pat Kizo's bum as he sits down. My words don't sound very sincere.

A low humming starts and spreads throughout the crowd. Two women, Molap's sister and Dzil, step into the center of the plaza and face each other.

"Dzil will represent Tuss in the finding," Kizo leans and whispers in my ear. "And Molap has asked his sister to defend him, but she is no match for Dzil." He scrunches up his face and shakes his head.

"Why are both representatives women?" I whisper back.

"Because women are experts in these arts. Very few men have the capacity, and even fewer are foolish enough to take the risk."

I watch Dzil, who looks like a champion fighter warming up for a prizefight. I shiver out of sympathy for Molap.

Drums sound, the women make that shrill noise, then everyone falls silent. The finding begins with Dzil singing and wailing an incomprehensible dialogue. Molap's sister follows with tears and sorrowful moans.

I lean against Kizo and whisper, "I can't understand a thing they're saying."

"That is because they are not speaking words."

"Then what's going on?"

"They are expressing only what is inside, those feelings that cannot be given words. Words are forbidden during a finding, because once a word is spoken, it becomes real, and like poison, words can kill."

After my encounter with Tukuman, I realize truth on the island is not always found in words. As the finding proceeds, I understand why Dzil is considered such a dangerous woman. The range, volume, and intensity of her vocals rival the great Maria Callas. Her performance is accompanied by a repertoire of gestures and gyrations that even a Russian gymnast couldn't match. All the while she never utters an actual word.

The opera continues for hours, late into the night, sometimes angry, sometimes sorrowful, always tragic. By the end we are all crying. Tuss, sobbing uncontrollably, reaches out and embraces Tiki's younger father, Den. They cling together. Molap has thrown himself to the ground facedown, moaning pitifully. It's truly the saddest public display I've ever witnessed, yet not a single word has been spoken.

Finally Kyle rises and speaks. "And so the finding is concluded."

The men and women, still crying, try their best to collect themselves, many embracing one another. It's the first time I've ever seen men and women make physical contact. Kizo and Pico pull me into their crying circle, and I find myself surrounded by men and women embracing me in a way that I interpret as gratitude for my attempt to help Tiki and sympathy for the pain and guilt I have for having lost him.

"What will happen to Molap?" I whisper to Kizo.

Kizo looks stern. "The original arrangement with him has been dissolved as if it had never existed. Molap will now wear a name of shame. He must return any gifts that were given him. No man will fish or make sex with him. No woman will trade potatoes or accept his juice. Den has already left him. He has lost everything."

"Harsh." I clench my teeth.

"It is our way," Kizo says.

I feel a gentle hand on my shoulder, and a woman's voice calls my name, or at least the name everyone now uses for me, Yabai. I turn and face Kyle. She smiles at me like we are old friends. She takes my hand, places something in my palm, and wraps my fingers over it. Still cupping my hand in hers, she says, "Brother." She clasps the back of my head, drawing me downward as she stands on her toes and touches her forehead to mine. Then she turns and walks away. I stand motionless for a few seconds, not knowing how to react and fearing I might do something out of protocol. I examine what she has placed in my hand. It's a simple seashell on a hemp cord, just like the one Nando always wears.

"She is giving her approval." Kizo grins.

"Her approval? For what?"

Kizo flexes his eyebrows. "For Nando."

I put the necklace on and smile, but a lump rises in my throat as I think of him still lying unconscious in his hammock.

It's late and the finding is over, but as we are about to return to the men's side of the village, we are startled by a loud, throaty roar from Luca as he appears on the top platform directly above us. Everyone stops talking and looks up toward him. He stands like an Olympian with his legs spread wide and his arms over his head. His body is smeared with what looks like greasy fish blood, and his hands are cut up. He's wavering unsteadily and has a crazed look on his face. I suspect he's high on grog. He's holding something over his head shaped like two bows. I stare up at him, trying to figure out what he is holding.

Kizo and Pico dash up the steps toward Luca. Pico jumps up and grabs the bow-shaped thing out of his hands and runs off behind the mound. Kizo scoops Luca up and sweeps him away toward the men's village. It happens so fast that Luca doesn't have the chance to resist. But it's too late. Everyone has already seen the thing he's holding: the jaw of a large shark—Rufus!

An expression of sheer horror splashes across Tuss's face as she stands and watches.

I close my eyes in dread. "Luca, you macho idiot," I mumble to myself. "What have you done?"

*

Guy sat in silence. The mechanical click of the wall clock dominated the room.

Richard waited a few minutes before speaking. Then he said, "So death comes to the island. You told me your parents had passed away during your final year of university."

"Yeah, they died in a car accident driving home from a vacation in Florida, back in 1970."

"Do you want to tell me about that?"

"After they died, I was all alone."

"Did you have any other relatives you could turn to?"

"Well, I did have an aunt who lived in Saskatchewan, Aunt Emmy, my mom's sister. She was a close friend of the living Jesus, and we didn't see eye to eye on a lot of things. The last Christmas I spent with her, I mentioned Darwin over turkey and mashed potatoes and was accused of blasphemy. If only she knew, evolution was the least of my transgressions."

"My parents' funeral was her first time back east since she'd been married. Truth is, she had always been envious of my mother and never liked my father, but she took on her role like a true drama queen, dabbing tears with one hand while serving finger sandwiches with the other. My parents' church had received advance notice of her arrival and instructions. A SWAT team of local church ladies were waiting for me when I arrived by train from Montreal. They had pretty much arranged everything. I remember the people all dressed in black and the long somber expressions on their faces, the sermon in the church and the graveside prayer. The minister said, 'The Lord giveth and the Lord taketh away.'"

"And what about you?" Richard coaxed.

"I did my best to hide in a corner, poking at tuna sandwiches with no crusts, guzzling warm soft drinks, and trying to figure out how to say words with *eths* on the ends. Every time I popped a gooey sandwich in my mouth, someone would come up and offer their condolences and sympathies. By early evening, I was bored shitless."

"Did you resent your aunt?"

"Not really. I didn't begrudge my aunt her moment of glory nor mind the invasion of the Bible-thumpers. They saved me the bother of dealing with it. But my folks were dead, and nothing would change that, full stop."

"And how did you react?"

Guy's lower lip trembled. "I managed to make my escape by assuring my aunt that I just needed a little time alone. I hopped the first train back to Montreal, got stinking drunk in the bar car on the way, headed straight down to the docks, and got fucked repeatedly."

"That was very self-destructive."

"I guess everybody handles grief in their own way."

"Did you blame yourself for your parents' accident?"

"I don't know, Doc." Guy stared at the wall above Richard's head and said nothing more. Minutes passed, and he remained transfixed and silent. Then Guy turned toward Richard. "Doc, you ever had anyone close to you die?"

"Yes." Richard nodded slowly. "I lost my best friend to AIDS a year ago."

"People still die from it, don't they?"

"The cocktail doesn't always work," Richard said.

"People should come with airbags," Guy said flatly. He dropped his head, grabbed the hair at his temples, and pulled.

"Might make life a little easier," Richard said. He pressed his lips together tightly.

"I've got to go." Guy got up and hurried out the door.

"See you Monday," Richard called after him.

Chapter Twenty-Two

Babo Ceremony

The rubber soles of his high-tops squeaked on the freshly polished linoleum as Guy walked down the corridor, rounding the corner toward Richard's office. Up ahead, he spotted Armando with his head poking partway inside Richard's doorway. Guy stopped and stepped backward, around the corner and out of Armando's sight. He listened to their voices rolling lazily back and forth, although he couldn't quite catch what they were saying. He heard Armando laugh, followed by the sound of his footsteps. Guy stepped around the corner.

"Good morning, Mr. Palmer," Armando said as they passed each other. "How are you today?"

"Not nearly as good as you." Guy grinned.

"Oh, thanks for the tickets to the awards ceremony. Linda says thanks too."

Guy winked and made a clicking sound with his tongue. "Think nothing of it, Kiddo."

"The doctor's ready. You can go on in." Armando dashed off toward the nurses' station.

"How was your weekend?" Guy said as he entered the office.

Richard was sitting with his chair leaning back against his desk, smiling and looking out the window at two squirrels chasing each other around the base of a maple tree. He hadn't switched on his computer yet. His gym bag was in its usual place, wedged between his desk and the wall, but it was dry and zipped tight. Richard sat upright and stretched his arms wide. "Great. The celebrity dinner on Saturday was a smashing success."

"I'm sure it was." Guy grinned.

"We sold out. It's a shame you couldn't get tickets all the same," Richard said.

"Oh, I had tickets. They send them to me every year. I'm what you might call a patron of the Center."

"Well, then, why didn't you come?"

"I gave my tickets to a fishing buddy of mine. I much prefer an intimate Sunday brunch for two over a crowded dinner with a bunch of strangers." Guy twitched his eyebrows.

Richard said nothing for a moment. He squinted and carefully studied Guy's face. "You're a clever old fox, aren't you, Mr. Palmer?"

"A good fisherman never tells the fish where and when he will place his hook, does he?" Guy shrugged. "But enough about your little prom night. I'm in the middle of a very important part of my story."

*

I would like to tell you that when I return to the cottage I kiss Nando and he awakens, but that would be too sticky-sweet for anyone to swallow. Besides, I think Disney corporation owns the copyright to that story line. Even though I've gone through the rites of passage for him and he is now officially a man, Nando is still motionless in his hammock, and I don't know if he will ever get better.

Pico and I are staying at Kizo's cottage in the village while we wait for Nando's recovery. I'm now back in society as Yabai, and as before, I go fishing with Kizo, Pico, and sometimes Lalli in the morning, and often spend the afternoon cleaning fish and bathing at the pool with Pico.

After the incident with the jaw of Rufus at the finding, Kizo says it's best that Luca stays at their camp up in the hills, at least for the time being. I know Luca was only trying to help by avenging Tiki's death, but some things can never be set right again.

In the evening I sit alone at the signal fire, watch the sun sink into the sea, and question what I'm doing here on this island. I wish Luca were here to put his arms around me and say, 'Don't worry, Kiddo. It'll be all right.' But Luca is lost in the grog, and I don't know how to reach him anymore.

I close my eyes and picture Tiki's face smeared with clay when we were making pots together. I think of how proud he was when he gave me that little squirrelfish at the beach in front of the other boys. But Tiki is gone now.

Most of all, I think about Nando, still in a semicoma. I imagine his warm breath against my ear as he whispers those promises that only lovers share. I'm not sure when it happened or how, but his smile, his touch, his smell has made whole in me whatever was missing and incomplete.

Then I open my eyes and look out at the white strip of surf beating against the purpling expanse of sea, and I feel truly lost and alone in paradise.

But as they say, dawn follows darkness, and soon Nando opens his eyes. He looks up at me and smiles weakly as I crouch next to his hammock and caress his face and smooth his hair. I want to hold him in my arms and make him better. He doesn't speak yet, but the glimmer in his big brown eyes assures me he has come back to me.

Kyle, who has been presiding over him like a head nurse, allows me to visit only for short periods, hustling me out the door before crazy Tukuman arrives for his daily visit. Although Nando remains in his hammock, with each passing day his strength and senses grow. Little by little, Kyle allows me to stay longer, until eventually Pico and I move back in and Kyle retires to her home in the women's village.

Finally one day, as Pico and I climb the steps after returning from fishing, I see Nando through the open doorway, fussing around the cottage, straightening up and cleaning. My first instinct is to grab him and smother him in kisses, but as we burst in through the doorway, I see the expression on his face is more perturbed than amorous.

"When I was out of my head, did you two do any cleaning?" he says.

"I swept a few times, and I recall Pico fluffing a pillow." I point to Pico, while he points back at me.

"This place is a disaster."

"We brought fish," I say brightly, and Pico holds up a group of mackerel strung together through their gills.

"Both of you, go away so I can clean and make something to eat." Nando points out the door and scowls, trying his best to suppress a smirk.

"Drop the fish, Pico, and run! Don't think of me, save yourself!" I grab Pico around the waist, and we scoot out the door. "Oh yeah." I swing around, clutch the doorway with both hands, and lean my head back inside. "Welcome back."

Nando comes running toward me, swinging the broom.

I hop down the steps after Pico. "I love you!" I holler back loud enough to startle the cattle egrets roosting in the nearby tree. I freeze in my tracks. It just kind of slipped out, but there it is. I've finally said it. I stand there on the bottom step with my mouth hanging open.

Nando is standing on the terrace looking down on me. His face is beaming. He pounds his chest twice over his heart, which means 'I love you too.'

Just then Pico comes running back and grabs my arm and pulls me ahead. I break into laughter, throw Nando a kiss, and follow Pico reluctantly. Nando holds his fist firmly over his heart, watching as we dash off.

By the time we leave the bathing pool, the sun has set. My heart is jumping like a fish and I practically skip back home, leaving Pico behind.

As I rush in through the door, I call out, "Daddy's home!" Man, I can't believe I actually say that. I look around. Our cottage is clean and neat, food is set out, but Nando's gone.

A few seconds later Pico wanders in, casually munching on a mango.

"Where's Nando?"

"Babo festival," he replies with a mouth half-full of mango.

"Fuck," I mutter through my teeth.

Pico looks at me and smiles widely with mango smeared all over his mouth.

That evening the full moon seems especially large and bright as we head out the door—Pico, hopping and bouncing, and I almost jumping down the steps. The other men have already gathered on the steps at the foot of the pyramid mound. Tukuman sees us and signals for us to climb up and sit next to him. *Oh great*, I think, *I'm going to spend the evening sitting with my schizophrenic father-in-law.*

As I prepare to sit down, Tukuman greets me in the traditional manner, grabbing my package and shaking it gently, which kind of translates into, 'How's it hanging?' I jump, then try to smile as warmly as I can. Tukuman, enjoying my modesty, bursts out laughing. Pico climbs onto his lap, and in a few minutes the ceremony begins. Drums pound and grog gourds are passed all around. Everyone is bristling with anticipation. Fathers are unashamedly sticking out their chests and waving their torches.

Finally, the babo, or should say young men, come out in procession into the central plaza, and as they say, the crowd goes wild. The Red brotherhood is first, followed by the Blue and then the Green, each dressed in exquisite, feathered capes the colors of their brotherhood. I see Smiley with the Reds and Bright Eyes amongst the Blue, and I cheer and wave. Then I spot Nando amid the Green procession, and as I do so he looks up at me and beams. I join in with Pico and Tukuman, who are bouncing wildly and chanting his name.

Once all the babo have collected in the plaza, they form a giant circle and begin to dance. The greatest performances, however, come from amongst the spectators: raining down flowers, making birdcalls and animal sounds, yodeling, dancing and gyrating and, oh yes, exposing their asses and farting as loudly as possible. Even though they do not actually clap or yell bravo, the message is essentially the same. Tukuman, a man of infinite talents and resources, bends over, bares his ass, and blows a fart that echoes off the plaza walls. I'm thankful for the heavy use of incense during this auspicious occasion.

Desperately wanting to join in the festivities, I do an awkward hippy dance and squeak out a belch, which causes Tukuman to almost fall over laughing. Then as I'm reaching for the grog, I witness a sight I only heard about in school and believed was nothing more than an urban myth—a Blue Angel. Pico, with a torch in hand, holds it next to Tukuman's exposed ass just as he releases his second opera. The gas ignites, sending everyone close by scrambling to safety. I can see the tears in Tukuman's eyes and smell the scorched hair, and I'm sure he'll have trouble sitting for the next few days. Like true adolescents, they roar with laughter and begin farting in rhythm to the beat of the drums. Encouraged but physically and emotionally unable to join the duet, I settle for playing bongo drums on their asses as they bounce them high in the air.

As the festival reaches hysteria, from out of nowhere, in the courtyard below us, Luca appears, waving a drinking gourd in his hand. He staggers into the center among the babo and begins to move like he is doing a rain dance from an old western film. The music and dancers stop. I look up at Kizo on the adjacent platform. He drops his head and looks at his feet. The cheers turn to low grumbles.

Luca stands facing the gathering with his arms spread wide. "I thought you said this was a party?" he yells up to us in a drunken slur. Some of the men stand up and cross their arms tightly. "Some party. I can tell when I'm not wanted." He makes an exaggerated gesture with his middle finger—of course, it has no meaning to anyone but me and Tukuman—and he staggers off behind the pyramid mound.

The music, dancing, and cheering have just resumed when suddenly everyone is distracted again by the wild screeches of Luca as he races across the corner of the plaza. A hailstorm of stones and obscenities coming from the women's side follow him. Men sitting on the edge of the platform scramble toward the middle to avoid being struck by flying stones. Everyone is silent. Kizo tries to make himself as small as he can. Without a word, he gets up and follows Luca. After a few uncomfortable moments and more low grumbles from the crowd, the music, dancing, and cheering start over again.

At some point in the evening, the music changes and the drumbeat slows to a heartbeat. Taking their cue, the babo cease dancing. They cast off their capes, pull off their loincloths and many of their more cumbersome decorations. Naked, they form a grand circle, butts to dicks, and undulate their hips slowly and rhythmically. The crowd falls silent. One by one each young man penetrates the young man ahead and is penetrated by the young man behind. There are a few tears and some whimpers, but there is ample coconut oil for lubrication. Bright Eyes is particularly well hung and proves to be a bit of a problem for the young man ahead of him. After a few unsuccessful tries, he trades posts with Smiley, who parks Bright Eyes's monster.

With the circle now complete, the drumbeat meters out the thrusts and undulations, accompanied by moans and groans. As I watch, I recall the first time I got fucked. It was by some nameless, faceless sailor down at the docks in Montreal. I knew none of the relaxation and breathing techniques I know now, and spit was my only lubrication. It hurt like hell, and I bled for a day afterward.

The drums reach a frenzied pace, along with the humping and moaning, and it's not long before the first young man pulls out his dick and shoots his load across the ass of the young man he has been fucking. This has a sort of snowballing effect, and all the young men climax, shooting as far as they can. The crowd chants, "Cum, cum!" When the final young man shoots, he accidentally catches one of the other young man in the eye with sperm. Again, the crowd dissolves into an arrested adolescent hysteria, cheering, laughing, and dancing like eels on acid.

Suddenly the drums stop, and the young men lock arms, forming a circle. The crowd edges toward the lower steps.

"What's happening?" I yell at Tukuman above the noise.

"When the conch shell blows, run like hell and grab Nando," Tukuman yells back. "If you want him, you had better be fast."

He barely finishes his words when the conch shell blows, and the audience spills down from the pyramid mound. I leap over Den's shoulders who is ahead of me, and scramble across the plaza. Pico, whose agility is superhuman, passes me, both of us heading in the same direction. Just in front of us, the superbly athletic Lalli is obviously also headed for our target. This is no time for fair play. I leap forward and grab him by the back of his loincloth, wrenching it up as hard as I can and sending him into a tumble. Without a pause, I run on, but Mazu and Jab are fast approaching Nando from the side.

"Pico!" I holler. Without further instructions, he flies through the air, pounces like a cat on top of Mazu and Jab, and sends them hurtling to the ground. I slide like a baseball player coming into home, smashing up against the cluster and scrambling to get my arms around Nando's legs. Hands, feet, and knees are everywhere. I hang on tight while Pico pulls off other would-be suitors. I haul Nando over my shoulder and do my best fireman's dash across the plaza, up the terrace steps, and to the safety of our cottage, losing Pico somewhere in the pandemonium. At last we are alone, a little dusty and battered but together.

We stand there in the doorway clinging to each other, our chests heaving as we try to catch our breaths. But now, after everything I've been through to have Nando, rather than ravishing him with my passion and desire, I feel awkward and self-conscious. My nervousness makes Nando uncomfortable, and that makes me even more nervous. I'm sure once I have quieted down after the excitement of the evening, everything will flow naturally and smoothly. I embrace him tighter, and we kiss and caress each other. And... nothing. Nothing swells, nothing becomes engorged. There is no bone, no ramrod, no throbbing member.

As I'm becoming increasingly distressed and desperately trying to hide my predicament, I feel Nando's hard dick, pressed against my leg, beginning to soften.

Oh no, I think, *this is a complete disaster*. I want to tell him this has never happened to me before, or I must have drunk too much at the party.

Just as I'm about to explain, a shrill animal cry pierces the quiet of our room and Pico leaps in, slamming into the two of us and toppling us onto the floor.

*

"Doc, you know that final climb on a roller coaster where the little train labors up the steepest hill and then drops over the edge into what seems like eternity? You feel like your insides are being turned inside out. You lose all sense of what is up and down?"

Richard smiles and nods.

"Let me just say, with Nando, I finally got my ride on the roller coaster!" Guy made a sweeping wave with his arm.

Richard looked with a frozen expression at Guy. "Spoken like a true Freudian." Then he chuckled.

Guy grinned and wobbled his head back and forth. "You know, sometimes a cigar is not just a cigar." Guy got up from the sofa. "See you next week." He left the room.

Armando was leaning over the nurses' station, humming to himself and writing something as Guy silently walked up to him. Guy leaned across the counter and sniffed.

Armando jumped back. "Ahh! Mr. Palmer. You scared me. I didn't hear you."

Guy said nothing. He cocked his head sideways and sniffed again.

Armando pulled back nervously. "Everything all right?"

Guy studied Armando's face.

Armando averted his gaze. "Are you sure you're okay this morning, Mr. Palmer?"

Guy smiled, reached over, and patted Armando gently on his head. "Good boy," he said. "You've netted your fish."

Armando looked bewildered for a second. Then his face turned red like an embarrassed little boy.

Guy winked, turned, and walked toward the exit.

Chapter Twenty-Three

Luca's Arrangement

As Guy rounded the corner to Richard's office, he saw Armando up ahead closing the door behind him. Guy stopped and watched. Armando headed down the corridor in the opposite direction. He was light on his feet, almost bouncing.

Guy continued down the corridor. He opened the door carefully. Richard was staring blankly at his computer screen.

"Here's your cappuccino. Oh yes, and I brought you something," Guy said excitedly, as if he were a schoolboy who had brought something for show-and-tell.

"A gift?" Richard closed his screen.

Guy placed one coffee cup on the corner of Richard's desk. "No, no, don't worry. It's just a simple drawing." Guy dug in his pocket, pulled out a crumpled paper, handed it to Richard, then went over and sat down on the sofa.

Richard got up, followed, and sat down in his swivel chair. He unfolded the sheet and examined it. "It looks like a drawing of a fish. Is this an archaeological pictogram?"

"Sort of," Guy said. "Tell them it should be about six centimeters long and in black ink only. Maybe your right pec or left glute would be a good spot."

"I'm sorry. I don't follow you."

"For your tattoo!"

"My tattoo?" Richard snorted. "I'm not really a tattoo kind of guy."

Guy wrinkled his face. "But tattoos are the way you record important things that have happened to you."

"Tattoos aren't the only way to remember important things in your life. Have you ever tried photos?"

"You can't wear a photo on your skin." Guy began to gesture and speak more rapidly. "A photo can never be a part of you. Take this one here." Guy pulled up one side of his T-shirt and pointed at one of the designs on his stomach. "It's Rufus." Guy lifted the other side of his T-shirt. "And this bird represents Tiki. They're gone now, but I still wear them on my skin. They're a part of me."

"But a tattoo is just an image," Richard said.

"Yes, but fantasy is a seed from which reality grows. Sometimes you have to help it a bit."

"I'm sorry. I don't follow."

"Put the fish on your bum and you'll give your fantasy form and space."

"It sounds like you're selling magic this morning."

"Magic? Call it what you want, but we do this with words all the time. You imagine something and then you tell someone, and by telling them you start to make what you imagined real. Words are just arbitrary sounds that have been given meaning and turned into symbols. Sometimes words are inadequate tools to do the job. Why is it so strange to think you might be able to achieve the same thing with another type of symbol—a tattoo?"

"But you're stuck with a tattoo for life," Richard said.

"You're stuck with the experience for life. The tattoo is only a symbol of that." Guy paused. "If you think about it, that's all life is—a series of experiences."

"I guess you have a point, but I'm still not convinced I need a tattoo."

Guy shrugged. "Suit yourself." He paused again, as if he were looking for something else to say. Then he exhaled slowly. "Like I was telling you on Monday..."

*

As I walk up the path toward the signal fire, I see Jab standing on the edge of the cliff looking out to sea. His head is drooping, and his arms are hanging limply at his sides.

"Jab!" I yell.

He swings around and looks at me with an expression of fright. "I don't know anything!"

I walk up to him, grab him by the back of his hair and his arm, and lean him over the edge of the cliff.

"I didn't do anything! I swear. It was Mazu."

"Where is Mazu? I want to have a little talk with him."

"There." He flails his arm out toward the reef.

In the distance, I see Mazu paddling a canoe loaded

with bundles.

"Where's he going?"

Jab looks at me with pleading eyes. "He's leaving for the Far Island."

"The Far Island. Why?"

"Everyone is saying that Mazu did some magic on you and Nando," Jab blubbers. "He may have given Nando puffer fish venom to drink and put poison wood sap on your chest!"

"Why would he do something like that?" I spit.

"Because he was jealous of Nando and he wanted you. And now Tukuman is looking for him too."

I haul him back from the edge and push him up against the rock face. "If Mazu knows what's good for him, he'll stay on the Far Island forever."

"But what about me?" Jab makes a long sniffle. "He took my canoe, and nobody will take me out fishing with them."

I sneer. "Ask Molap. I hear he's looking for someone to go out with him. Now get out of my sight before I change my mind and throw you off this cliff."

Jab runs down the trail without looking back.

Later as I enter our cottage ready to tell Nando the news about Mazu, I see from the furrows on his brow that something is bothering him. "What's wrong?"

"Nothing, why?"

"Well, if you keep frowning like that, you're going to get premature wrinkles."

He forces a smile. "Oh, you're just saying that to be

nice."

It's easy to forget that signs of aging are considered beautiful here. "Nando." I take his hands in mine. "C'mon, tell me what's wrong."

He breathes in deeply. "My sister."

"Is she okay? She's not sick, is she?"

"No, it is not that." He looks to the ground. "Dzil has broken the arrangement with Lalli and made an arrangement of her own without Kyle." Nando pulls his hands from mine and clasps his head.

"Who did she make the arrangement with?"

Nando looks as if he is going to burst into tears. "She has made an agreement with Luca."

"With Luca?"

"Yes, yes. Kyle discovered this from Kizo. It is not right to make secret arrangements without your mate. It is not right." Nando drops his head and shakes it vigorously.

"Calm down, calm down." I hug him. "I'm sure they will work it out. Luca may be able to give her the juice, but I don't think he's the best choice of father."

Nando plunks down on the platform bench, flops over on his side, and lies in a fetal position. "Everyone says as soon as she becomes pregnant, she plans to discard my sister."

I sit down beside him. "That's just malicious gossip." I gently rub his buttocks and back. "Dzil's a hard woman, but I'm sure your sister is able to reason with her."

"The shame Dzil has brought upon my sister is

unbearable." Nando remains curled.

"Maybe your sister would be better off without her." I move both hands up to rub his shoulders.

"Kyle will lose everything: the baby, the home she built, the land she cleared, and most of all, respect among other women." He lifts his head to look at me. "Everything goes to the birth mother. A child must always be protected."

"But Dzil is not acting in the interests of the child. She is playing political games." I shake my head.

"It happens that way sometimes, and Dzil is a descendant of Tara, the deceiver. She knows how to arrange things for her advantage. When Kyle and Dzil became partners, the old people said she only wanted to use my sister's good name and status. Now she will destroy it."

I stop rubbing and hold his shoulders. "We can take care of your sister if this happens."

"Yes, it is a brother's number one responsibility to take care of his sister, but a woman must remain among the other women with her shame." Nando sits back up.

"Your poor sister." I cup the back of his neck.

"I had hoped that someday we would make an arrangement together." He looks straight into my eyes, as if he is looking for my reaction.

Suddenly Kizo bursts through the doorway of our cottage. "You must come. Luca is not well. He needs you."

"Is he hurt? Is he ill?" I ask, trying not to sound too concerned, but Kizo looks so desperate I can't refuse.

The climb to Luca and Kizo's camp is steep, and Kizo, even though loaded with supplies, practically runs up the hill. I'm dripping with sweat by the time we arrive at a clearing with a little thatched hut built close to a fresh stream and a splendid view of the bay and fishing boats below.

"Did you bring more grog?" Luca hollers from his hammock. "We are out, and I'm getting thirsty. I can't spend the whole day in this hellhole without something to numb the boredom."

Kizo smiles at him, swings his heavy pack to the ground, then leans over to kiss Luca. Luca turns his face and pushes him away.

"If you want to be my bloody wife, then act like one and get me and my dear friend here a fresh gourd of grog."

Kizo obeys, serving him a gourd, then handing one to me. I remember Larry's father and how hostile a drunk can get if you refuse to drink with him, so I play along, taking tiny sips.

"What are you, some kind of old lady drinking tea? Drink that shit like a man."

"You called me up here to tell me how I should drink?" I place the gourd on the ground and turn and start to walk away.

"Ah, come on, come on. I was just having a bit of fun with you."

I turn back, throw him a sour grin, and pick up my gourd. "And it's good to see you too."

"Yup, I got a pretty nice little setup here. You're welcome to move on up anytime, Kiddo. Tin Man here is not much of a conversationalist, and I could use the company."

"Thanks, I'll keep that in mind, but I'm more of a beach boy, not really a mountain man. Besides, I've got the signal fire on the cliff to tend to."

"Oh I forgot, you got your own cozy deal with Nando. Wouldn't want to interfere with the honeymoon couple."

I ignore his jab. "So I hear you've made an arrangement with Dzil."

"Not bad, eh?" He pushes his hammock and swings lazily. "My juice for her potatoes and coffee. That's me, just an old milk cow." He winks. "Or the only bull in a pasture full of steers. Depends on how you want to look at it."

The muscles in the back of my neck tighten. "I hope you know what you're doing. Dzil's not a woman to mess with."

"She's just a twat. I know a lot more about how to handle a twat than you do, fairy boy."

"Can't argue with that one." I grab the cord of his swinging hammock. "So what's so urgent you needed to see me?"

He grabs a nearby bamboo stalk and halts his swing. "Gold!"

"Gold? Are you still on that?"

"You bet I am. You know how Tin Man here likes to run around in that stupid chest plate half the time?"

"Yeah."

"Well, that chest plate is decorated with gold." Luca holds his gourd up. "Gold! You hear me?" He takes a big swig. "Seems like a long time ago a Spanish galleon smashed up on the rocks here. The thing was full of Inca gold headed for Spain. It didn't sink right away, and the natives had the good sense to salvage the gold and store it in a cave just up the coast, not too far from here." He beams and holds up his gourd for a toast.

I make no move to reciprocate. *An old Spanish wreck*, I think. That explains two pieces of the puzzle: one, why they have gold when they neither mine nor have metallurgical technology, and two, why so many of the villagers look Hispanic and can speak some Spanish. There has been contact, though obviously limited and a long time ago. I don't bother to explain any of this to Luca, as he clearly has only the gold in mind.

"Great." I shrug. "But what does that have to do with me?"

Luca takes another swig. "Do I have to spell it out for you?" he yells, spitting grog on his chest. "We load up as much gold as we can carry in the lifeboat and get the fuck off this rock. We'll be rich as kings. When we get back, we'll buy a ship and return for the rest, tax free. Tin Man here tells me the calm season is just a moon away, and that's when we head out." He points over his head toward the sea. His arm is shaking and he's dripping with sweat, probably the effects of the grog. "Once we're in the shipping lanes, we'll be spotted."

"What if you aren't picked up?" I ask. "You could die out at sea." Luca doesn't seem to notice I said "you" and not "we."

He waves his hand back and forth. "We'll take plenty of fresh water and supplies. I know how to navigate by the stars, and we can't be too far from Florida or Cuba." He slaps his chest. "Besides, the time has come. We either take our chance at sea and get rich or spend the rest of our lives rotting here like savages on this island."

I'm silent for a moment. I wish I didn't owe him my life. Then I look at him and say, "The gold is not yours to take."

"What the fuck are they going to do with it?" Luca sits upright, his legs straddling his hammock. "It's not like they have anything to spend it on. They won't even know it's gone. Look, there's enough gold for both of us."

"Forget it!" I shake my head and stick out my chin. "I'm not going to be part of your little scheme to rip them off."

"Fine, Kiddo, just don't start crying the blues when I'm living like a king and you're kicking yourself for not knowing a gift for the taking. Just remember..." He jabs his finger in the air. "I saved your ass. You owe me."

"Yes, I'll help you get home. That's all." I place the gourd on the ground and turn and walk away. This time I have no intentions of being coaxed back.

"You'll change your mind once we get rescued," he calls after me. "Then you'll thank old Luca for saving your ass and making you rich. You just be sure the lifeboat is ready to go."

I'm fuming. I want to... really, I don't know what I want to do. I hate Luca for what he has become, for what the grog has done to him, but at the same time, I realize that I can't hate him just because my paradise is his hell. How did my hero become my nemesis?

"Kizo, go back with him and get some fresh fish for

dinner," he yells. "I've got some things to take care of, and I don't want you hanging around."

Kizo catches up with me, and we walk in silence along the path until he passes me.

"Kizo, wait up. Your legs are longer than mine. Slow down."

Kizo slows slightly, and I trot up to him and grasp his elbow.

"Why do you let him talk to you like that? You're not his bloody servant, you know."

"He does not mean it. It is just the grog. He is worried." Kizo avoids my eyes.

"Worried about what?" I stop abruptly, pulling Kizo to a halt. "He's sitting on his fat ass all day in a hammock drinking like a fish. What has he got to worry about?"

"Fish do not drink." Kizo looks to the ground.

"It's an expression, and besides, you are trying to avoid my question. Why do you let him treat you like that?" I reach up and gently lift Kizo's chin.

"I love him." Kizo's eyes briefly meet mine, and then he looks down again.

"That's not an answer. That's an excuse." I lift his chin again.

"He loves me. Really he does." Kizo speaks quickly. "I have made an arrangement for him to have a child with Dzil. He did this to show me he loves me. I am his man." Kizo pulls away and walks ahead.

I want to tell him he's being used, that Luca is only trying to prove to himself that he's not homosexual. And now he has gold fever. But I know anything I say to Kizo will not make it better, and I don't want to hurt him. I also know what happens to the bearer of unwanted truths. I'm totally dependent on the people here, and I can't afford to fall out of favor with Kizo.

"And when the time comes for him to leave?" I call after Kizo.

"I go too. He needs me, and I cannot live without him," he calls back without turning to look.

It's pathetic really, but there's nothing I can say or do. I run up to him and put my hands on his broad shoulders. "Kizo, wait. You are as much my brother as he is. You know that. And you also know that I'm as worried about him as I am about you. I desire only goodness for both of you."

Kizo stops and turns. "Also me. I desire goodness for you."

We say nothing more and continue in silence.

Not too far along the path, in the soft mud, I see a small set of recent footprints. I'm sure Kizo sees them too. They're too large to be a child's, too small to be a man's. Petite really. The only person I know of with such petite feet is Dzil. Something in my gut tells me trouble, big trouble, is brewing. Why would Dzil be visiting Luca? Why indeed? I pray my worst fears are wrong.

Then an idea occurs to me, slightly self-serving and manipulative, and I feel a little guilty for conceiving it. In all fairness, if Kizo is intent on following Luca to the ends of the Earth, and let's face it, he is an infinitely more skilled seaman than I am, then maybe a solution has presented itself. If Luca leaves as soon as possible with Kizo, perhaps trouble can be avoided before whatever secret things going on between Luca and Dzil become public knowledge.

I resolve to go ahead and prepare the lifeboat and supplies: water and food. The gold is Luca's affair, not mine. It's more than obvious he needs to leave, and if a little gold will hurry the process along, so be it. Again, simple village life has become far from simple, and I have a lot of work cut out for me. Time is running out. So much for fishing, feasting, and sex. Am I sacrificing Kizo in my own interest to stay? Do I want to stay and maybe end up as crazy as Tukuman? If things continue as they are headed, sooner or later everyone will pay a price.

*

"Words like 'I love you' fade the instant they are spoken," Guy said casually, as if he had not been staring at the far wall and talking for the past forty minutes. "A lover, a friend, an important event, they're all here." Guy swept his flat palms over his chest and shoulders.

"Are we still talking about tattoos?" Richard asked.

"Every experience—every person you know—they all leave a mark, a tattoo, or a scar."

"True, but do our experiences always need to be displayed?"

"They are, one way or another."

Richard nodded thoughtfully.

"Look at the way you dress, for instance. You obviously know the difference between quality Egyptian cotton, rami, and linen. And not only do you have an eye for fabric, but you also appreciate craftsmanship. All of that had to come from somewhere."

Richard snorted an uncomfortable laugh. "You don't miss a thing, do you? I guess that's something I inherited from my father. He started out as a salesman with nothing, and now he has one of the best men's haberdasheries in the north end of the city."

Guy nodded. "So even though you didn't follow in the old man's footsteps, in a sense, the clothes you choose honor him and the tradition he dedicated his life to. See, you already wear your father's tattoo."

"I've never really thought about it that way." Richard smiled. "I have to admit, we have that in common. We both like nice clothes."

"By the way, nice watch too. Was it a graduation gift?"

Richard took a quick look at his Rolex. "Thanks. Well, sort of. I bought it with some of the money he gave me for graduation."

"Strange, how when a father gives his son a watch it validates who he is and who he is trying to become, whereas a check feels like he's just paying off an obligation."

Richard flinched.

"A son who is never able to get his father's approval," Guy continued. "I guess that's an old story, isn't it?"

"What are you really trying to say?"

"Nothing." Guy lowered his head, raised one eyebrow. "I thought we were discussing your tattoos."

Richard closed his eyes and raised his palm sharply. He breathed in deeply and tensed his jaw. "Guy," he began carefully. "One of the reasons you have difficulties with people is that you say things that are invasive and offensive."

Guy shrugged. "But is it true or not?"

"That's not the issue here, Guy," Richard said. "The issue is that your comments are neither requested nor desired." Richard cleared his throat and continued. "In your story you describe Luca as a man who is also quite invasive and offensive. He has all but destroyed his relationship with Guy and has ended up marginalizing himself on the island."

Guy looked up. "You really don't get him at all, do you?"

"Why don't you explain him to me, then?"

"He's not a bad person. All Luca wants is to be wanted and needed, but every time he tries to reach out, he makes a mess of things."

"And why is that?" Richard said.

"Because he hates himself too much to allow anyone to love him."

Richard continued, "On the other hand, Guy in your story is a man who cultivates the love of others and has become completely integrated into the society."

"Yes, that's the way it was." Guy nodded.

"One character resists while the other embraces. One wants to leave while the other wants to stay within the fantasy. Yet neither character is able to let go of the other." Richard held out his right palm as if he were offering Guy something.

Guy looked at his empty palm.

"Both of these characters are really you, aren't they?"

Guy opened his mouth to speak, but no words came.

Richard waited a minute, but Guy remained silent. "It's time," Richard said as he glanced at his watch. "But I think you should reflect on how both Luca and Guy in your story really describe you and your struggles."

Guy said nothing, got up, and left the room.

Chapter Twenty-Four

Baby Leo

Guy arrived at Richard's door a few minutes early. He leaned against the wall and waited. Inside he could hear Richard and Armando talking in low, lyrical tones.

"Now get out of here before I throw you down on the sofa and commit some unspeakable violation of workplace etiquette," Guy heard Richard say.

"And you know who would walk in and catch us, don't you?" Armando said.

"Oh, that would be all we need." Giggles. Then the type of muffled silence one hears when two people are secretly snogging.

Guy covered his mouth and snickered like a schoolboy as he made a stealthy retreat down the corridor around the corner. When he heard the door open, he casually started back toward the office.

"First one home makes dinner," Armando whispered back through the door. He closed the door and turned to leave.

Guy was standing a few feet behind Armando. "Good morning, Armando."

Armando jumped. "Oh, good morning, Mr. Palmer."

"Sleep well last night?" Guy smirked.

"Not at all." Armando fought back a yawn.

"Good boy." Guy entered the office.

"Here's your cappuccino, Doc."

"Oh, thanks. I could really use another cup of coffee this morning." Richard sat up. "A suit and tie? You're very elegant today."

"Meeting at the university after our session." He pulled the lapels of his Gucci suit, straightened his Armani tie, and sat down on the sofa. As Guy crossed his foot over his knee, Richard quickly glanced at his Prada shoes—no socks.

"What's the meeting about?"

"Disciplinary committee." Guy reached into his pocket and pulled out a rather flattened croissant. He took a large bite and continued to speak as he chewed, crumbs falling onto his lap.

Richard's stomach growled.

"Oh, sorry, would you like a bite?" Guy held out the half-eaten croissant.

Richard waved no. "Do you want to tell me about it?"

"I teach a course about shamans, herbalists, and *curandero*." Guy stopped, held open his mouth, pounded his chest, and belched. "Students come with their tofu bars and homeopathic remedies." Guy shrugged, took another bite, and continued to talk and chew. "They want to hear that the chicken bone magic they buy in trendy alternative shops will instantly bring them peace, harmony, and understanding." He waved his hands and fingers as if he were miming an Indian dance. "That's not science, it's magic." He spread his arms, scattering crumbs on the sofa and floor.

Richard sat back and held his chin. "But isn't it your job to help them understand the difference?"

"They only want to hear about noble savages and Don Juan mumbo jumbo. To make a long story short, I told them they were a bunch of muffin heads, and they went crying to the chairman." Guy spotted a crumb sticking to his finger and licked it off.

"Is offending your students the most productive way to teach?"

"Probably not." Guy paused. "But the university no longer teaches students how to think critically. It's a service provider interested only in consumer satisfaction." Guy popped the last piece in his mouth, then proceeded to pick crumbs off his lap and eat them.

"I'm sure that doesn't apply to everything at the university." Richard spoke slowly, elongating some of his vocals.

"Hey, take psychiatry—why don't we just resolve all our problems with an outpouring of fuzzy, warm emotions followed by a group hug?" Guy waved his hand dismissively. "But enough about this boring stuff. Can we return to the island, please?"

*

It's a day like any other day in the village: sun shining, people smiling, birds singing, flowers blooming. I spend the morning fishing with Kizo and Pico while Nando remains in the village instructing the children, as usual.

As Pico and I trot home with our catch, I have the distinct impression that people are looking at me and smiling the way people do when they know something that you don't know. I think, well maybe I just look particularly nice today, or maybe there is going to be some special festival, and everyone is excited.

When we arrive at our cottage, Nando's sister is here. Pico bounds over and hugs her around the waist. She holds his head close to her breasts and strokes his hair. Since a man must always show humility in the presence of a woman, especially a woman as important as Kyle, I lay my catch of fish at her feet and stand against the wall. She greets me formally, bowing her head slightly, then uses the familiar greeting, patting her heart, which is usually reserved for close family members.

I respond formally, saying, "It would honor me greatly for the respected sister of Nando to take as much of my miserable fish as she desires."

She clasps both her hands over her heart. "It is I who am honored that the one who is so loved by my little brother accepts these humble gifts from the soil which I tend." She gestures to a cornucopia of corn, beans, squash, and fruit carefully arranged in the corner. It's more than obvious that she has not just popped over for tea and a little gossip.

I look at Nando, who's grinning impishly.

Then with a serious tone, Kyle says, "Sorrow and joy are often mixed. As you know, after Tiki's birth mother died, Tuss never took another mate, and she raised Tiki alone. She always wanted a baby brother for Tiki. Finally, she has given birth to a wonderful man-child, yet she is still without a partner. I have always held the goodness of Tuss above all other women but dared not speak of it because Dzil was my partner. Dzil has little use for me now. It is well known that she intends to dismiss me."

"I'm sorry," I say.

"Do not be." Kyle touches my forehead. "I am old, well beyond the years I could bear a child, and Tuss is alone with a child and she needs me. I have confessed my love for her, and she has accepted my offer to share the child." She smiles. "And you see, joy has grown out of sorrow."

"That's wonderful news. Isn't it, Nando?" Again, I look to Nando for some kind of confirmation that it is in fact wonderful news and that I'm responding in the appropriate way. By now he's beaming.

"What about Dzil?" I ask.

"She is free to choose another mate. Of course, people will say I dismissed her because she has not brought me a child." She pauses. "I will now accept a small basket of your glorious fish," Kyle says with a tiny smirk.

Pico leaps over, grabs a basket, and quickly fills it with the largest, fattest fish in the catch and hands it to her.

Kyle holds Pico's face in her hands and touches her forehead to his. "I go now so that you and Nando may discuss more important things than fish and vegetables." She balances the basket on her head, turns, and seems to float out of the doorway with Pico following.

Nando is bouncing and smiling so hard he looks as if he's going to pee.

"Okay, what's going on?"

Nando starts slowly and hesitantly. "Tuss respects you and wishes to honor you for your goodness toward her poor Tiki. With your permission, she wishes to name the child Yabai," Nando says.

"I would be honored." I suspect he has not told me everything yet.

"Tuss has suffered great sorrow," Nando says. "As the Daughter of the Moon teaches us, joy can grow from sorrow."

"Stop telling me myths and let me know what's going on."

He breathes in deeply, then almost blows out his phrase in one breath. "The man-child Tuss gave birth to has pink skin, green eyes, and yellow hair—just like you, Yabai!"

I look at him with my mouth hanging open. It has finally happened.

"You are white with excitement. I can see that."

"I think I'm going to pass out." I sit down on the platform.

"Oh yes, it is so wonderful, but there is more to tell."

"More?" I moan and flop backward.

"My sister and Tuss desire to make an arrangement."

I sit upright. "Are you asking me what I think you are asking?"

"I am asking you to be a daddy with me."

Now I'm the one who's smiling so hard tears come streaming down my cheeks.

"Come over here," I command. "I see a daddy I need to kiss." I stretch my arms wide.

Nando climbs up on the platform and straddles me. I grab his wrists and flip him over on his back. Now straddling him, I hold his arms above his head and lean over and lick his nose. He laughs and turns his head to one side. I lightly bite his earlobe. "Nando, can we give our baby another name?" I whisper.

"What name do you wish to give him?"

"Leo."

*

Guy turned his head and stared out the window at the deep-orange leaves of the small maple tree that stood against a steel-gray Toronto sky. He spoke in a slow, measured pace without turning back to look at Richard. "It's not the whirl of my hair or the tone of my skin, but it's written in my DNA. It's not the language I speak but the way my tongue and mouth form the sounds and my hands follow as if they already know what I'm about to say. Whether I face the east or splash myself with water, it's the altar at which I worship. It's how my feet touch the ground and carry me through space or move me to the rhythm of music that flows inside my head. It's in the way I hold my eyes when I look at you and the world around me, and it's what whispers to me when I close my eyes to sleep."

"Who said that?"

"I did. I wrote it a while ago when I was feeling really bad about things. It was supposed to be my eulogy, but I didn't have anybody who would read it for me at my funeral."

Richard sat quietly, watching as Guy continued to stare out the window. A man in a charcoal business suit talking on his cell phone walked along the sidewalk, gesturing wildly as if he were directing air traffic. A couple of young women, still in their teens, dressed in black, their pallid skin offset by their shiny, black-dyed hair, came from the opposite direction and passed without taking particular notice of him or his strange public dance.

Guy slowly turned his head back toward Richard. "Men? Women? Bisexual? Pansexual? Metrosexual? I don't know what any of it means. My whole life I've fought to be homosexual for myself, gay to my friends, and a faggot to the rest of the world. Now what am I? What is anyone, anymore? I miss the days when we were perverts, Nancy boys, fudge packers, and fairies, and only we shared the secret, shadowy corners."

Richard smiled delicately. "I know it sounds trite, but be gentler with yourself, try to forgive yourself, and learn to love the person you are."

Guy smiled back, looked up at the clock, and rose with both hands pushing against his thighs. "You know what they say. Coming out is never a single event. It's what you do every morning of every day for the rest of your life."

"I guess we're both working on the same thing, aren't we?"

Guy nodded and walked out of the room.

Chapter Twenty-Five

Time Runs Out

"Hey, you're back in your regular outfit this morning. Where's your suit?"

"At home. Waiting for my funeral."

"What happened at the meeting?"

"The chairman told me I had to make an official apology."

"Did you apologize?"

"Yes." Guy pursed his lips and nodded sharply. "I said I was officially sorry that they were a bunch of muffin heads."

Richard placed his coffee on the desk. "Was that the wisest thing to do?"

"Probably not, but I'm not going to lie." Guy shrugged.

"I'm sure they are not all a bunch of muffin heads."

"Look, Doc, we're scientists." Guy sat forward in the sofa and rested his elbows on his knees. "It's our job to say things that people don't like."

"So what now?"

"All my courses have been canceled." Guy waved his hand. "I've got more free time now."

"Maybe you can use the extra time to publish some articles and work on your CV. There are other universities, you know," Richard said calmly.

"Actually, I'm planning a little getaway. Teaching would have interfered with my schedule." Guy wormed back and forth on the sofa like he was trying to make a smooth spot in the sand with his butt. "Now, can we return to my story? It's almost finished."

*

So Dzil was thrown out, and Tuss and baby Leo have moved in with Kyle. Dzil complains loudly about how she was deceived and has suffered a great injustice, but few people are willing to listen to her, and some even laugh at her behind her back. She's now alone and still not pregnant.

In the meantime, I've become a father, and by the next moon, Nando and I undergo the formal arrangements with Kyle and Tuss. Somehow, it's just assumed by everyone that Pico is part of this arrangement too. The three of us are well on our way to settling into domestic bliss. With lots of hungry mouths to feed at home and with Pico's help, I'm fast becoming an adequate fisherman. Nando continues to do most of the domestic stuff, as he has always done. Leo is the focus of our lives. Nando and Pico seem to know exactly what to do with a newborn, while I, on the other hand, have no experience and am nervous. I spend hours staring at him, and whenever I hold him, I can't stop myself from playing with his toes. I count them over and over again—with my fingers, my nose, and my mouth.

"Yabai," Nando calls from inside while I'm out on the terrace with Leo making farting sounds on the bottom of his foot as he gurgles. "Take baby Leo out of your mouth."

"Yes, dear, I was just counting his toes."

"I'm sure he has the same number of toes now as he did this morning."

That afternoon the four of us head off to the bathing pool. After his swimming lesson, Nando lounges on the sand while I stand knee-deep in the water swishing Leo back and forth and making motorboat sounds with my lips.

"I want Leo to be the best swimmer on the whole island." Nando thumps his chest. "I don't want him to be afraid to become a man like I was."

"You may have been a slow starter, but you've more than made up for it." I blow him a kiss. Pico swims over like a frog, and I lower Leo onto his back. Then I lift Leo up in the air into a strip of sunlight beaming through the breadfruit tree, and I gaze up at him.

"Are you trying to teach baby Leo to fly now?" Nando says in jest.

"No." I lower him and kiss his belly. "I'm eating the moon."

As the sun starts to sink and the shadows become long, Nando takes Leo back to the village, and Pico and I go down to the beach to finish preparing and provisioning the lifeboat. Kizo is still committed to leaving with Luca, and their departure is on the next full moon, only a couple of days away. Everything is falling into place.

Then that evening it all starts to unravel.

I'm up on the cliff with Pico tending the signal fire when Den finds us. He's out of breath and so badly agitated it's difficult to follow what he's saying. Eventually we figure out that Molap saw Dzil making secret trips to Luca's camp, and he followed her there.

"Molap is angry with her for what happened to him at the finding, and he wants to have his revenge," Den explains. "So he ran back to the village and told everyone he saw Dzil having sex with Luca."

"I knew this would lead to trouble." I slap my forehead.

By the time we get back to the village things are far worse than we expected, and both men and women are gathered in the women's plaza. Nando, Pico, Den, and I peer around the side of the pyramid mound and see Dzil standing in the center of the plaza. She throws herself on the ground and writhes around like she is having a seizure while she screeches at the top of her lungs.

"This is bad, very bad." Nando shakes his head. "She is accusing Luca of raping her."

"Of all the stupid things Luca has done, this is the worst."

Kyle climbs to the upper terrace and calls for reason, but Dzil continues to screech and dance around the plaza. People stand on the steps and terraces and watch intently. After the shark incident and his other drunken escapades, many villagers are not too sympathetic toward Luca. A couple of women cry out for Luca's skin. Kyle, doing her best to contain the situation, raises her arms and rules that before a decision can be made there must first be a formal finding.

"Nando, you and Den stay here and try to help Kyle calm everyone down. I'm going to Luca's camp to warn him his time has run out." I place both hands on Pico's shoulders. "Pico, make sure the lifeboat is ready to go." I dart down the steps and head across the plaza toward the trail leading into the hills.

"Why are you here?" Luca yells as I approach his camp. "Did you start thinking about my gold and decide you wanted to come along?"

"Dzil has accused you of raping her. Is it true?"

Luca spits out a laugh. "I haven't set foot in the village for weeks. She's the one who's been coming up here. I guess she wanted her juice fresh from the tree." Luca grabs his package and jiggles it.

"Guilty or not, I'm here to warn you." I hold my arms out, pleading to him. "Dzil is coming with a group of warriors, and they want your blood. The lifeboat is ready and Kizo is going with you, but you must leave now!"

"A pack of dykes with wooden spears don't scare me. I'm not going anywhere without all my gold." He holds up one of the sacks he has just prepared.

"Luca, Dzil is out to kill you!"

He plops the sack down on a small pile in front of his hut. Then he turns and grabs a gourd, takes a swig, and holds it out to me in a way that is more like a challenge than an offer.

I hold my hands up in surrender. "Please, just take your gold and go."

"Look, in case you forgot..." His words are slurred, and he's wavering back and forth like he's blowing in the wind. "The minute I set foot on firm soil, they'll arrest me for abandoning ship during my watch. The crew drowned, and I could spend the rest of my life in prison." Luca takes another swig and wipes his mouth with the back of his hand, flicking the drool onto a bush. "I need you to testify that the captain was on the bridge when we hit and that he ordered me to abandon ship and get you to safety."

I stand defiantly with my hands on my hips. "I can't lie, and I won't abandon my family!"

"Fine, Kiddo, if you're not gonna help me, I'll just leave you to rot on this stinking island for the rest of your stupid life. Ha! You know, I've got half a mind to go back, steal your squeaky-clean life, and pretend like Luca never existed!"

I shake my head. "Luca, I don't even know who you are anymore." I turn and start down the path to the village. "I have a family to think about now!"

"Family?" Luca calls after me. "Three faggots, two dykes, and a little bastard—now there's a laugh."

Luca may be a lot stronger than me, but at that moment with the rage I feel boiling, I would really like to hurt him.

"C'mon back," he begs. "I was just having fun with you. You can't leave me. We're supposed to be brothers!"

I keep walking.

The following night, Pico and I are on the cliff tending the fire. For the life of me, I don't know why I continue to tend the signal fire other than out of habit. The nearly full moon is shielded behind a cloud, giving everything a soft silvery glow. It's Pico who sees them—a canoe coming from the Far Island, gliding silently through the darkness out along the reef's edge, then turning in toward our bay.

"Tara," Pico says in a low voice and makes a low growl in the back of his throat.

I don't witness most of what follows, so I am telling you this as accurately as I can, given the circumstances. Dzil, it seems, ignores Kyle's ruling to wait for a finding. With the help of three Tara women, she sets out to find Luca. Dzil wants to use Luca's alleged rape to demonstrate that Kyle has lost control and is no longer a good leader. Once she has created havoc in the village, Dzil will attempt to establish herself as the new Big Woman.

In the meantime, Luca and Kizo have just stored away most of the sacks of Spanish doubloons in the lifeboat and are returning to camp when Dzil's hunting party comes upon them. For all his size and strength, Kizo, forgive me if I say, fights like a fairy boy, and it doesn't take them long to subdue him and tie him to a tree. They net Luca and carry him off. It's the next morning before Kizo manages to struggle free and find his way to us.

Although it's unlikely we can get anyone to help rescue Luca it's essential that we get him away before Dzil can create a climate of complete chaos. Nando, Pico, Kizo, and I head up the hill toward Luca's camp. Our intent is not to do combat, but to free Luca and run. We have surprise on our side, and Kizo knows the hill paths well.

As we creep into Luca's camp, there are only three guards there, who are quite drunk, and there is no sign of

Dzil or the others. I suspect they are headed toward the village to create more havoc. A smack across the back of the head with a log takes out one guard, while Pico and Nando gag and bind another. The third proves to be more difficult and screeches for help before we can subdue her.

We find Luca tied naked and spread-eagled on the ground in front of his hut. He has been beaten badly and is unconscious. Kizo drops to his knees and sobs.

"Cut him loose and let's go!" I call.

Kizo frees Luca, slings him over his shoulder, and we run down the hill trail headed for the beach.

I really think we've made it by the time we load Luca in the lifeboat and push it into the surf. Then as Nando, Pico, and I stand chest-deep in the water steadying the craft, Kizo, that big idiot, jumps out and wades back to the beach to grab two remaining bags of gold.

"Forget the gold, Kizo. Leave it," I yell. "Get in the stupid boat!"

Kizo opens his mouth to speak, but before he can say anything, I see a spear fly through the air and lodge firmly in his shoulder. He falls over backward onto the sand with a thud and lies motionless face up, the spear pointing skyward. I look to where the spear came from and see Dzil and her band standing on the edge of the cliff overlooking the beach. They appear as shocked as we are. For a moment, no one moves; no one speaks.

Then Dzil screeches like an insane woman, and her small band of warriors hurl spears and rain stones upon us. I yell to Nando and Pico to push the boat out. We shove hard and scramble aboard. Pico jumps into the stern and holds Luca, who is laid out among his sacks of gold. Nando positions himself in the bow. I bear down hard on the oars and row. Once we are out beyond their range, Nando crouches behind me and places both hands on my straining shoulders. "As long as Luca remains, this madness will not stop." Then he hugs me and kisses the back of my neck. "Both for Luca and the village, you must take him away."

"For Luca and the village?" I choke out the words.

"Yes. This responsibility belongs to you. There is no one else."

"Come with me, both of you," I plead.

Nando presses his cheek against me and speaks into my ear. "We cannot. We have Leo now."

I drop the oars and turn to face him. He holds my sweaty face and kisses me deeply before I can say any more. We stand and cling to each other, rocking to and fro with the undulating sea. I can't let him go. I can't go on without him.

Pico scrambles forward, sobbing uncontrollably, and hugs us both. Tears come streaming down my face. Then Pico grabs Nando by the arm and pulls him from mine and they jump overboard. How I hate myself for teaching him to swim. I grasp the gunwales to stop myself from jumping in after them. "I'll come back," I call out through my sobs and reach toward them. "I'll come back."

Nando sputters and coughs as he attempts to call out something above the thunder of the waves pounding against the outer reef. Then he throws his fist in the air and splashes widely as he thumps it twice against his chest. I make a fist back at him and hold it firmly against my heart. As Nando and Pico swim back toward the shore, I stand and watch my world drift away.

I drop onto the bench and begin to row with fury toward the break in the reef and out into the open sea. Here I am back where I started, in a lifeboat with Luca, not really knowing where we are headed. But this time it's Luca who is unconscious and it's me who must save him.

*

Guy breathed in and out. Sounds and voices outside in the corridor wafted in.

"Is that it? The end of your tale?"

"Oh no, not yet." Guy waved his finger back and forth. "But you'll have to wait until next week for the exciting conclusion." Guy pushed himself up off the sofa. "Hey, I see your sister gave your cat back, eh?"

Richard looked at him curiously. "How did you know that?"

Guy reached over and whisked Richard's sleeve lightly with his hand. "Cat hairs, what else?"

Richard chuckled. "Sometimes you scare me, Mr. Palmer."

"And what about those other stray hairs in the bathroom sink and the shower? Not to mention the razor and the toothbrush." Guy flexed his eyebrows.

Richard squinted and scowled.

"It's a big step—making space for someone else, isn't it?" Guy walked out of the room, pulling the door closed behind him. He strolled down to the nurses' station, where Armando was busy typing something into his computer.

"Oh hi, Mr. Palmer," Armando said brightly.

Guy said nothing. He reached over the counter, took Armando's hand from the keyboard and carefully inspected the scratches on the back of his hand and wrist.

"I got into a fight with a cat. I lost, obviously." Armando made a little chuckle.

"He's a territorial animal. If you don't assert yourself, he'll never respect you," Guy said decidedly as he released Armando's hand.

"She's an old cat. I guess she's a little cranky."

Guy gave Armando a friendly pat on the cheek. "Who's talking about cats, Kiddo?" Guy turned and walked away.

Just around the corner out of sight, as he stopped to read the *In Case of Fire* instructions on the wall, he heard Armando pick up the phone and dial.

"Doctor, I would like to make an appointment."

Pause.

"Yes, it's serious. I'll need a complete examination with follow-up therapy."

Pause.

"He already passed by. Yeah. He asked me about the scratches on the back of my hand. Why is everyone so interested in the cat today?"

Pause.

"Speaking of the cat, I want to have a dinner party next Wednesday."

Pause.

"Both your parents and my mom."

Pause.

"I'm not just an overnight guest, you know."

Pause.

"Yes, you've been bad, and I'm going to discipline you later tonight."

Giggles.

Guy whistled a little tune as he sauntered down the corridor and out the exit.

Chapter Twenty-Six

The Story Ends

Balancing two cups of coffee on a small cardboard box, Guy carefully maneuvered the door open. Once inside he pushed it closed with his backside. "Here's your coffee, Doc."

"Thanks." Richard carefully lifted both cups off the box lid and placed them on his desk.

Guy opened the box and held it toward Richard.

"Croissant, too, this morning? Ah, don't mind if I do." Richard took a croissant in his fingers, and the flaky crust crackled. "What are we celebrating?"

"The conclusion of my tale." Guy smiled. He placed the box on the corner of the desk and looked at it. "*Fresh doughnuts,*" he read out loud. "The label on a box is never quite the same as the contents inside, is it?"

"Doughnuts or people?" Richard took a bite, and a large greasy piece of croissant fell on his tie.

"People. Our place in society—race, ethnicity, gender, age, and even who we desire. Boxes that tell us who we are and who we are not." Guy pointed at Richard. "You've made a grease spot on Mr. Armani's tie."

Richard looked down and whisked the crumb off with the back of his fingers. He held up the tie and examined the spot. "Do you feel like you are in a box?"

"Sometimes, and the label says, Caution: silly, old, tattooed faggot inside. Use at your own risk."

Still holding his tie, Richard snorted. "You know, I don't know why I wear a tie with some man's name all over it who I've never even met." He undid the knot, slid the tie off, and tossed it on the corner of his desk.

"So how was the Bion conference?"

"The conference? It went well. Boston is a wonderful city." Richard sat back and stretched. "How was your weekend?"

"Good. I had a little weekend getaway." Guy nodded. "And what about your paper? How did it go?"

"I think it was well received. I got a lot of questions afterwards, which is always a good sign."

"Delusional Retreats and the Claustrum. Great title."

"Wait a minute. You weren't at the conference, were you?"

"Yeah, how else would I have heard your paper? I was a little disappointed you didn't use me in any of the case study material though."

Richard breathed in deeply. "I'm not sure how comfortable I am with this."

Guy clasped his face. "What? Did I do something wrong?"

Richard raised his hand and opened his mouth to speak, but the words dissipated in the air, and his hand fell back onto his desk.

Guy raised his eyebrows. "The conference was open to the public, you know."

"You're absolutely right." Richard exhaled the words.

"I guess the reason you didn't talk about me is because I haven't finished my story yet."

Richard shook his head and gestured with his left palm. "Go ahead."

Guy licked the crumbs off his fingers and began.

*

I row until my arms ache, and I continue to row, inflicting as much physical pain on myself as I can. A day out to sea and we become engulfed in a fog. Without any sense of direction, rowing is futile, but I continue until I collapse with exhaustion and despair. The whole time Luca remains unconscious in the bottom of the boat. By the second night the fog begins to clear, and the sea becomes choppy. I'm an experienced seaman now, and I steer with the current.

Suddenly a strange storm appears all around us and I hear a great explosion. Far off, in a silhouette of light, I can make out a ship—our ship, the *Crescent Moon*. And again, another explosion and the silhouette slips below the waves. For a brief moment, I think I see a small craft rowing away from the scene, but then I lose it in the darkness.

By early morning the storm has subsided, the sky is blue, and the sea is gently rolling. Luca never regains consciousness, and his body has grown cold during the night. I tie a bag of his precious gold around his feet, kiss his forehead, and whisper, "Good night, Boy Scout." Then I slip his stiff body overboard and, like an image from a dream, watch as he slowly sinks through the ribbons of light and disappears into the infinite blue. It would have been pretty difficult to explain what a half-naked tattooed man is doing in a lifeboat from a lost ship with bags of gold and a dead comrade. It's better this way. There will be no inquiry into Luca's responsibility for abandoning ship and crew—the *Crescent Moon*, lost at sea, with all hands on board.

As for me, I'm well provisioned, and after a week I eventually spot the coast, off the Florida Keys. I beach the lifeboat under the cover of darkness and stash the gold. The rest is not important. For the next few years, I sail around the Caribbean and Latin America until I eventually find my way back to Canada.

I've lived mostly off the gold, and my life has been comfortable. I've moved from one man to another, never staying long. But as I get older my time is running out. Every moment of my life, even my dreams, are filled with my obsession to find my way back to the Islands of the Stars.

*

Guy stopped and drew in a deep breath. Then he placed his hands on his lap and sat very upright, beaming like a small child. "Well, Doc, that's pretty much it," he almost chirped. "That's my story. What do you think? Am I crazy? Are you going to lock me up and throw away the key?"

Richard stared at Guy with his head slightly cocked. He held his fist up to his chin and rubbed the stubble but said nothing.

"Remember our deal, Doc? I'm straight with you and you're straight with me."

Richard's hands were now poised in front of his face in a kind of prayer position, and he wore an expression as if he were trying to decide what to say and how to say it. "Okay, here goes the clinical speech. Fantasies are important. The major difference, of course, between a person who has a fertile imagination and one who is suffering from a psychosis is, the psychotic person can no longer distinguish between reality and his fantasy world. As the fantasy seduces him and colonizes his mind, he deteriorates, spending more and more time in his fantasy world and shunning reality. He eventually becomes antisocial and dysfunctional."

"That's what the textbooks say, but what do you think?" Guy yawned and rolled his eyes.

Richard leaned back in his chair and put both hands behind his head. "You've constructed a very elaborate fantasy world based on your personal experience and your knowledge of anthropology. At times this fantasy world has created problems for you. You've had problems with alcohol and drugs. You have trouble forming relationships, difficulties at work, and problems creating a life that is satisfying and fulfilling. Even so, you are remarkably logical and clear thinking. You certainly do not fit the profile of a borderline psychotic." Richard paused. "Next week, I want to look into the reason why you created this fantasy in the first place. This is the key to liberating you from your dependency on it. Maybe then you will be better able to integrate into the real world and interact with people."

"And the truth, without shrink talk?" Guy said calmly.

"The truth?"

"Remember what Bion said about truth being food for the mind."

Richard breathed in deeply. "I don't even know where to begin or how to digest all of this. That's the truth."

"Thank you for that, Doctor. I knew I could trust you." Guy pushed himself up in the sofa.

"Before you go, there's one more thing I think I need to point out," Richard said firmly.

Guy sat back down like a schoolboy who was caught trying to leave class before the bell. "What's that?"

Richard looked directly at Guy with a flat expression. "In everything you've told me, you have a very unusual way of presenting yourself."

"What do you mean?" Guy averted his eyes from Richard's.

"The Guy I see before me is gregarious, extroverted, witty, self-centered, and at times polemic and aggressive, but the Guy you have described to me on the island is shy, socially awkward, altruistic, and mostly passive."

Guy grinned widely. "Now I know you really were listening to me."

Richard stared at Guy as if he wished he had the power to penetrate the surface and see who lay beneath. "Who are you really?"

"Isn't that what you're supposed to be helping me discover?"

Richard slowly blinked and continued to study Guy, but he didn't respond.

"Doc, I had that dream again last night, but this time it was different. This time, in the dream I am floating in a rubber raft toward a beach. There are two, beautiful, naked, young men playing together in the surf. One is smaller and blond and the other very large and muscular. They see me and start to jump and wave. The larger man dives into the surf and swims out toward my raft. The smaller one darts out of the surf and runs down the beach, waving and calling to an old man who is sitting on a cliff watching. 'Grandfather, Grandfather,' he calls. 'He has come back home!'"

Richard looks at his watch. "We need to discuss this next week."

"Oh no, sorry, Doc. I can't next week." Guy stood up. "I've booked a small sailing trip for a couple of days, just to relax and get a little sun and fresh air."

"I'm envious. I could use a short vacation." Richard swiveled around in his chair as Guy moved toward the door. "We'll see each other the week after then. Have a good trip."

"I plan to," Guy said brightly. "Thanks again for the truth."

"Guy." Richard spoke his name as if they were old friends.

Guy paused.

"Thank you too." Richard threw him a quick wink.

Guy bowed his head, then disappeared out the door.

Chapter Twenty-Seven

The Letter

Bermuda, October 5th 2009

Dear Doc,

I am writing to let you know that our appointments are indefinitely canceled.

You kept your word and gave me the truth, so I think you deserve the same.

I may have filled in a few details and embellished some events here and there that I didn't actually witness, but other than that the story I told you was exactly the way I remember it—except for the ending.

As you know, when Molap told everyone about the little tryst between Luca and Dzil, the shit hit the fan. But the big joke was on Luca! After all his ranting about wanting to be 'a real man,' he couldn't even keep his erection long enough to put a bun in Dzil's oven. She was pissed to say the least. That didn't stop her from taking advantage of the situation and accusing Luca of trying to rape her.

Dzil and the Tara, however, didn't find Luca up at his camp, because he and Kizo were already down at the beach stowing away the last of the gold. They had just pushed off and climbed into the boat by the time everybody caught up with them. That's when Dzil, or one of her crazy warriors, launched a pig spear directly at Luca. Kizo, that fool, saw it coming and took the spear for Luca. Luca just kept rowing as the lovesick Tin Man fell overboard. He didn't even pause to see if Kizo was alive or dead. Regrets or not, he made his escape and left everyone else to clean up his mess. He rowed out past the reef and out to sea until he was swallowed by a curtain of fog.

After about a week of drifting around he spotted land, one of the small islands off the Florida Keys. Even though he had arrived back safe and sound, he still faced some serious charges for abandoning ship, and he probably had some hard prison time to do, not to mention a lot of other questions about the gold he could not and did not want to answer.

Guy, on the other hand, was a blank sheet, white as the driven snow. After all that time on the island together and all those evening talks on the cliff, Luca knew practically every detail of Guy's life. It was Luca who had been watching Guy from the shadows with voyeuristic fascination. Luca thought, why not borrow Guy's identity and start over? Heaven knows Guy wouldn't be back again to use it.

In those days, identity theft was a lot easier. A few letters to Guy's crazy aunt professing his commitment to the living Jesus and explaining his missionary work with the 'heathens' of the Caribbean got her signature on a Canadian passport application. The rest was child's play.

Not knowing what else to do, Luca decided to pick up where Guy left off, and he went back to school as a mature student, got a PhD in anthropology and a job at Toronto University.

But he couldn't let the past go, and he wallowed in his remorse. Every anthropology text he read brought him back to the island. For all his bullshit about being bisexual and all his self-loathing, he finally had to admit that he had only ever been in love with two men and there had only ever been two men who had loved him.

As the years went by, each new face and body he woke up with seemed to look more and more like that big, sweet Tin Man on the island. He probably would have ended it all, except one thing kept him from doing it. He had to get back. He had to know what had happened to Guy. He had to know if Kizo was still alive. It gave him a reason to keep going.

So there it is, Doc. Now you know the truth. Luca grew up alone and had never had anyone who truly loved him. When he washed up on the shores of the island, he finally found two people who were willing to sacrifice their own lives for him. But how could anyone love him when he hated himself so much? So he dumped them both for some sacks of gold coins.

Even when he got a second chance for a new life and came back as Guy, he wasn't able to do much better.

By the time you read this, one of two things will have happened. Either I am floating facedown in the sea somewhere, or I have found my way back to the Islands of the Stars.

Remember the fourth principle of lying. It doesn't really matter if anyone else believes my story, as long as I do. But thanks for listening anyways.

Your patient, Luca

P.S. In this packet you'll find a key to a box in the Royal Bank, Church and Wellesley branch. The box number is 1066, in your name. There is enough gold left to take Armando to a tropical island somewhere. Bon voyage.

Epilogue

Toronto Daily Mail, October 7, 2010.

A twenty-six-foot sailing boat leased to Canadian Dr. Guy Palmer, part-time anthropology professor at Toronto University, was found adrift off the southern coast of Bermuda with no one on board. Meteorological reports show brief localized tropical storm activity in the area, and the life raft was missing. There was no sign of foul play, and after four days, Bermudian and American coast guards have called off the air and sea search. Dr. Guy Palmer is missing and presumed dead.

Acknowledgements

Thank you to Nancy Feyen, Phil Haddock, Robert Morley, Andrea Elizabeth Smith, Madeleine Johnson, and Eleonor Shannon, the members of the Milan English Language Writers Group, for the encouragement, criticism, and guidance they gave me during the very long process of writing this manuscript. Also thank you to my other friends, Howard Leviene, Raymond Doyle, Yanne Harrington Salomonsen, and Amanda Davis, who read and commented on various versions of the manuscript. Most of all, thank you to my husband, Piero Salvioni, who has always given me his love and support.

About Mark David Campbell

For the past twenty years Mark David Campbell has been living in Milan, Italy where he writes, paints, and helps Italian academics and business people prepare presentations and compose papers in English. Prior to moving to Italy, he spent twenty years studying and working in archaeology and anthropology in Canada, Central America, Jordan, Egypt and Greece. He earned his Ph.D. in social cultural anthropology from the University of Toronto and taught as a part-time professor.

In addition to writing, he has shown his paintings at numerous individual and group shows in Toronto, Canada and throughout Italy. In his spare time, he likes scouring second-hand stores, boating on Lago Maggiore and eating pizza and drinking beer with friends.

Facebook
Mark David Campbell

Coming Soon from Mark David Campbell

Secrets of Ishtabay

Young Elio shivered and pulled his knees in closer, becoming almost fetal as he remembered kicking in the back door of the church and taking the wooden statue of San José. But he couldn't remember where they had taken it.

Elio sniffed his shoulder and the back of his hand. The musky odor of sex still lingered on his skin. Yes, they had been to Coco's, too. He also remembered the sound of smashing glass. But that was all he could recall.

Still half-drunk, Elio finally rose from his hammock and poured himself a cup of scorched coffee. After breakfast he'd wander down the dirt path to the river to bathe. Chinche and Tigre would already be there. He reached over to grab a couple of warm tortillas from the pile his mother had left on the little wooden table. As he reached, it felt like his shirt was stuck to his body, probably dry sweat or vomit. He took his shirt off and looked. It was blood!

Frantically he checked his body and arms but saw and felt nothing—no cuts, no wounds. He exhaled with relief. But if it was not his blood, whose was it?

Elio tried to think clearly, but his head was still spinning and everything was a jumble. He stood there trembling, not knowing what to do next.

Suddenly, he remembered Chinche yelling, "Let's cut off his gringo balls and stuff them in his mouth."

And he wasn't sure if it was something Chinche had only said or something he had actually done.

Elio panicked.

He found a pair of his father's britches and a fresh shirt hanging on the line. He scooped up the rest of the tortillas and wrapped them in a red handkerchief, then filled a gourd with water. He rolled his blood-covered shirt in a tight ball and stuffed it into an old paper bag he had found in the kitchen. He'd throw it away somewhere where no one would find it. Then he grabbed his straw hat from the nail where it was hanging, pulled it low over his head and quickly darted out the gate towards the trail that led into the bush to his father's milpa. If there had been trouble the night before, the bush was the safest place to hide.

"Ahh," Elio half sighed, half grunted as he drifted back from his thoughts. That was so long ago and it was best not to try to remember things he could not change. What was done was done.

Also from NineStar Press

Left in the Dark by Zev de Valera

Cal Restrepo, victim of a road rage automobile accident, emerges from unconsciousness into a world he does not recognize.

Under the care of the doctors at Wending Hills and the help of his friends and neighbors, Cal gradually recovers his memory and the full use of his body. Yet, so many of the memories do not fit what he feels is the "real" Cal.

Are his memories still clouded and unreliable, or was the Cal Restrepo who existed before the accident someone entirely different than the man who survived?

Killing Games by Reis Asher

Edgar Tobias works as a freelance computer programmer in the city of Anver. Desperate to escape his deceased fathers' fame as a hit singer-songwriter duo, he left the city of Kasyova and the arts behind. He doesn't know he's about to be targeted in a vicious murder game where the prize is a million dollars in cryptocurrency to the first person who can capture his murder on video.

Reis Asher lost everything in the Anverite civil war ten years ago, including their mother. Their father created the agreement known as Unification, which joined Anver and Kasyova to create the Twin City-States of Anver-Kasyova, ending the civil war and ushering in a new era of peace and prosperity.

When they discover the Killing Game, they know that it represents a threat to everything they hold dear and set out to stop it. But powerful forces are at work that refuse to be undermined by one stubborn soul and their sense of justice.

Someone wants Edgar dead, and they'll stop at nothing to see him six feet under… even if that means Reis and other innocent bystanders get caught in the crossfire.

Birthday Presents by Dianne Hartsock

Crimson loves to dance. He adores watching the pretty boys grind to the frantic beat of the music and picking out his lover for the evening. But more than that, he lives for his birthday, that one day a year he gives into his darker impulses: choosing a young man to lure into the alleyway with promises of sex, then slitting his throat in the midst of their passion and reveling in the hot blood on his hands.

For Tracey Winston, life has become a nightmare. Kidnapped from a nightclub in Boulder, Colorado, brutalized and raped by Crimson, he's held captive in a cabin in the Rocky Mountains along with sweet Kyle, a young man Crimson keeps chained to his bed and is slowly torturing to death. Though Tracey manages to escape with Kyle's help, he has to leave Kyle behind in Crimson's cruel hands.

Detective Gene Mallory has never stopped looking for his brother Kyle, kidnapped from a nightclub seven months previously. The case breaks open when Tracey Winston comes forth at the urging of his new boyfriend, claiming to have knowledge of where Crimson is hiding out. A manhunt begins with Crimson continuously slipping through their net. Lives are on the line, with both Gene and Tracey being targeted by the killer. A traitor in their midst tips Crimson off to their plans.

Crimson's birthday has come and gone, and he will kill again.

Connect with NineStar Press

www.ninestarpress.com

www.facebook.com/ninestarpress

www.facebook.com/groups/NineStarNiche

www.twitter.com/ninestarpress

www.instagram.com/ninestarpress

www.ingramcontent.com/pod-product-compliance
Lightning Source LLC
Chambersburg PA
CBHW030229100526
44583CB00013BA/603